DATE			
OCT 23 '80			
APR 29 '82			
FEB 7 '86			
NOV 0 6 1990			
OCT 15 2008			

Persons

Contributions in Philosophy

The Platonic Method: An Interpretation of the Dramatic Philosophic
Aspects of the "Meno"
Jerome Eckstein

Language and Value
Charles L. Todd and Russell T. Blackwood, editors

Inquiries into Medieval Philosophy: A Collection in Honor of Francis
P. Clarke
James F. Ross, editor

The Vitality of Death: Essays in Existential Psychology and Philosophy
Peter Koestenbaum

Dialogues on the Philosophy of Marxism
Society for the Philosophical Study of Dialectical Materialism
John Somerville and Howard L. Parsons, editors

The Peace Revolution: Ethos and Social Process
John Somerville

Marx and Engels on Ecology
Howard L. Parsons, editor and compiler

The New Image of the Person: The Theory and Practice of Clinical
Philosophy
Peter Koestenbaum

Panorama of Evil: Insights from the Behavioral Sciences
Leonard W. Doob

Alienation: From the Past to the Future
Ignace Feuerlicht

The Philosopher's World Model
Archie J. Bahm

Persons A COMPARATIVE ACCOUNT OF THE SIX POSSIBLE THEORIES

F. F. Centore

Contributions in Philosophy, Number 13

GREENWOOD PRESS

WESTPORT, CONNECTICUT • LONDON, ENGLAND

Library of Congress Cataloging in Publication Data

Centore, F. F.   1938-
  Persons, a comparative account of the six
possible theories.
  (Contributions in philosophy; no. 13 ISSN 0084-
926X)
  Bibliography: p.
  Includes index.
  1. Philosophical anthropology. I. Title.
BD450.C42   128   78-74653
ISBN 0-313-20817-4

Library of Congress Catalog Card Number: 78-74653
ISBN: 0-313-20817-4
ISSN: 0084-926X

First published in 1979

Greenwood Press, Inc.
51 Riverside Avenue, Westport, Connecticut 06880

Printed in the United States of America

10 9 8 7 6 5 4 3 2 1

To all who cherish
their freedom and who do
not want to see it lost.

Contents

Preface

Someone once said that if you could teach a parrot to repeat "resultant of forces" over and over, sooner or later some university or other would award it a Ph.D. in physics. A parrot saying "status and role" often enough would be similarly honored in sociology. Likewise in biology for a bird repeating "natural selection" a sufficient number of times. In philosophy I guess something like "know thyself" would be required. If one may judge by the way philosophers are typically represented in the popular media, an imitation of Socrates would seem to be the perennial expectation.

Such statements are, of course, rather gross caricatures. Nevertheless, they do contain a large kernel of truth. It would appear to be the case that in each discipline there is some central theme which dominates the whole enterprise. In the subject of human personhood, regardless of the special discipline involved, the "know thyself" approach does seem to have a certain universal flavor about it. Human beings have always been a mystery to themselves. People never tire of studying themselves. Always an object of wonderment, the human person has always, as far as recorded history can tell us, possessed a decidedly narcissistic bent. Undoubtedly it will continue for a long time into the future.

Under the circumstances, one more book on the meaning of the human person is not too much for the world to take, especially when the aim is not an evaluation of the various possible meanings but simply an attempt to reveal to the reader what they are. What does calling a creature a person mean? How many possible positions are there? All too often efforts along these lines have been superficial, confused, or both. My aim is to delineate carefully the possible root positions on human nature so as to cut through much of the haphazard and extraneous information and observations often found surrounding this particular subject matter.

It is easy enough to recite fact after fact, to index heaps and heaps of data, and to mention the results of thousands of individual experiments. However, organizing the material, most of it interdisciplinary, into some sort of enlightening whole is not so easy. Yet, to arrive at the meaning of being a human person is what the data collecting is ultimately supposed to be all about. What is the meaning of human existence? What difference does it make whether I'm a "person" or not? As we shall see, the answers to these questions depend upon one's view of the whole reality of the universe. Each of the different possible positions is part and parcel of a comprehensive and all-encompassing world view.

In the process of fulfilling this book's purpose I will be referring to the work which has been done, and which is still being done, in various scientific fields of study insofar as the information and the procedures they provide for saying something about the human person are pertinent. In this sense my work may be called a synthesis. Rather than taking each science as separate from all others, I look at each in order to determine how what it says is related to the subject of human nature. This, of course, is no easy task, and the result is not perfect. Nevertheless, the attempt at integration is as important today as it ever was in the past. As the old saying goes, if eating to stay alive is at all important, then half a loaf of bread is better than none. In a similar fashion, any serious effort to say something enlightening about the ways in which the fundamental theories of the human person really differ from each other should be welcomed by anyone interested in the history and destiny of the human race.

Consequently, the fields of psychology, biology, chemistry, and physics must be made to give up their pertinent treasures of information on this subject. An overview then becomes a real possibility. Such an overview, however, cannot be a mere summary of scientific texts. It must rather be, if it is a true synthesis, an overview animated by its own unifying principle. This unity of direction and purpose must be clear throughout the whole of its development. In a word, it must be philosophical.

Does this mean that this analysis cannot be considered a ''scientific'' work? Not necessarily. As we will see later, the nature of science is itself a philosophical question. The advocates of the various views on the human person both agree and disagree on the meaning of science. For the moment, though, there is one view of science which would tend to support the claim that this work is scientific.

According to Karl R. Popper, a work is scientific (or rational) if it is open to refutation via any sort of intersubjective human experience. This is the main point of his work *Conjectures and Refutations* (2nd ed., London, 1965). In this summary of his lifetime of study he has rightly given up trying to specify exactly and precisely from whence come scientific theories in the first place. Such theories exist now and have always existed in one way or another in human history. Nobody can say exactly from what source or sources—tradition, personal experiences, experiments, and so on—they first take shape in the human mind. You can just as well call them conjectures, guesses, or hunches as anything else. According to Popper, good ideas remain good ideas regardless of their source.

Once present, however, they should be open to criticism and positive refutation based upon public information. This is the sign of their rational or scientific nature. I believe that this work fulfills this criterion. It is a well-founded, systematic presentation of the various possible theories on the human person which goes to the root of the matter.

The significance of such a study in the practical order, if it can be successfully carried to completion, hardly needs mentioning. The world today is beset with a whole host of problems, all closely connected with the status of the human person. Some parts of the world are grossly overpopulated; others vastly underpopulated. Everywhere, it seems, there is a problem with the pollution of the environment— from tin cans to chemical and atomic wastes that simply refuse to go away. Economic problems abound also. Much of the world is saddled with both monetary inflation and industrial depression at the same time. Nevertheless, some nations are still relatively rich while others are desperately poor. Even in the rich nations, though, there are many people who worry about being able to stay that way. We must constantly face the question of whether we want more "socialism" with higher and higher taxes or more "capitalism" with taxes held to a rather low level. The shortages of renewable energy resources and the numerous ideological wars of words are, of course, only added concerns. Where will it all end?

Each of these issues is directly and immediately connected up with the answer to the question "Who am I?" Lean one way in your answer, and get the majority of the world to go along with you, and you may at long last come close to developing a real heaven on earth. But, lean another way, and before long you may have the whole world crashing down around your ears. The big question is: Which is which? This book at least makes a contribution to a better understanding of exactly what the problems are in the process of reaching a decision.

Several further points remain to be made. First, the vast majority of quotations from Plato, Aristotle, Lucretius, and Aquinas are based as far as possible upon the original language used by each of these thinkers.

Secondly, I wish to thank John Kuntz for his help with some of the translations; Joseph Owens, C. Ss. R., of the University of Toronto, and José Huertas-Jourda, of the University of Waterloo, for several suggestions and comments which have helped improve the text; and Larry Azar and John Coffey, two past teachers who have greatly contributed to my appreciation of the history of philosophy and science in my search for the meaning of the human person. Also, my many students over the years, who have helped me hammer out the contents of this study by their intelligent questioning, deserve my thanks.

Last, but certainly not least, I want to thank the members of the College Board of Governors for their generous financial support during the year of my sabbatical leave. With their aid I was able to devote myself full-time to this work.

Persons

CHAPTER 1

An Overview

PROBLEMS

Saying that the riddle of the Thebean Sphinx was easy compared to the riddle of the human person would be an understatement. Ask either ordinary people or expert professionals in some particular field of knowledge "Who am I?" and you are more than likely to receive a portentous array of answers.

Is the human person distinguished by his or her intelligence, and, if so, where does it come from? The brain? Does being a genius have to do with the number and depth of the folds in your grey matter? If so, why is it that the brains of great mathematicians such as Gauss and Einstein are no different from the brains of ordinary, uneducated, day laborers? And what about the small brains of little children? Are they a sign that they lack humanity?

Maybe it is not just the brain but the overall mechanism of the body which accounts for "mind." The human body, some might say, is like a greatly refined computer. What, then, are we to do with all those inferior computers which still run on electricity rather than hamburgers and french fries? Should we take steps to be friendly with them and maybe show them some real affection? Is destroying one of these beautiful creations as bad as killing a human being? Or worse?

Then again, maybe humans are created by some "Divine Force" over which we have no control. "The Lord giveth and the Lord taketh away.'' Or are we the result of some alien invasion from outer space which briefly visited our little planet countless years ago? For those who do not believe in God but do believe in Martians, Galactic Battle Ships, and UFO's, this may be the answer. The Olympic gods, once thought dead and gone forever, seem to have made a big comeback in the form of Superman, Batman, and Wonder Woman. Is this our destiny also? Just think about modern evolutionary theory which teaches us all about differential reproduction and the never ending ''progress'' of the human species.

So what is mind? Are we to take seriously all the current publicity about ''out-of-body'' experiences? Can you die and come back again, maybe in a different body? Are all those who claim ESP powers either liars or ignoramuses? How can there be perception without some intervening medium between the person and what is perceived? Not even to mention the question of the authenticity of miracles.

Speaking of evolution, just how do we know a human being when we see one? Should we look to dolphins, porpoises, and chimps to help us find the answers? Of what help are detailed mathematical measurements of physical traits? Is there any physical measurement that can be made upon one individual that can also act as a standard for everyone else in the species? Size? Weight? Color? If changes in the color of butterflies and pigeons can justify placing some of them in a different species, why do we not do the same with people? And besides, how do you know what to measure in the first place if you do not *already* know what is and what is not a human being? When the census taker asks about ''family members,'' should the cat and dog be included?

Maybe it is a mistake to use physical traits to determine what is or is not a human person, but what about some special ability or activity? Let's try something like the power to use some simple reasoning power, such as an elementary syllogistic form. Ask a baboon if it comprehends ''All baboons are mortal, Boom Boom is a baboon, hence Boom Boom is mortal,'' and you'll likely get a blank stare or maybe a banana peel in the face. But then, ask a one-year-old human child the same sort of thing and all that's likely to happen is that you'll be drooled upon, or maybe have a cookie thrown at you. Not a very promising situation.

The confusion with respect to the human, the social and political animal, is no less. Socialism is noncompetitive; capitalism is competitive. You would think that a political system based upon evolutionary theory would be competitive, while one based upon Divine Creation would not be. But in fact in the world today it's just the other way around. The Western democracies praise capitalism, while the Eastern socialists insist upon a policy of "power from above" with unified central planning and no strikes by the workers.

The whole area of male-female relations is also a thorny one today. Are males really superior to females and, if so, in what way or ways? Or is there a strict equality in everything? And, if there is, shouldn't this be reflected in the laws of the land? And, if there isn't, shouldn't this also be legally recognized? Is having more rights for females really unjust? After all, what does justice mean: Dividing up the pie so that everyone, regardless of his or her needs or contributions, gets exactly the same amount, or, giving each person what is due to him or her, which could well mean an unequal distribution? Maybe "women's rights" means that women *should* have *more* rights than men because of their greater contribution to the upbringing of society's future citizens.

The list of important questions is long, and the possibilities for conflicting policies are many. If females are on a par with males, and maybe even of more importance to society, how is it that magazines which consistently depict them as mere lumps of flesh, mainly suited to be sex slaves to males, are allowed to flourish? As soon as someone suggests outlawing them, however, some well-meaning people start shouting "persecution!" and "censorship!" Yet the lawmakers have no qualms whatsoever about controlling all sorts of other things—from "hate literature" directed against various minorities in society to information about what is really going on in government. Why not adopt the *laissez faire* principle with respect to these latter categories as well as with respect to the pornography business, especially in view of the fact that "hate literature," for instance, usually affects only a small percentage of the population while the pornography magazine philosophy affects fully 50 percent or more of the population? Could most of these problems have something to do with our view of what it means to be a human person?

Another currently contested issue is that of capital punishment. Are we to agree with Hegel that a criminal has a right to be punished and that the government has an obligation to punish? If so, how, and to what extent? If each human being can look ahead to a "morning after," would it not be proper to let the criminals among us receive their various suitable punishments then? On the other hand, if there is no continuation of human existence beyond the grave, would it not be proper, in order to make sure that criminals receive their just deserts, for governments to insist that the worse the criminal the more severe the punishment, perhaps even going so far as to torture some of them to death? It could well be consistent with certain theories of the human person to punish now in order to make sure that the criminal really suffers for his or her crime. Again, it all depends upon your view of the human person.

Getting back to evolution again, can we really take seriously statements about some primeval amino acid *striving* to reproduce itself *ad infinitum?* Can the primitive "soup" really be thought of as *willing* the evolution of higher life forms? Isn't this all very "anthropomorphic"? And isn't "anthropos" just the Greek word for "man"?

Is there any way out of such a labyrinth? Yes there is, and the rest of this book represents an effort to provide at least an outline for any future resolution of this most pressing of human problems.

THE NUMBER OF POSITIONS

There are six, *and only six,* possible positions on the place of human beings in the universe relative to other species. These six positions range from the extreme of complete materialism to the extreme of complete spiritualism. In between there are four possible "mixtures" of matter and spirit.

The six positions may be arranged on a line, either horizontally or vertically, with the totally materialistic view at one end and the totally spiritualistic view at the other end. However, for the purposes of this exposition, the six positions should preferably be arranged around a circle. In this way one can see more clearly the actual relationships among them. As possible positions the two extremes are not really so far apart. They do in fact merge or transmute into one another.

Historically the completely spiritualistic extreme arose out of, and as a direct consequence of, the extreme of complete materialism. The same situation exists today, and probably always will. The intellectual necessities of the situation are such that the circle arrangement will remain accurate and contemporary for as long as human beings continue to contemplate their own nature.

THE POPULARITY OF THE SIX POSITIONS

The popularity of each of the six views has not been uniform through the ages. At one time or another one or more of the possible positions will be more popular than others. These shifts in the popularity of one or more view in relation to others is a part of history discovered through the common media of any given age. By looking at the literature, plays, and folk stories, one can see that at one time a more spiritualistic view of human existence prevailed than we find today. Perhaps at some time in the future the situation will change back again. With respect to the present, though, future historians will look back upon the literature, plays, television stories, and radio programs of our own century and note how we tend towards the materialistic extreme in our view of human nature.

However, in any age the historian may care to investigate, at least several of the six possible positions exist together, simultaneously. Every age has both its materialistically inclined thinkers and its spiritualistically inclined thinkers. This, of course, is just as true of our own century as of all past centuries. This is not to say that each of the six possible positions can be found explicitly stated and defended in any given period of human history in the manner in which they are presented here. Indeed, at least one of the views seems to be a rather special product of modern times, while another one is so peculiar that some historians doubt whether its author of two and a half centuries ago really took the position seriously himself. My only point is that these are *possible* positions, all of which must be discussed if the field of basically different views on the human person is to be exhausted. Furthermore, in terms of the extremes of complete materialism and complete spiritualism, no one age can claim a monopoly on tendencies in one direction or another.

A COMMON PITFALL AVOIDED

This exposition of these six views avoids the confusion one usually encounters in the study of human nature, that caused by what the logician refers to as a "cross-division." One frequently finds the nature of human beings discussed under a whole series of headings which take no cognizance of the most elementary rules of logical division and presentation. For instance, headings such as Humanistic (perhaps the most abused term in this area), Existential, Pragmatic, Christian-Stoic, Scientific, Transcendental, Materialistic, Analytic, Monism, Dualism, Epiphenomenalism, and Interactionism are still quite common today.

But as anyone versed in elementary logic knows, this is like dividing "food" into subclasses such as salty, served on a paper plate, hamburgers, eaten in New York, and the like. Or imagine dividing up "humankind" into the subclasses of tall, fathers, bricklayers, Americans, baseball fans, and so on. The overlapping of categories destroys at the outset any chance for a clear understanding of the various alternatives to be found under the main heading. A basic and primary rule of logical division is that one and only one criterion be used when making the division. By jumping around from one standard, or basis for division, to another, the whole list becomes badly muddled and uninformative. This presentation attempts to avoid this shortcoming all too often found in the study of the human person.[1]

The intention is also to avoid a common variation on the cross-division approach to the subject of the human person, which is simply to snip a little here and a little there out of the great wealth of written material on the nature of human beings. These passages are then collected together and presented to the reader in some kind of chronological or alphabetical order. Somehow or other these anthologies are supposed to be useful and helpful to someone trying to understand the human person. In fact, however, they are not.

At best, long anthologies can do no more than provide a certain amount of raw material to be analyzed and ordered into some truly comprehensive and useful form. The editors of these anthologies rarely attempt such a move. Most often one is left on one's own to make some sense out of the many and various opinions. And if and when such a comprehensive appraisal is attempted, it usually ends up representing a retrogression to the cross-division type of subgrouping mentioned earlier.[2]

THE ONE CRITERION

The central problem one must seek to resolve with respect to the human person is the status of human beings as a species. Mankind is one species among many in the universe. What is the relationship of the human species to other species? Is there a continuity with other species, especially the "higher" primates? If so, in what respect? Is there a discontinuity with other species, again especially with respect to the great apes and monkeys of the world? If so, in what way or ways are human beings as a species different from their fellow creatures in the world?

At the outset there certainly seems to be some kind of overlapping of other species with humans. Does it make any sense to ask whether people are superior or inferior to other kinds of living things? Are not all creatures ultimately on a level? Is an individual human being really any better than his or her pet dog or cat? Our problem then is one of attempting to determine what criterion would cause the human species to be ranked in a hierarchy above or below the other creatures in the biosphere.

Historically speaking, this criterion has always been sought in the area of mind, reason, and spirit. When humankind as a species has been compared with other species, it has always been mind, reason, or spirit which has been either exalted or suppressed in the comparison process. Consequently, to be true to the history of the subject, this is the aspect of human nature upon which attention must be concentrated.

The key questions then become questions about the nature and extend of mind. To what extent is mind or spirit or soul to be identified with the body? How many basically different ways are there of distinguishing mind and matter in human beings? How much reality is to be attributed to mind as separate from matter?

As it turns out, there are six basic ways of answering these questions. Each of the answers proposes a different way of viewing human beings in relation to the other creatures in the material world. They range from the extreme of complete materialism to the extreme of complete spiritualism. That is to say, there is a complete denial of soul at one end of the spectrum of views and a complete denial of the very existence of body, or indeed any matter at all, at the other end. In between appear the more commonly held and widespread positions.

My intention is to look at each one separately in order to determine its central doctrines, to say something about its origins and background, and to list some of its major consequences in the worlds of science and society. In the process I hope to be able to state exactly how the six positions differ from each other, especially with respect to the positions juxtaposed on either side of any one given view. In this way the reader will be able to see easily and quickly the options open to someone interested in finding a place for himself or herself in and among the many other creatures in the world. This work will put you in a position to decide for yourself what you are as a human person.

RESTRICTIONS

These pages are meant as an essay concentrating on only one aspect of human nature. They should not be taken as a complete compendium of everything and anything there is to say about humankind, not even of everything important which can be said on the subject of the human person. When the subject is human nature, the idea of a definitive treatment within the covers of one book is beyond imagination. Where human beings are involved, everything is related to us in one way or another. The investigator who thinks all the answers can be found within the psychology department of a large university will soon be disappointed and would quickly discover that every other social science has a sizable contribution of knowledge to make to a more complete understanding of what being a human being means.

But no sooner has this been revealed than the investigator would also be informed that the biology department has no intention of being left out of the picture. To the extent that biology is dependent upon physics and chemistry, these two subjects also become important. At this point the investigator would have to take into account a great deal of mathematics as well, since a knowledge of mathematics is essential to any of the physical sciences. And even then the task would not be finished. After mathematics had been mastered the theologian would be waiting to have a say in the matter. By the time the investigator had finished following one lead to another, he or she would have worked around the whole circle of human learning. Quite obviously, then, my essay on the various views concerning the status of persons cannot hope to do any more than barely fulfill its self-imposed limitations.

Another type of self-imposed restriction must also be mentioned. The reader will find that I have, in the interests of staying uncluttered and conserving words, followed the wide and steady courses of the mainstreams of thought. This may be most obvious in my treatment of the fourth view, wherein I stick rather closely to the ''Toronto School'' of Thomism as represented by E. Gilson. Without a doubt, *each* of the mainstreams has numerous tributaries and rivulets attached to it, and to try to discuss every one of them would require more words than any sane person would be willing to wade through—*quot homines tot sententiae*. The thousands of subschools, accidental variations, and dissident positions are quite impossible to manage with any degree of care. Consequently I will not even attempt doing such an impossible thing.

NAMES AND LABELS

What shall we call the six possible positions on the human person? Since the imposition of names or labels is a strictly arbitrary affair, I have tried to pick out names which are somewhat descriptive of the positions for which I mean them to stand. If such titles are unpleasant, in the sense of conjuring up images and notions which are not considered to be honorable or even honest, I am perfectly willing to alter them. However, will their replacements really be any better in view of what the doctrine itself stands for?[3]

One way around this problem might be to give up names altogether and simply stick to using numbers. This is possible but unnecessarily sparse and colorless. More descriptive labels do serve at least a minimal pedagogic purpose. They can alert the reader to inherent differences among the various views, as well as serving as a basis for comparison when attempting to fit in some thinker's view not explicitly mentioned in these pages. All in all, then, it would be helpful to anyone interested in the question of human nature to have the possible positions set out in the following fashion:

1. *Reductionistic Materialism.* This is the most extreme view of the human person at the materialistic end of the spectrum. It attempts to analyze all human experiences in terms of matter in motion. Those who advocate such a position, such as B. F. Skinner, believe that this approach to human nature is necessary for scientific reasons. As a result, any reference to "mind" or "soul" or "spirit" as a true causal agent in human affairs must be ruled out as mere superstition.

2. *Nonreductionistic Materialism.* This represents the next step up the scale and around the circle away from a complete, that is, reductionistic, materialism. Those in this camp, such as John Dewey and Karl Marx, regard references to mind or spirit as quite respectable from the scientific viewpoint. Such references are in fact necessary if the scientific investigator is to remain true to the facts of human experience. Human beings do possess a "soul." However, the existence of such a thing as an important aspect of the human person is not to be taken literally. That is to say, talk about the soul should not be interpreted as indicating the existence of something really immaterial and existing, even for a while, as really distinct from the material components of the body.

3. *Psychosomaticism Without Immortality.* This position represents the continued "dematerialization" of the human person. This, however, is not to deny the facts used in support of the previous view. True, the human being is *both* body and soul. However, it is also true according to this view that the soul is really distinct and immaterial with respect to its body. The mind or soul or spirit of a person cannot be regarded as merely a function of the body. It exists in its own right as the organizing principle of the body. It is what gives unity to the organism. Indeed, the term "organism" cannot even be used unless the existence of the immaterial soul is admitted. Nevertheless, the soul is not immortal. Body and soul die together.

4. *Psychosomaticism with Immortality.* In this position the soul advances to the point of being a true substance in its own right. It is not only the "form" of the body but is also subsistent. While alive the body and soul constitute one organism, just as maintained by the previous position. The body is neither some unnecessary accident temporarily connected with the soul nor is the body the source of the mind. Rather, it is the other way around. The soul is the cause of its organized body. The soul, which can exist alone, is the source through which the body exists as a body. Since the soul does not depend upon the body to exist, but vice versa, it can survive

the body. Hence, at least the immortality of the soul is guaranteed. In addition, however, since the soul and body constitute one natural union, the religious doctrine of the resurrection of the body, to reconstitute one human being in the future, becomes a reasonable expectation.

5. *Vitalism.* In this position the soul does not become any more spiritual, but it does alter its relationship to the body. The body now becomes unnecessary, and even an evil, with respect to the soul. The soul and body are no longer one thing in life, but two things forever separate and opposed to each other. On this view, the preexistence of the soul becomes likely. Moreover, it would then also make sense to speak about the transmigration of the "person" from one body to another in some future life, or series of lives, until some final rest and salvation is achieved.

6. *Reductionistic Immaterialism.* This position takes us full circle. The reverse side to the completely materialistic view of the human person is the completely spiritualistic view of human nature. Beginning where the reductionistic materialist leaves off with respect to the stages of the argument used to establish the first position, those in the sixth position go ahead to develop an argument to show that precisely the reverse is true.

The result of this line of reasoning, from the point of view of the human's place in the universe relative to other things, is that the body is utterly denied as possessing any real existence independently of the mind. Instead of a war between the body and the soul, with each soul occupying the place of the only and true person, it is maintained that there is no body at all in any material sense. As an extreme position the sixth view is comparable to the first. Yet, surprisingly enough, it is as serious and respectable a piece of "scientific" reasoning as is the first position.

The various views may be set out in the fashion shown in the chart on page 14.

Each heading is subdivided into two subheadings. This process is continued until the six basic positions on the human person are reached. These paradigms constitute, so to speak, the "lowest species" with respect to the essentially different views on the human person given the standard of division which I have chosen to use. As you will note further, it is possible to draw a line from position one to position six so that the extreme views are at each end of the line. This physical arrangement reflects what each one in fact purports to repre-

A CHART OF THE SIX THEORIES

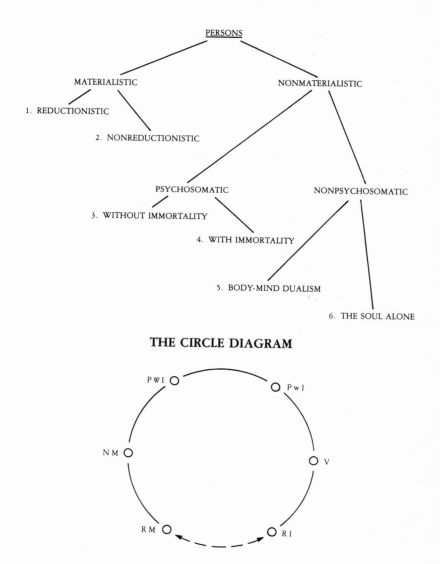

PERSONS

MATERIALISTIC   NONMATERIALISTIC

1. REDUCTIONISTIC

 2. NONREDUCTIONISTIC

   PSYCHOSOMATIC   NONPSYCHOSOMATIC

3. WITHOUT IMMORTALITY

   4. WITH IMMORTALITY

   5. BODY-MIND DUALISM

     6. THE SOUL ALONE

THE CIRCLE DIAGRAM

P w̄ I   P w I

N M   V

R M   R I

sent concerning the human person, that is, the extremes are truly at the extremes.

Now let us take this line and bend it into a circle and see what happens. This produces the circle diagram mentioned earlier. This arrangement, as we will see, has the advantage of illustrating how positions one and six transmute into one another due to their own internal necessities. Although, ontologically speaking, the extreme of reductionistic materialism is certainly essentially different from that of reductionistic immaterialism, the *methodological* problems involved in defending either one are such that we can never be sure that we have established one to the exclusion of the other. This circle diagram would appear as shown on page 14.

It must be emphasized that each of these theories or paradigms is separate and mutually exclusive with respect to each of the others. As the following chapters will show, it makes no sense to try to lump together the reductionistic materialism view and the nonreductionistic materialism view. Even though, at first sight, they may appear to be merely variations on a pantheistic worldview, in fact they are quite different. Whether or not there are, objectively speaking and independently of the investigator's own mind, real hierarchies in nature is a question of crucial importance. A nonreductionistic materialist takes the hierarchies of nature quite seriously. To say otherwise would be an insult to such a thinker. Even though both are only matter, a human being *is* better, truly and objectively, than a dog or cat. To deny this would be completely false—and unscientific. In other words, there are materialists, and then there are materialists.

In the same way, those following the psychosomaticism with immortality paradigm would be very uncomfortable, indeed downright upset, over the prospect of being lumped together with those in the psychosomaticism-without-immortality position. There is just no way in which the immortality of each human being can be arbitrarily eliminated. As we will see, there is no room for an intermediate position between these two theories. An immortal human person suddenly becoming mortal, or vice versa, simply does not make any rational sense. Those in both of these juxtaposed camps know this full well and would strongly resist an attempt to marry them—with or without a shotgun.

The same is true of the last two possible theories, except that here it is much more obvious. Nobody could miss the difference between those who say human beings have three-dimensional, extramental material bodies which exist independently of any mind whether human or divine, and those who deny it. Regardless of what may be explained, or explained away, as being mere appearance, when it comes to an understanding of the way things *really* are, vitalism and reductionistic *im*materialism are separated by an insurmountable barrier.

If you consider the situation with respect to the second and third theories and the fourth and fifth paradigms, it would be the same. Nonreductionistic materialism and psychosomaticism without immortality want very little to do with each other. Indeed, if each remains true to its own inner necessities (as with all the other views), they *cannot* get together. The radically different ways in which each explains the fact of extramental hierarchies in nature rules out any bridge between the two positions. You may *change* your position, but you cannot unite the positions.

The psychosomaticist with immortality and the vitalist are in the same boat. Both place a heavy emphasis upon the very special and distinctive character of the human soul. Yet neither one would want to be seen keeping company with the other. The former would feel denuded by the vitalistic denial of the importance of the body. The latter, on the other hand, would feel contaminated by the former's insistence upon the unity between body and soul.

Nevertheless, despite their essential difference, both views are such that no other view can intervene between them as long as we continue to stick to our single basis for division. The nature of the soul is such that it must remain immortal once in existence. Both parties would regard any doctrine teaching that there could be a sudden shift from immortality to mortality as unthinkable.

So, to expand a little upon what was said at the beginning of this section, it is possible to object to so-and-so's being placed in a certain "school," but it is impossible to do away with classification altogether. Some modern commentators may object to the "labeling" or "pigeonholing" of the great thinkers of the past and present into various "schools" or "isms." Nevertheless, a study of these same great minds makes such labeling inevitable because one of the things revealed by such study is that, although some moderns may object to the very idea of classification, the great thinkers of the past and present themselves never harbored such misgivings. In fact, in contrast to those who may hold such fears, in the vast majority of cases the thinkers themselves were very careful, within the purview of their knowledge at the time, to situate their own position relative to others.

CHAPTER **2**

Reductionistic
Materialism

THE POSITION

Man and Nature

The central doctrine of reductionism as it applies to human nature is that there are no essential differences among things which exist in the universe. This is a truly radical view, certainly not the commonsense view of anybody living in the world, not even of the scientist studying human beings. To the ordinary person in his or her ordinary life the world is composed of hierarchies in which some things are in essence truly and really superior or inferior to other things. The differences are not merely matters of accidental degrees. Rank on rank the many and various species of mineral, plant, and animal, and finally humankind, rise up to form a pyramid of increasing excellence in the universe. There are truly qualitative differences of type existing up and down the scale of creatures around us. For someone to say that it is not really so strains the imagination of the average person.

Even those who make such claims do not come upon this conclusion by way of ordinary observation. The reductionist must reason his or her way to the reductionistic position. As an ordinary person he or she lives in the same world as his or her next-door neighbor. But as a thinker he or she can view the universe quite differently. A good example of a reductionist in the twentieth century would be B. F. Skinner, the noted psychologist.

After many years of thought and contemplation, not to mention numerous research projects, Skinner wrote *About Behaviorism* as a summary of his lifetime of study. Skinner is very self-conscious about the radical nature of his proposed program. "As the philosophy of the science of behavior," he tells his readers, "behaviorism calls for probably the most drastic change ever proposed in our way of thinking about man."[1] The drastic change of which he speaks is precisely the reductionistic view of human nature. Human beings, despite appearances to the contrary, are on a par with everything else in the universe. The elements of matter which go into the constitution of the moon and Mars are the same ones which go into the constitution of human beings. For this reason, a scientist should analyze a human person in the same way as a worm or monkey. "I know of no essentially human feature that has been shown to be beyond the reach of scientific analysis," asserts the Harvard psychologist.[2]

As a result of the totally materialistic evolution of the material parts of the universe, the human species has been formed by the pushes and shoves of one part of matter interacting with other parts. Today we are still dominated by pushes and "drives" which propel us forward along life's path. The secret of success in human affairs is to utilize this knowledge of what we really are in order to control the future destiny of the human race. This is our only hope for salvation in the world today. We cannot depend solely on the physical and biological sciences which have so dominated our recent past. They have only served to create for mankind more problems than they have solved in destruction, pollution, and selfish, self-satisfied ways of behavior. The future belongs now to the science of behavior. If the physical sciences have failed to save us, the social sciences are ready and willing to take over. They, at least, cannot be said to have failed, states Skinner, because they, and especially behaviorism, have "scarcely been tried."[3]

The Three Steps

The movement from ordinary observation to the scientific understanding of the way things really are with respect to human beings proceeds in three steps or stages. First comes a definition of the scientific method, then a statement of its consequences in general, and finally an application of its consequences to the human species.

Reductionists insist upon the need to be scientific. By science they mean the pragmatic results of concrete experimentations. For them the scientific method is the experimental method conceived in strictly material terms. To classify as a truly scientific experiment, the work must possess certain traits which will always and everywhere serve to distinguish science from mere emotional opinion. These features are repeatability, intersubjectivity, and the scope of applicability to things of the same nature. In other words, anyone familiar with the techniques of a given scientific field must be able to repeat a colleague's work in the area in which it was originally performed, as well as extend the same techniques to similar areas within the same field, and get the same results. There is no room in science for the purely subjective experience. People who claim purely private results for their work may qualify as mystics or poets or the like, but they cannot be called scientists. The purely autobiographical statement is fine in literature, but it must not be allowed to penetrate into science. Everything in science must be public, open, and above board.

True science is not afraid to submit its results to impartial and objective inspection by others in that field of study. For someone to claim that he or she has made a tremendous scientific discovery and then refuse to allow anyone else to check the results in a public manner would be the very negation of the scientific attitude. No one of any intellectual status would allow himself or herself to be fooled by such a claim. People would immediately recognize the person making the claim as a charlatan and proceed to expel that person from the scientific community. This course of action would be the only one open to the true scientist.

As a deduction from this starting point it follows that subjectivism is the one great enemy of true science. There is no room in science for mysterious forces which cannot be made public through measurement and physical observation. Appeals to the unseen in any form must be rejected as being outside the pale of true scientific behavior. This ban would of course apply to human feelings and emotions. Private experiences of any kind may be important to the individual having such experiences, but they cannot be of any value whatsoever to the scientific community. Unless the experiences can be made public and open to measurable observation by all, they must be kept out of any scientific appraisal of the situation.

Quite obviously, then, as the third step reveals, any reference to unseen forces or causes in human behavior must be rejected as prescientific. This would be especially true of the mind (or the self, soul, psyche) in human beings. "There is no place in the scientific position for a self as a true originator or initiator of action," Skinner states quite consistently.[4] He certainly cannot allow the existence in human beings of something which must be rejected from every other area of the universe. It follows, therefore, that the truly scientific social scientist must rigorously adhere to the same scientific principles as all other reputable scientists in the world.

Hence, since he is forbidden to make any reference to mind, he is forced into the position of replacing all references to mental states by descriptions of the behavior by which they are known to the investigator. Such descriptions would be open to public inspection, open to repeated testing, and capable of being recorded for the use of future investigators. In other words, behaviorism (reductionism) is not simply a possible scientific approach to the human species; it is the *only* approach worthy of the name.

Yet Skinner does at times reject the title "reductionist." The word has sometimes been used in a derogatory way to describe his philosophy of behaviorism. To avoid such derogatory connotations, he would just as soon not be known by that title at all. He even attempts to remove the label from behaviorism. He tells us that behaviorism does not attempt to *reduce* feelings to bodily states, or thought to behavior, or morality to various features of the social environment. Instead, it simply affirms that bodily states *are* what is felt, that thought can be analyzed in terms of behavior, and that the social environment has "always been responsible for moral behavior."[5]

However, an objective appraisal of Skinner's rebuttal would have to say that rather than denying his own reductionism, he is affirming it. What he is saying in effect is that there is no need to reduce anything to anything else because it already exists in a reduced state. By following the scientific method in a consistent and unflinching manner, he has arrived at the correct conclusion concerning human nature, so that there is no need to start at some higher level in order to reduce something to something else. He has arrived at the something else directly and smoothly with one grand sweep of the scientific method.

The argument, therefore, is airtight. It may be rejected, but not on scientific grounds. It may even be regarded as irrelevant to the ordinary nonscientific person. As far as the average person is concerned, or even as far as the scientist in off moments is concerned, things can go on as usual. Even though reductionism is the proper scientific position on humankind, "Yet there is nothing in a science of behavior or its philosophy which need alter feelings or introspective observations."[6] The facts of experience could very well always remain the same. What must change, however, is the old-fashioned view of what *explains* the facts. The true explanation, derived from the true scientific method, is reductionism.

BACKGROUND

Method and Nature

At this point one might wonder why making a philosophy of human nature out of a scientific method is necessary. Strictly speaking it is not. In fact, though, the step from method of procedure to fact of nature has been taken in the past. Indeed it is very hard to resist taking such a step. The point of the meaning of science is to be pragmatic, concrete, in the world, productive. It is not merely an interesting intellectual game one plays on Sunday afternoons. If science cannot tell us what is true about the world, reason the reductionists, then it is no better than the old armchair philosophies of the world conjured up in prescientific days.

This at least was the attitude of John Broadus Watson, the Johns Hopkins University psychologist who has pretty well set the tone for all of twentieth-century reductionism. He explained at one time how behaviorism, in its early days, always had to be on the defensive. It was very new and radical, and many of the orthodox psychologists of the time found it highly obnoxious. One way of escaping much of the adverse criticism was to say simply that behaviorism, with its stimulus-response experimental technique, was only a methodology. It made no claims about the true nature of things. It was merely a successful device for investigating psychological phenomena and nothing more. But after a while the situation changed. The shoe was on the other foot. No longer need the reductionist be ashamed of his views. He could now launch a counterattack. Let the critics prove, using the scientific method, that they had anything of value to offer on the nature of mankind. Where is the objective evidence for mind and consciousness? There is none. It is time then to stop pretending that S-R is only a method. Rather, it must henceforth be regarded as the fact of nature and not just as the tool of science. So argued Watson.[7]

The Two Levels

Historically speaking, of course, the reductionistic position is much older than the twentieth century. Its roots lie far back in history. In its conclusions modern materialism is but a variation on the ancient materialism of several Greek thinkers, such as Democritus (480-390 B.C.) and Epicurus (341-270 B.C.), and the Roman poet-philosopher Lucretius (99-55 B.C.). As a matter of fact the ancient doctrine of atomism was an attempt by some Greek intellectuals to circumvent the problem of change in the world bequeathed to them by that great father of all Greek philosophy, Parmenides of Elea.[8] Parmenides reasoned in the following manner:

1. Only intellect can be trusted to tell us what is true about the universe.
2. Intellect tells us that when something has real existence, it must be totally and completely actual.
3. But then it follows that such a thing cannot change in any way. To change means to become something it presently is not. It makes sense for a sitting person to stand up (a form of not-sitting) but not to change to a sitting position. Likewise for everything in the universe.
4. The only way to get around this problem is to talk about nonexistence as real. But this is impossible. Nonexistence can neither be known nor expressed. Hence, all change, motion, and alteration is a deception; a mere appearance shown to us by the one unchanging Being.

The ancient atomists took Parmenides seriously. Their doctrine was not the result of any kind of inspired guess. They could think of no way out of his argument except by affirming the real existence of nonexistence, which they called the empty, the void, or empty space. What Parmenides referred to as the one unchanging real existence, the atomists made into the atoms. Each atom is eternal and unchanging. It is possible, though, for there to be many different atoms with different sizes and shapes. By changing their positions relative to each other, these "uncuttables" would lump together to form the bodies we observe in the universe. By simultaneously affirming the existence of the little specks of matter which differ only in size, shape, and position and the existence of the *inane* or void (nonexistence), these thinkers thought they could save the appearances of change in the world.[9]

The Main Point

The important, pertinent point to be noticed here is the way in which all reality of a positive nature is regarded as being built up out of tiny specks of matter all of which are on a par. No one speck is ultimately any better or worse than any other one. Precisely here do we find the root of all reductionisms. Even later in history, when the atoms become much more complicated, this basic notion was preserved. It was even preserved when some later thinkers wanted to regard the universe as made up of a continuous mass of matter, a pure extension with no voids or gaps between the parts.[10] Even here matter was considered all on a par. Whether the universe is composed of one matter (extension) or many (atoms), then, the results are the same: Ultimately all the material parts are of equal value. Everything observed comes about by a combination of the internally unchanging, unobserved, and equally noble minute parts of matter.

A Secondary Point

There is also another important point to be noted here. In fact this point played the central role in the deduction of the total immaterialism of George Berkeley, who added further steps to the chain of reasoning after the reintroduction and widespread acceptance of at least a methodological materialism during the European scientific revolution. As the ancient atomists fully realized, their doctrine necessitated a separation between the primary qualities of matter and the secondary sense qualities of material things. The microcosm and the macrocosm must each possess different features. The traits of shape, size, and position are really in the particles of matter which come together to form the observable bodies of sense experience. All other qualities, however, such as color, smell, taste, hardness and roughness, temperature, and so forth, are not really in the material body. They exist only in the observer. As Lucretius states:

> Now pay attention to what I have figured out, and don't think that the bright things you see are white because they are composed of white parts, or that black are black because they are made up of black parts, or that things of any color whatsoever are composed of parts bearing that color. For the bodies of matter have no color at all either like or unlike the things you see as colored.[11]

And furthermore: "But lest you unfortunately suppose that this is true only of color, know also that atoms are totally devoid of warmth, cold, and violent heat, and are barren of sound and drained of moisture, and have no scent of their own."[12]

This assumption was not gratuitous, hasty, or unnecessary on his part. It was dictated by the very nature of the subject matter. The basic principle at work here is that the principles of explanation must not bear the same qualities which they are supposed to explain. It is a universally accepted principle of reason regardless of the age of the thinker. No scientist, for instance, would dream of explaining the green color of chlorine gas by saying that it was made up of little green parts, each of which in turn was composed of little green parts, and so on *ad infinitum*. This is something known to all reasonable reductionists, both past and present.

During the later Renaissance Lucretius was reintroduced to Europe after many centuries of neglect. His doctrine gradually built up a large following. His followers, at least as far as the physical sciences are concerned, included Gassendi, Boyle, Newton, Dalton, Gay-Lussac, Ampere, Avogadro, and many others. When this influence in science was combined with the equally great contemporary philosophical influence of René Descartes during the same period, the trend towards reductionism could not be stopped. Even though Descartes did not allow for the existence of voids between material particles, his continuous matter (extension) possessed the same mathematical qualities as the atoms when it was broken up into pieces and regarded as moving around. Viewing all of material nature as being on a par soon became the only respectable scientific approach. There is only one type of matter, each part of which is equal in dignity to every other part. Hierarchies in nature are secondary. They are constructed out of minute parts of matter and *ultimately* are reducible to those parts with nothing left over. This is reductionism, *the* scientific view of nature. Combine this background with Skinner's view of *the* scientific method, which is equated with public retestable experiments demanding nonsubjective factors, and the reductionist program is perfectly consistent with modern science.[13]

In this sense Skinner is part of the "physics" tradition in psychology. This tradition, in modern times, began with the French materialists of the eighteenth century who discarded the minds or souls which Descartes had placed in his material human bodies. In the nineteenth century this approach to "man the machine" was given added scientific support with the introduction of experimental techniques designed to test human beings as a physicist might test some material subsection of the universe. Psychology became the province of the physiologists. This school has continued through to the present time. G.T. Fechner, Ivan Pavlov, John B. Watson, and B.F. Skinner are some of its well-known members.[14]

That the influence of this school of thought has become deeply ingrained in all aspects of modern life does not need much defense. Everything today *must* be reduced to numbers and formulas. The omnipresent computers which so dominate all aspects of contemporary life cannot be spoken to in any other language. This is certainly obvious enough in the physical sciences, as it is in the social sciences which so much desire to emulate their elder relatives.

Even without being a professional in some scientific study, though, one can see this easily enough, at least those who know what they are looking for can. Some examples would be the rapid growth of public-opinion polls as every media organization and every political party strives to put numbers on its popularity. Any doubts about whether or not you can be sure that what people *say* will coincide with what they *do,* and whether or not a few samples from here and there are really representative of the masses, are pushed aside. Even more obvious is the typical evening news weather report which tells you that there is a 10 percent chance of rain tomorrow. The reporter could just as well say that there's a 90 percent or a 1 percent chance of rain. He can *always* be sure he's right—*regardless of what actually happens!*

The modern approach to reality seems to be to use numbers simply for the sake of using numbers. Why? Because this is the *only* way you can handle a reductionistic universe. Not to use numbers is to admit that you are not scientific, something no self-respecting prognosticator in any field would ever want to admit. The background to this situation, however, has nothing to do with whether or not careful measurements are really useful and informative in many cases. It has rather to do with a view of the universe, a view *deduced* from a definition of science, not induced from any set of numerical data. In contrast to the other paradigms, then, for reductionism mathematics and physics are the king and queen of the sciences.

SOME CONSEQUENCES

The Atoms Blindly Run

In 1795 the French mathematician Pierre Simon de LaPlace wrote the first edition of *A Philosophical Essay On Probabilities.* It has since become a classical statement of the first and primary implication of reductionism in the material universe. At the beginning of chapter 2 he states that everything that happens has a cause and that it is an illusion to think that something can happen without some previously given set of determining factors. These factors may be obscured and hidden from the direct view of the human observer. Nevertheless, they are there and acting all the time. We may be ignorant of the exact nature of these hidden forces, but we cannot deny their existence on account of such ignorance. As time goes on, and as our ignorance is progressively dispelled, the material universe will become less and less mysterious. Theoretically speaking there is no reason not to suppose that in the future every secret of the universe will be revealed. Perhaps within the compass of one formula the scientist will be able to comprehend all the causes propelling bodies along their respective ways and thereby also be empowered to predict with great exactness and precision their every future movement and disposition.

According to LaPlace, given a super intellect able to gather and analyze all the data on the universe at any one instant of time, the whole universe would become an open book. Encouraged by Newton's great accomplishment a century earlier, LaPlace can imagine a situation in which *everything* in the universe, not just our own system of sun and planets, would be comprehended in one set of laws. In that day "nothing would be uncertain," and the whole past and future of the universe would appear as "present."[15]

What does this mean with respect to human nature? Anyone who proposes any view at all on human nature would agree that human beings are alive. Every investigator would also agree that the differences among living things go deeper than their external appearances or morphology. Furthermore, when considering nonliving things in comparison with living things, everyone would affirm that there, too, vast differences exist. What everyone is concerned with, therefore, is not the fact of differences but the "how" or "why" of the differences. In a system which reduces biology to physics, namely, reductionism, the "how" must be explained in terms of the minute particles of matter moving around in space. By regarding mind, as well as every other observed difference, as merely the results of material rearrangement, it could be eliminated altogether. All mental activities, as well as all vital and nonvital activities, are caused by some physical change in the underlying material structure of the body exhibiting such activities. Given such a view, human beings, like everything else, become a part of quantitative nature. As simply another part of nature the various physical sciences should, in theory at least, be able to explain human activities without the help of any other kind of knowledge, such as mind as a causal factor. Even psychology cannot be considered a separate science.

Predictability

Obviously, then, there is no more room for any kind of true freedom in human beings than there is in the stars or the ocean waves. In the same way that a physicist would study any other sample of matter in motion, the reductionist would consider all human activities, even the most exalted types, as merely mechanical processes shared to one extent or another with all other creatures. Thinking itself becomes a mechanical transformation of stimuli into responses, of nerves and fibers and electrons, of input and feedback mechanisms. Where among all these moving little parts can freedom creep in? Nowhere.

Skinner himself is well aware that a complete denial of freedom is a necessary consequence of the reductionistic position. Others may shun this consequence, but not the strict scientist. In an earlier work, *Beyond Freedom and Dignity,* he tries to make precisely this central point. A sentimental approach to human nature may be able to maintain some semblance of the old-fashioned respect for individual human freedom, but the least familiarity with the scientific method and its necessities soon destroys such out-moded sentiments and feelings. "A scientific analysis of behavior," reasons Skinner, "dispossesses autonomous man and turns the control he has been said to exert over to the environment."[16] Human beings do not really choose what they want, they are pushed into what they get by the blind forces of nature. The scientist knows this. The unscientific, sentimental person does not. "The direction of the controlling relation is reversed: a person does not act upon the world, the world acts upon him."[17]

The strict behaviorist is not so naive as to believe that he can always isolate a simple one-to-one correspondence between one stimulus and one response. There is, rather, a complex of initial events leading to other events. Rather than a one-to-one relationship there is an association of various stimuli and responses built up over a long period of time. The response, therefore, will often appear to be greater than the immediate cause even though no mind or soul underlies the reaction. The investigator must work with sets of things, not merely single triggers and reflexes. Nowhere in this system, though, is there any room for freedom. Ultimately, human beings are just as predictable as anything else in physical nature. Appeals to reason, conscience, inner feelings, and so forth are really a waste of time.

The task of the modern scientist is to get on with the business of determining in detail what conditions give rise to what behavior and then to change the conditions to elicit the behavior society desires. A recognition of the truth of reductionism is the only scientific salvation for the modern world. Only then will social reformers be in a position to stop wasting time, money, and effort on approaches that are sure to fail. As long as true science is ignored, society will continue to stumble along, its legs hobbled by the illusion of freedom. The road to a healthy society, one capable of walking straight and tall, is to realize once and for all that mental events are simply built up out of certain sets of physical events. These physical events can be controlled. In other words, the first step is to admit the truth of reductionism. The second step is to act on it. This is what science tells us.

Consistency

In the sense that Skinner is willing to do away with any real freedom, novelty, and objective unpredictability in the world he is far more consistent than his predecessor Lucretius. The ancient reductionistic view covered everything in the universe from the Greek gods to the human mind or soul. It was said that only the very finest of atoms go into the constitution of the distant and indifferent gods which inhabit the empty regions between the worlds and also into the constitution of the mind. The mind is a balance of atoms closely resembling those of air, wind, and fire, plus the "nameless" atoms. These exceedingly fine atoms are concentrated in the chest area, but they also spread throughout the whole body.

On the surface it would appear that Lucretius has outlined a strictly deterministic system. Pieces of matter are pushed and pulled around by physical forces without any overall direction except for those laws of nature which have accidently been worked out over the centuries. When the temperature rises above a certain level, ice melts. Ice never says, "No, not this time." Nevertheless, Lucretius bends over backwards to modify his system to allow some degree of freedom for people. The rigid cause-effect relationships found in material interactions must somehow be broken. He accomplishes this in the following way.

All cognition is supposedly the result of sense impressions. Atoms peeling off from the surface of objects literally travel through space to the human sense organs. They are then transferred to the region of the heart and finally to the "nameless" elements within the mind. Here ideas are formed by combining and separating images.

The process may also work in the opposite direction. An image may originate in the "fourth" or "nameless" nature, be transferred to the rest of the mind atoms, and finally reach the body atoms. How are these reverse processes begun? There is, first of all, sensory stimulation from external causes. But there is also something else. Within the soul there is an uncaused motion of atoms: They "swerve." This strange innovation is totally unexplained. It is just there, even though not directly experienced. In order to give people freedom Lucretius finds it necessary to balance his doctrine of absolute determinism against a doctrine of absolute chance.[18]

George Sarton, the modern father of the history of science in the English-speaking world, describes these two qualifications (the "nameless" and the "swerve") of the reductionistic system as nothing less than "extraordinary."[19] And indeed they are. They go against everything Lucretius thought atomism stood for. In order to endow humans with freedom, he introduced into his system the same kind of thing he was originally so much against, namely, unexplainable, mysterious forces. This time, however, such forces are completely at variance with his system and must be thrown in as a stage trick in a last desperate attempt to save the human ability to choose freely.

This may sound rather old and out-dated. Nevertheless, a review of twentieth-century literature shows that it isn't. Take, for instance, the relatively recent *The Concept of Mind* (1949) by Gilbert Ryle. In the tradition of Ludwig Wittgenstein, this well-known English thinker wanted to regard philosophy as primarily a vehicle for clarifying language. Originally very much interested in scientific language and in the creation of artificial languages which would keep all communications neatly scientific, the Linguistic Philosophy Movement soon turned to "ordinary" language as its base of operation. And what does one immediately discover about ordinary language except that, due to its usually confused and ambiguous condition, it is eminently unsuited to scientific and philosophical discussion? Perhaps the modern professional philosopher should concentrate on clarifying ordinary language and thereby the very old human problems in philosophy.

Ryle was concerned with the ancient dichotomy between mind and body. Could such a paradigm be nothing more than a "category mistake," that is, the failure to realize that the way we talk is primarily responsible for the impression, however untrue it may be, that the body and mind are really two separate and independent entities? Ryle thought it was and proceeded to explain how language can be altered to do away with such a dichotomy. Although it would be going too far to simply identify "thinking" with "talking," "thinking" as a term of human discourse should not be taken to refer to the function of a special part of the human person. In reality all such references can be replaced by descriptions of how people behave in different ways.

Mind-related terms only describe certain aspects of a one, unified human being which, as far as observation is concerned, is a totally material entity. In the final analysis there is no mysterious, superior, and immaterial mind-substance underlying human actions.

If Ryle had stopped here, he would have been a consistent reductionist of the more sophisticated type. But after nicely doing away with mind and freedom in his linguistic or "logical" behaviorism, he bent over backward to reinsert it. He asked himself if a universe in which everything observable is governed by the laws of physics can still have any room left over for human freedom and answered in the affirmative. He justified his positive attitude with several illustrations.

Consider, for instance, a chess game. Once in motion the course of each piece is fixed according to certain rules. However, there is no necessity that any particular piece be moved at any precise time. There is no pre-ordained pattern of play. The players are free to choose their moves, and so there can be as many different games—some good, some bad—as there are individual players.

Similar observations may be made about writing a book, playing billiards, and playing a game of golf. In all cases the governing rules are necessary but not sufficient to explain what is actually observed to happen. At each stage of the game individual initiative and freedom are intermixed with the iron rules of science. And thus it is also with human actions.

But what is the explanation, within the human person, of this freedom within necessity? Would Ryle be willing to agree with the explanations of some others, such as Saint Thomas Aquinas, who would be happy to admit the compatibility of just such a combination? Ryle refused to say, but he did assert that it was proper for the investigator to stop asking about the chain of causes and effects when he has reached the level of mind. In this way he can stick to observations about what actually occurs and leave aside any consideration of what goes on in the mysterious pre-operational area of mind.

A very convenient ploy, yet one which is obviously quite arbitrary. What Ryle has done in effect is to throw freedom out the front door only to usher it back in rather gratuitously through the rear. The insistence that "Humans are humans because humans are humans and humans are free because humans are free" may be fine for a certain type of mentality, but it can hardly be considered an advancement in human thought. It's understandable that someone should want to preserve the appearance of freedom; it's a fact of experience. But why someone should wish to preserve the fact of freedom in an otherwise strictly scientific system is quite another matter. Ryle, like Lucretius, should have been either consistently "scientific" or have left open the door to other explanations. However, he did neither and as a result did nothing significant, except perhaps show us once again the dangers awaiting anyone who attempts to penetrate the meaning of the human person.

The intellectual glass mountain leading to an understanding of the human person is slippery at best. Nonetheless, why should one take pride in tumbling down its side and landing in a mess of tautologies? Is not such an attitude a little bit too much like the elegantly dressed lady who fell into a mud puddle, and then strutted off telling her companions how much better she looked, to be regarded as anything other than plain silly by the ordinary person using ordinary language?

The key question here isn't whether or not it's possible to force ordinary language into behavioristically sounding molds so as to get it to fit a pre-established theory about the nonexistence of mind as a separate entity; it is instead whether or not there is evidence from ordinary experience for the separate existence of mind. If there is some prima facie evidence, which Ryle himself admitted there is, it should be evaluated in as fair a manner as possible. This would be a significant endeavor. But to struggle mightily with semantics in an effort to show that mind-terms might be verbally "reduced" to observable physical functions is to sidestep the whole issue. And to then gratuitously reintroduce free choice as an unjustified, and unjustifiable, fact can only serve to make matters worse. If Ryle were truly a staunchly scientific observer, he would have had nothing to do with such antics.

Human Worth

True reductionists like Skinner will have nothing to do with such backtracking. Once the scientific course is set, the faithful captain of the scientific ship must see the journey through to the very end. Skinner has done this with respect to freedom. Another necessary end product, though—yet one which many reductionists, including Skinner, do not yet seem ready to accept fully—is the destruction of the idea of a unified human race. Are all human beings equal? Maybe yes and maybe no.

Certainly they are not equal when viewed from the strictly physical point of view. Years ago it was said that the average 150-pound person was worth about ninety-two cents. That was the market value of the various chemical ingredients which made up the average body. But that was before inflation. It is now said that the price of a human being has increased by more than a factor of six. Yet the principle remains the same. Human worth is determined solely by the body. There is nothing else for the reductionist to appeal to. How, then, can the unity of the human species be maintained? The only answer is that it cannot.

If you are to be sold by the pound, then obviously, on average, males are "superior" to females; Westerners, on average, are "better" than Orientals (unless he happens to be a sumo wrestler), and so on and so forth. In effect each and every human being becomes unique, not only in terms of occupying his or her own set of space-time coordinates, but essentially. Everything becomes individualized to the point where no one can claim to be in the same species with anybody else. The human race is fractured billions of ways at once. All the human factors which count for anything in interpersonal affairs, for example, beauty, intelligence, skill, become matters of chance and heredity. There is nothing else to appeal to.[20]

Skinner himself admits that what constitutes the essence of the species is not yet understood. He hints, though, that when it is finally comprehended, it will be explained as a combination of genetic and environmental forces.[21] The question is whether or not such a thing is possible even in principle. Are not gene structures as material as anything else in nature? How can the internal structures of one's cells be used to explain the unity of the species when it is our very material constitution which renders each of us different from everyone else in the universe? The same would hold true for environmental forces. Each human being is subjected to different environments from the moment of conception. These forces make people different, not the same. They tend toward separating individuals rather than toward unifying them. Within certain subgroups of individuals some influences may be sufficiently constant to produce a relatively stable "culture" for short periods of time. But these cultures can just as easily war as cooperate with each other. In fact, of course, as history shows all too well, the former phenomenon has dominated the history of the world.

All in all, then, since no two bags of chemicals are exactly the same, there is no possible way in which our chemical constitution can be used as a basis for grouping all human beings together in the same species. Similarly, since no two bags of chemicals are subjected to exactly the same pushes and pulls, neither can environment be used for the purpose of unifying the race. No, the final conclusion must be that each and every individual thing in the universe, including each human, is in no way naturally connected with any other one except in some superficial morphological manner. A full realization of this consequence of reductionism is the ultimate psychological barrier to be overcome in human life. Once this fact of nature is openly admitted, the work of reconstructing society according to scientific principles can begin in earnest.

Behavior Modification

Thomas Hobbes was a leading atomistic reductionist of the seventeenth century. Although he wrote a great deal on many subjects, he is remembered today primarily for his political philosophy. Perhaps someday the same will be true of Skinner. According to Hobbes's view of human nature each individual is in a state of war with every other individual. Left alone, each human being would lead a beastly and crude life. Each individual's drive for self-preservation naturally forces him or her to sacrifice others in order to fulfill his or her own needs. Such a situation would have soon destroyed the human species, reasoned Hobbes, if something else had not acted to counteract it. In a nutshell, then, a necessary consequence of reductionism is social chaos.

Hobbes's solution to this state of affairs was to introduce behavior modification in the form of the iron-willed, absolute sovereign. The "body politic" for Hobbes was literally a material conglomeration of bodies held together by force. Given his view of human nature, Hobbes found it very easy to justify the English monarchy. It was in fact not only justified but made an eternal necessity dictated by a scientific understanding of mankind. The only way to prevent chaos and destruction is to put all power into the hands of the sovereign whose word is law. Although Hobbes liked to talk about the arrangement as a deal or contract between the people and their ruler, in practice it was a one-way street. The origins of society were hypothetical. The practical situation in Hobbes's own day was not. The kings ruled with an iron fist—or at least they wanted to. Not surprisingly, although suspected of atheism, Hobbes was still a favorite at court.[22]

Skinner finds himself in the same situation, intellectually speaking, in the twentieth century. And he knows it. He is constantly under attack as a would-be dictator, lacking only the political power to put his views into practice. He has even been caught, in *Walden Two* (1948), daydreaming about what he would do if he in fact possessed such power. Behavior modification through operant conditioning will work, he insists. He has no doubts that since it is theoretically correct, it must be practically effective.

What is lacking is something more than mere lip service for the virtues of the behavioristic program. The charge that it would be inherently cruel if actually put into practice is categorically rejected. After all, behaviorism *is* true here and now. It is not a thing of the future. It is a scientifically accurate description of what is presently true of all culturally determined human affairs. What is lacking is not scientific confirmation of behaviorism but a unified direction to operant conditioning.

We see, then, two points. One is that S-R is *already* a fact of nature. The other is that of all the forms of operant conditioning only a few are cruel or punitive. These should be eliminated, Skinner asserts. What is left over, however, would still be forms of behavior modification. These points are summarized for us in a letter he wrote to the editor of *Science* in response to what he considered to be a misuse of the term "behavior modification." He tells the readers of *Science* that the term originally arose as a way of describing a system of positive reinforcements deliberately designed to replace punitive techniques. It certainly is true that various cruel methods will modify behavior. But why use cruel means when culturally determined behavior patterns can be changed by noncruel methods? Do we not in fact use such methods all the time, for example, in the form of "religious rituals," "lotteries," "traffic signs," and "price controls"? Of course we do.[23]

These points are often overlooked by the critics of the behavioristic program of social ethics. Although well-meaning, what the critics fail to appreciate fully is the inherent consistency of the system. Once the starting point is granted (and who with any respect for science would deny it?) the remainder of the system follows quite naturally and necessarily. It is, therefore, useless to hurl accusations of a "humanitarian" nature against the walls of behaviorism. Such accusations simply bounce off like peas from a peashooter directed against the walls of Fort Knox. There can be nothing "inhuman" about the consequences of reductionism, since, by definition, this position on human nature is the scientifically true and proper position about humans in the first place.

Individual Unity

Is it not possible to be a nonauthoritarian reductionist? Consider Hume. It might be supposed that because David Hume regarded his primary objective in life as being to become a famous man of letters rather than a seeker after truth, he can be easily rejected. It is true that he does say of himself in his brief autobiography that literary fame was his "ruling passion" and that he moved to the city in 1751 because such was "the true scene for a man of letters."[24] This has led some commentators to reject him as being a basically dishonest, though long-winded, thinker who obstinately refused to examine his own first principles.[25] Nevertheless, as far as he would allow his thinking to go, he did make a real effort to be consistent. Insofar as his efforts concerned reductionism and behavior modification, he is of interest here.

Hume made no bones about the fact that he was a reductionistic atomist. Towards the end of his *Inquiry Concerning Human Understanding* Hume imagines a conversation between himself and an Epicurean. In the course of the conversation Hume says to his imaginary alter ego, "...you insinuate yourself into my favor by embracing those principles to which, you know, I have always expressed a particular attachment."[26] According to these principles the whole universe is composed of discrete particles of matter which combine in different ways to produce macrocosmic entities. The same must be true of what is usually called "mind" in ordinary language. The mind, like everything else, must be composed of parts. Everything that exists, explains Hume, is discrete and particular, "and therefore it must be our several particular perceptions that compose the mind. I say *compose* the mind, not *belong* to it. The mind is not a substance in which the perceptions inhere."[27]

What we see here, of course, is basically the same situation as presupposed by Skinner and Hobbes. But is there any way out of the social consequences of such a situation other than that envisioned by these two men? Hume thought there was. What Hume proposed in effect was a sort of natural moral law doctrine, although he did not call it that. Humankind is guided, he thought, by certain inborn tendencies, inclinations, and sentiments which lead individual human beings constantly to readjust their behavior to suit their changing social circumstances. Over a long period of human history, after much experience in interpersonal relationships, certain rules of behavior have been developed which serve the needs of people better than any other rules. Human reason, applied to repeated experiences, is capable of deciding among good, better, and best modes of behavior in human affairs. Within the very experiences of social affairs, toward which we are naturally inclined, we can discover the correct rules for utilitarian, enlightened self-interest modes of behavior.

In the long run, all people in all societies will come up with the same basic set of rules of behavior. All that is needed in order to have this happen is to allow great freedom of thought and practice. Through free experience everyone will converge on the same set of conclusions. "I never balance between the virtuous and the vicious course of life," affirms Hume, "but am sensible that, to a well-disposed mind, every advantage is on the side of the former."[28]

The question now arises of whether or not Hume can offer an appeal to certain common and stable elements in human nature in order to establish a nonforced type of behavior modification. The answer must clearly be no. There can be no appeal to the natural laws of human nature when there is no such nature in the first place. The problem of individual personal identity was always a serious one for Hume. He felt he was somehow *one* thing, a unified whole, but his doctrine on how things really are in the world told him that this was impossible. Predictably enough, the best he could do in the matter was to throw up his hands in despair.[29]

This state of affairs has been well described by the well-known and influential German biologist Hans Driesch. In the early part of the twentieth century his attack on materialistic reductionism took the form of emphasizing how it failed to account for the unified existence and behavior of organisms. Although primarily concerned with the typical classroom version of Darwinian evolution as taught at the time, what Driesch pointed out can be applied to all members of this school of human nature. According to Driesch:

> Darwinism dealt with variations occurring at random; the organic form was the result of a fixation of only one kind of such variations, all others being extinguished by selection. In other terms, the specific organized form, as understood by Darwinism, was a unit only to the extent that all its properties related to one and the same body, but for the rest it was a mere aggregation or summation. . . . where every single character of this unit, in every single feature of form or of quality, is the result of factors or agents each of which is independent of every other.
>
> To this sort of contingency of being, as maintained by Darwinians, criticism has objected, as we know, that it is quite an impossible basis of a theory of descent, since it would explain neither the first origin of an organ, nor any sort of harmony among parts or among whole individuals, nor any sort of restitution [regeneration] processes.[30]

In the end, regardless of appearances, we are still dealing with a bag of chemicals. Hobbes, Hume, Darwin, and Skinner must all agree on this. There is, therefore, no real and objective unified nature to human beings. There is only an accidental and very temporary congruence of material parts. Such an understanding of what nature really is cannot be used as a foundation for any kind of social system based upon the inherent qualities of human nature.[31]

Thus stands the modern form of reductionistic materialism. Born of an ancient attempt to overcome an old and serious intellectual conundrum, the doctrine faded from popular view only to be resurrected once again in modern times. Because it seemed to fit in very well with what many major scientists were doing during the European scientific revolution, it became almost synonymous with the scientific position on the way nature really is, independent of human sentiments and feelings. Although atomism as a doctrine of nature is now disintegrating, the connection between science and reductionism in the early twentieth century was strong enough to warrant a reversal in the equation such that reductionism could be regarded as the only possible result of the scientific method. This in turn gave rise to a series of deductions and consequences most widely known today under the heading of behaviorism in psychology.

Yet this view is not solely a product of the present time, nor of any other particular time in history. Reductionism, as a philosophy of human nature, is an ever-present possibility in human self-evaluation. It will always remain a possible way of looking at people. By the same token, since it necessarily results in social and political insecurity due to its wolf-man appraisal of human relations, it will always require some form of authoritarian behavior modification mechanism as an antidote. It is true, of course, that there may be some advocates of this paradigm who would *wish* to follow some other ethical direction, but the fact remains that their desires, however well-meaning, are in reality only an indication of a superstition carried over from some other model of the human person.

CHAPTER 3

Nonreductionistic Materialism

THE POSITION

Trouble in Paradise

When Parmenides defended his highly unusual view that there is in fact no change or alteration in the universe, he did it as part of a two-part poem. The first part was about the way things really are, the second part about the way things appear to be to the ordinary person who lacks the power of clear and precise logic. The second part incorporates various views about the changing material world of sensation. In it Parmenides purports to describe the way things *seem* to be.[1]

The atomistic reductionists adopted the same approach. The atoms are in principle beyond the reach of human observation via the senses. They are known through reason and through reason alone. Certainly, once known about, many sense observations can be brought forward to bolster the theoretical claim. The many sense experiences everyone has of porous objects, sounds traveling through walls, and so on, can now be explained by means of the atomistic theory. Nevertheless, the gap between the way the world really is and the way it appears to us (as continuous in some respects, as colored, as textured, and so forth) will always remain very wide and deep.

Modern reductionists have not been able to avoid this situation either. The language of behaviorism is full of talk about the way things really are as opposed to the way they seem to be to us. This conclusion is inevitable once the thinker starts down the reductionistic road.

From the point of view of many scientists in the world, however, both past and present, this situation is not a happy one. Can the reductionists really be right when they say that their position is the *only* scientific view? Are not scientists human beings like everyone else? Don't they have feelings and emotions and sentiments, including the strong sense of a personal freedom of choice, at least in some matters, like everyone else in the world? It would seem so. Also, what about the disastrous social and political consequences of a consistent reductionism? Is it really necessary that all true and respectable scientists be supporters of some form of centralized dictatorship, even if it is a benevolent dictatorship? And what about mind? Isn't it obvious that thoughts must mediate between the S-R limits?

Perhaps there is some middle path that a good scientist can follow. This path would have a nonreductionistic boundary as one parameter and a nonspiritualistic boundary as its other parameter. If such a path could be found, it would certainly be a great boon to people. For then, without getting back into such antiscientific ideas as spiritualistic superstitions, rational scientific thinkers could have the best of both worlds. On the one hand they could call themselves true and sincere scientists, people who really know what they are talking about when it comes to the physical world; on the other hand they could be truly "humanistic" human beings who would be completely justified on rational grounds alone in regarding the human species as unified and as possessing a special right to respect. The nonreductionistic materialists lay claim to having found exactly such a middle course. The secret of success in the new approach is the way in which modern science can be employed to show that the whole is greater than its material parts without having to affirm the real existence of anything in the universe except matter.

The Philosophers

According to the old-fashioned materialism of reductionism, explains Roy Wood Sellars, matter was thought of as being merely mass, movement, and blind mechanical processes. But now things are quite different in science. Now everything is thought of in terms of different levels of complexity and fields of interaction, rather than simple little pieces of matter moving around in empty space.[2] The old materialism, or reductionistic materialism, depended upon a view of the microcosm which closely imitated what could be observed on the macrocosmic level. The ultimate little parts of nature were supposed to be but small versions of the larger lumps of matter observed on the macrocosmic level. This is all now far behind us—or at least should be. No longer can science work with the products of a perceptual imagination, no matter how active and creative. Today we must contend with mathematical symbols, architectonic subtlety, inner dynamic qualities, and patterns of relationships in the analysis of the physical world.[3] In agreement with George Santayana and Sidney Hook, Sellars proclaims a new interpretation of materialism, to wit, that although matter is the only substance or power in the world, it is not the only reality.[4] Consequently, Sellars states, the new "materialism is not epiphenomenalistic and reductive after the fashion of the scientific materialism based on classical physics."[5] It is rather a modern form of dynamic thinking which allows for the true reality of human consciousness, feelings, and evolutionary novelty in the world. There are true hierarchies in the universe. Everything is not on a par, qualitatively speaking. The common perceptions of mankind are basically correct—all without any appeal to the incorporeal or metaphysical forms of the traditional antiscientific religious philosophers.

Another modern thinker, much better known than Sellars, is John Dewey. Dewey wanted to be a scientist or at least to be known as a scientific mind. At the same time he wanted to be a philosopher of democracy and freedom. How could he be both at once? In fact he could not according to the principles of reductionistic materialism. What he required was a new sort of materialism, one that would allow for the reality of mind, self-consciousness, and freedom. The key to this new kind of materialism was to be found in the doctrine of evolution. Morris R. Cohen has said that when the history of the twentieth century is finally written, John Dewey (along with William James) will be remembered as the first major philosopher to have worked out the repercussions and significance of Darwin's evolutionary philosophy.[6] Not only did he devote a great deal of thought to the practical effects of evolutionary doctrine, for example, in education and social affairs, but he was also very much concerned with its theoretical background and underlying assumptions. This was the work he began relatively early in his mature career while at Columbia University near the beginning of the twentieth century.

If evolutionary doctrine is to be taken seriously, if it is to have any real meaning and significance in the history of the world and the human species, it must be productive of real novelty in the world. In the evolutionary struggle there may be failures and setbacks, but there can never be the stagnation of hierarchical types found in reductionism. Overall there must be progress in the sense of higher and higher levels of complex perfection, culminating ultimately in the emergence of human beings. Dewey's own thoughts on the whole subject culminated in his work on mind and matter entitled *Experience and Nature,* the second edition of which appeared in 1929. This work has become a classic statement of the aim and position, as well as for some of the necessary consequences, of nonreductionistic materialism. More than a metaphysics, *Experience and Nature* is a whole cultural outlook—a religion even.

What concerns Dewey is not morals but metaphysics, that is, "the nature of the existential world in which we live."[7] He makes it clear in chapter 1 that his main problem in understanding the real world of experience is how the world of change can be reconciled with a world of permanence. How can becoming and being exist together in one universe? Taking his notion of "being" from the Greeks, who ended in a denial of full reality to the world of changing experience, Dewey gradually outlines for the reader an approach to the universe which eliminates Greek Being altogether. Even Aristotle must be included among those who insisted upon separating the world of becoming and flux from the world of permanence. "Aristotle," Dewey says, "acknowledges contingency, but he never surrenders his bias in favor of the fixed, certain and finished. His whole theory of forms and ends is a theory of the superiority in Being of rounded-out fixities."[8]

This same attitude, according to Dewey, persisted through the Middle Ages and entered the modern philosophical and scientific world through the works of Descartes. This Frenchman, with his reductionistic material world and his vitalistic mind-substances, which were all mutually exclusive with respect to each other and with respect to matter, is the person largely responsible for our fractured view of the world today. If we cannot get mind and body together today, the reason is the notion that mind is somehow eternal and absolute while body is changing and unstable.[9] If philosophy today has a bad press, the reason is that past philosophers have taken a nonempirical approach to the world, resulting in a denial of the truth of our ordinary experiences. Such dualisms must be avoided. And, since being and becoming are irreconcilable and all the modern developments of science support the reality of becoming, "being" must be eliminated. The universe must be explained in terms of change, development, evolution, and novelty. Science must be preserved, but at the same time the reality of human feelings and freedom must also be preserved.

According to Dewey's reasoning process, then, the need both to do away with the superiority of fixity and to regard fixity and flux as incompatible imposes upon the modern thinker a certain set of boundaries within which he must settle the nature of humankind. On the one side, in order to preserve freedom, he is not free to fall back into reductionistic materialism. On the other side, in order to maintain the scientific stance, he is not free to appeal to anything immaterial or spiritual in human nature. By so doing the modern investigator of the nonreductionistic materialism variety can regard himself as occupying the happy medium between two extremes. He cannot be accused of the crude materialism of the reductionists, and he cannot be accused of the antiscientific bias which infected thinkers of the past, especially religious ones. What was needed was a "new dialectic"[10] of interactional relations and, he claimed, the new materialism has found it.

Writing about the same time as the leader of behaviorism, Dewey, without calling anyone by name, makes it clear that reductionism is not for him. Watson had attempted to reduce thinking to the outward expression of thought, namely, language or the very act of speaking itself. Even today it is quite common to see psychologists confuse words and gestures with meaning as they test for language in primates. This will never do, thinks Dewey. In order to make sense of language, a word must do more than merely represent a one-to-one correspondence between itself and some physical entity. There is meaning present which goes beyond what can be momentarily pointed to. "The words make immediate sense," Dewey states, "as well as have signification. This something now present is not just the activity of the laryngeal and vocal apparatus."[11]

The basic reason for this type of mistake on the part of the reductionists is that they refuse to recognize any reality other than what can be measured. They keep thinking in terms of LaPlace's ideal formula. What can the future contain, they ask. Nothing but what was already in the past, they answer. Dewey does not think that this is right. At least it does not really take evolution seriously, regardless of how many times they use the word. If he objects to reductionism, it is not merely because of some feeling he has or because it offends his sense of beauty. No, it is because it does not do justice to modern science. Dewey states that the real objection to "metaphysical materialism" is neither moral nor aesthetic. Rather it is that the mechanistic doctrine (as distinct from "mechanistic science") makes two false claims: That matter is the efficient cause of soul and that "cause" is superior in reality to "effect."[12] In other words, if reductionism were merely a methodology (mechanistic science), it could be tolerated. But when it is presented as the way things really are in the universe (mechanistic metaphysics), it must be rejected as overlooking the whole point of evolution.

Dewey is just as strong in his rejection of the other extreme. Just as nonreductionistic materialism must avoid the mechanical view of the human person, so must it avoid any attempt to spiritualize human personality. The idea that humans are the result of a special creation by God and are thereby endowed with a special destiny of a spiritual nature is no longer acceptable. It cannot be said that the human race is going anywhere in particular, that it has some divine goal, or that it is developing according to the script of a divine writer. Rather than this sort of thing, humankind is writing its own story as it keeps adding to its own evolutionary history. As Dewey points out, *both* the traditional mechanical and the traditional teleological theories of the person suffer from the same failure, namely, they both use nonhistorical explanations. This old-fashioned "sense of causality" must be rejected.[13]

Once a balance between the two extremes is achieved, Dewey believes, a new harmony will appear in the literature of the world. The old war between the unchanging spirit and the forever changing world of existence will fade away. The many labels attached to one side of the fence or the other will disappear. There will no longer be any need for advocates of one world or the other to hurl derogatory remarks at each other. A kind of secular salvation will settle on the world. In that day neither the term "materialism" nor "spiritualism" will apply to the universal scientific doctrine. "Consequently," he quite seriously, honestly, and consistently affirms, "while the theory that life, feeling and thought are never independent of physical events may be deemed materialism, it may also be considered just the opposite."[14]

It must never be forgotten, though, that any talk about the spirit is only for the sake of showing the middle course of nonreductionistic materialism. After all, what evidence is there for the independent existence of soul? Dewey, like Skinner, cannot find any. True, scientists in this century cannot conclusively demonstrate that there is a continuity of type between body and mind. This will come in the future. But, until we have a demonstration of this continuity, we will have to be content with a piecemeal approach using whatever is the fashionable language of the time to express connectedness and unity.[15] Such language may even be religious in nature. However, the reality of the world is such that even religious language can give us only hints and metaphors about reality. What cannot be directly shown in detail by science now must nevertheless be accepted as basically true because of the way it fits in with the generally admitted truth about the ever growing, never finished process of historic evolution. It is not evidence, then, but only unfamiliarity with the requirements of evolutionary theory which keeps people from embracing nonreductionistic materialism *en masse*. "Unfamiliarity" and nothing else keeps us from viewing matter and mind as two traits of natural events, events in which matter expresses sequential order, and mind their logical connections and meanings.[16]

Such words are all well and good when making a presentation of the present state of affairs in the world, but how did such a situation come about in the first place? To Dewey's way of thinking there are two keys to understanding the genesis of mankind. In the first place comes the fact of organization. In the next place comes the fact of increasing levels of complexity. The difference between the physical and the psychic is not one of difference of kind or type but one of different operational levels. According to the way Dewey reads the results of science, there is no problem in relating the physical to the mental.

There are only certain empirical events marked by definite qualities and powers. And in the first place stands *"organization* with all which is implied thereby."[17]

Organization of material events into inclusive wholes on varying but interacting hierarchical levels of complexity is what accounts for the special nature of mankind. This is *the* answer to the perennial question about our status as a species in nature. To free ourselves from both classical reductionism and classical spiritualism, we must see things differently. Near the end of his chapter on the relationship of human beings to the rest of nature Dewey concludes that we must see the organism *in* nature, the nervous system *in* the organism, the brain *in* the nervous system, and the cortex *in* the brain in order to have *the* answer to the ancient body-mind problems which "haunt philosophy."[18]

The answer given by the advocates of this position depends upon the fact that there are different levels of organization in the material universe. If these organizations are analyzed, one discovers that they are arranged in a clearly discernible hierarchical fashion. The different levels of the system are then found to be associated with different types of activity. Such organization is not restricted to humans. It begins with the inorganic and moves upward through the organic to humans. At any one time, then, the world can be seen as composed of parts which form a continuum ranging from some relatively homogeneous elements, such as gold in the earth, to a very complex system containing systems within systems, such as a human being. This self-organization of matter is what explains people and all that they do.

In agreement with the reductionistic view, therefore, Dewey sees us as emerging from less complicated structures as part of a continuum in which there are no radical breaks. In disagreement with the reductionists, however, he wants to leave room for different kinds or sorts of inorganic elements and organic creatures that cannot be reduced to each other. All such differences in kind, though, as well as their attendant properties and behavior patterns, are to be ultimately explained as the resultants of physical forces.

Without any radical breaks in nature, disturbed states of inner equilibrium produce different kinds of organization from whence come different consequences. Generally speaking, in the case of animate bodies the equilibrium always tends to restore itself, whereas in nonliving things ordinary entropy is the rule. Depending upon the degree of intimacy of interaction among natural events of increasing complexity there is more or less life or soul or spirit in a body. Just as some bodies have conspicuously more fragrance, color, or solidity than others, so some have more organized unity (that is, life) than others. That is all there is to it. The organism is in nature, the nervous system is in the organism, the brain is in the nervous system, the cortex is in the brain, and thought is in the cortex. For Dewey, then, human beings truly possess the best of both worlds.

The Biologists

What do the biologists think of such a scheme? In a way the biologists, or at least the "naturalists" such as Charles Darwin, were responsible for the position in the first place. The philosopher can give the view the stamp of completeness in terms of its preconditions and consequences, but it was and is the biologist who gives it its stamp of scientific respectability. Although no statistics are available, it would be safe to say that the nonreductionistic materialism position is extremely common among biologists, undoubtedly because of the central position held by evolutionary theory in most phases of biological science today. At the same time, then, most biologists are not prepared to regard human beings as just so many bags of chemicals to be weighed and measured. There are many biologists who would say that organisms are not merely additive systems of independently acting parts. Merely reorganizing and rearranging material parts no more provides unity than collecting together all the highly organized members of an army would make the army one thing. Just like everyone else, reductionists are astonished at the way chemical changes, for instance, produce new substances with properties entirely different from those of the elements that go into them. But, the nonreductionists would claim, merely rearranging the elements is not enough to explain the phenomenon.

But how can this be? Once the reductionistic position is denied, are you not then committed to some form of immaterialism or spiritualism? Ernst Mayr, for example, would think not. There is no doubt in his mind that biology requires different principles of explanation than those found in physics and chemistry. But being different from the physical sciences does not necessarily mean being antimaterialistic. Living things have been subjected to billions of years of evolution. The result has been material systems different in kind from nonliving ones and immensely more complicated. However, they are not for that reason necessarily any less material or physical in composition.[19] From one point of view, this famous biologist goes on to say, human beings are merely higher primates. This at least is true from his perspective as an evolutionist. "But," he insists, "it would be totally wrong to say that man is 'nothing but a primate,' because man is a very special, a unique primate."[20] When considered in comparison with all other primates, or indeed with all other things in the biosphere, human nature is so special and distinguished that it is very hard sometimes to see human beings as continuous with the rest of nature. Nevertheless, it must be so. Although not the only reality, especially with respect to human existence, matter is the ultimate force or power in nature. Consequently, everything must be explained in terms of matter.

Yet the question of how such a vast difference in nature is possible without an appeal to something immaterial still presses in upon the investigator. One biologist, a rather famous geneticist named Theodosius Dobzhansky, has attempted to supply an answer. The answer he gives is basically the same one supplied by all nonreductionistic materialists either explicitly or implicitly.

When considered from the developmental point of view advocates of this position adopt the quantitative-qualitative jump language. Dobzhansky, for example, takes just such an approach. He sees the evolution of man as proceeding from lower life forms to higher life forms and to be one of gradually increasing complexity. The product grows with the instrument and the instrument with the product. In time, humans transcended their animal origins to become the most successful species of biological evolution. There was, in fact, a revolution in the case of humans. After achieving an upright posture, walking on two feet, using their hands to make tools, and somehow acquiring language, the almost-people were people. The light of the human spirit began to shine.

In this cosmic-biological-human transition there are no unbridgeable gaps to overcome. What is novel is not the components but the patterns. In people one finds a peculiar constellation. In principle, though, there is no radical break between humans as a species and lower species. Evidence for this, claims Dobzhansky, can be found in the way lower forms carry on to a lesser degree all of the important human functions, such as communication. Human ancestors contained the paltry beginnings of human faculties, which when greatly refined and reorganized quantitatively speaking, produced a qualitative difference, a new kind of being called human. Yet, states Dobzhansky, all the ingredients for such a leap forward were always there. "The transcendence does not mean that a new force or energy has arrived from nowhere; it does mean that a new form of unity has come into existence."[21]

The central point for him is that the human person is very special, even unique. He claims that to talk about the human person as a type or class separate from all other animal species is indeed justified. Furthermore, because people are so special, we owe to each other a special kind of consideration and treatment. How did such a situation come about? By way of certain undirected slow change processes which resulted in different degrees of complexity of material parts. Consequent upon these organizational changes were radical qualitative alterations.

None of this, however, involves anything really spiritual. You can insist upon having new and different principles of science over and above those used in physics and chemistry without implying anything literally immaterial in nature. All you need affirm is that the slow change processes have produced systems different in kind from any nonliving systems in terms of complexity. Such biological systems are not for that reason any less material or physical than those found in nonliving systems. All we must do is to realize, explains Dobzhansky, that "The differences between man and animals are, then, merely quantitative. This does not entangle us in a contradiction. Quantitative differences may grow large enough to become qualitative."[22]

Matter

When discussing the nonreductionistic materialistic position, there are two additional areas which deserve special attention. One is the way in which the viewpoint alters the reductionistic view of matter. The other is the way it recognizes and emphasizes the importance of unity in living organisms.

With respect to the definition of matter we notice two things. One is the way in which the investigator must give up the idea that matter is to be identified with the mathematical qualities of length, breadth, and width. The other is the way in which all the dynamic, active, and creative powers previously assigned to God must now be assigned to matter itself.

What is "matter" according to the new materialism? In Sellars' view it certainly is not what is perceived by some particular person. In opposition to Berkeley, he finds any concentration on the mental side of perception a very poor way to explain the meaning of matter. For scientific purposes matter cannot be regarded as what can be gleaned via individualistic sensations. On the contrary, says Sellars, "Matter is that which can be designated, located and manipulated."[23] This means that matter must be something public. It must not be defined in terms of subjective impressions but in terms of intersubjective data. Matter, therefore, is simply what scientists deal with as they move about the world. And this is as far as he can go in his definition of matter. To try for more would be to become *too* philosophical about it.

Yet what little we know is enough. If scientists can adequately designate things around their labs and confirm facts about them, that is sufficient. It teaches us to be as well balanced in our view of matter as we are in our view of the person. Matter is something between pure extension and subjective impressions. Sellars can agree with neither the reductionists nor the spiritualists. The former is too outdated and the latter is too subjective for science. The middle course is best, he thinks. Our concept of matter must be constructed over a long period of scientific experimentation. What we will finally have is now unknown, but we can be sure that it will not be the view of matter held by either extreme.

Dewey seems to be in basic agreement here. For Dewey both mind and matter belong to the complex of nature. On the surface this may appear to be saying that there is some mysterious third thing, some neutral Stuff, some great It, underlying both mind and matter. Such a view, however, of what Dewey has in mind is due only to our ingrained ways of speaking. Instead of trying to substantialize functions and events with nouns, we should rather speak of natural events using adjectives and adverbs. Instead of talking about the mind, we would then talk about nature in its conscious aspects, and so on. In other words, individual minds do not own ideas. Ideas are the property of nature. Rather than saying "I think a stone" or "I see a stone," it would be better to say that a stone is thought or seen by nature here and now in this locus. Such language would better reflect the true state of affairs in the universe.

The same sort of thing holds for talk about the material side of nature. The physical is as much a function of natural events as is the mental. If Dewey seems hesitant about talking directly about matter, it is because he fears being interpreted in a reductionistic fashion. Matter should not be considered as something independent, static, and separate when compared to mind. If it is to be defined at all, it must be defined in relationship to everything else that is going on in nature. "Matter," states Dewey, "or the physical, is a character of events when they occur at a certain level of interaction."[24] It is only interactional analysis which can distinguish among the simply physical, the psychosomatic, and the mental types of events. These are not separate states of being. They are different levels of complex organization and interaction in nature.

Consequently, matter is a low level of natural interaction. Furthermore, it is never really entirely divorced from the higher types of interaction. Matter and mind are both aspects of one world which goes on for ever and ever. If one should ask for a definition of nature, the best Dewey could do would be to indicate the vast array of human experiences open to us. Nature is the world of experience, vast and variable. Nobody can do any better in a definition of matter.

The first point leads to the second. One main emphasis of nonreductionistic materialism is the desire to keep mankind natural in the sense of rejecting anything supernatural or spiritual. Yet evolution takes place. New things are created. Progress and development are essential aspects of the natural world. How is this possible? Since, by definition, there is no supernatural force to account for change and development in the universe, the only place to look for the source of evolution is in the natural world itself. This is certainly the case with Sellars and Dewey. It is also the case with respect to many others who appear to be talking about something spiritual in nature. Edmund W.

Sinnott, for instance, a biologist of some note, is very much impressed by the way in which living systems show a purposefulness in their development. This is so in all organisms, especially in human beings who can study their own development in biology. The goal-seeking quality of life is in fact what biological organization really means. To be alive is to be adaptable. A push in one direction is rectified by a living movement in the other. List a thousand cases of this sort of thing and you have a textbook in biology.

But again the question of how this can be explained arises. Sinnott is ultimately unprepared to answer this question. However, he is sure that the best thing for the biologist to do is to avoid the extremes of mysticism and reductionism.[25] Instead of extremes one should pay attention to the basic matter of the universe for an answer. What the biologist wants to avoid is either making body and mind into separate and mutually exclusive entities or some sort of monism which makes either body or mind into the only essential reality. Rather, his view would regard "*both* as derived from something deeper than either."[26]

A new sort of monism based upon nature is what is required. Further on Sinnott states that this more basic reality gives rise to all human traits, from the most base and antisocial to the most exalted and sublime. Beginning on the animal level and working up to the human level can be found all those inner drives and emotions which constitute our jungle heritage. "But *from this same source,*" insists Sinnott, "let us not forget, are born man's deepest satisfactions, his cravings for beauty, his moral aspirations, his love for his fellows, and his reverence for something greater than himself in the universe outside."[27]

What is this basic stuff of the universe which can give rise to such contradictory manifestations as social and antisocial behavior? No one knows. However, if you wish to call it God, you may do so. It must never be forgotten, though, that the divine is never apart from nature. God is in nature. God is that basic force which organizes everything. Ultimately God is unnameable. It is that something which is the really real underlying both mind and body. Indeed, human nature itself is part of the divine. "Man's spirit, rooted in life, may actually be a part of the Universal Spirit, emerging from it and returning to it again."[28]

The views expressed by Sinnott are certainly not the views of just one biologist. They are in fact the views of many people from many walks of life. The philosophies of the ancient Stoics, Baruch Spinoza,

Georg Hegel, Herbert Spencer, Henri Bergson and perhaps Alfred North Whitehead, come immediately to mind, as do the religions of Hinduism and Buddhism. Many of the world's great writers have also expressed their view of human nature in such a manner. George Bernard Shaw, for example, in his play in praise of philosophy entitled *Man and Superman,* has Don Juan say:

> And I, my friend, am as much a part of Nature as my own finger is a part of me. If my finger is the organ by which I grasp the sword and the mandoline, my brain is the organ by which Nature strives to understand itself....Were I not possessed with a purpose beyond my own I had better be a ploughman than a philosopher;...This is because the philosopher is in the grip of the Life Force.

What ties all of these thinkers together, whether they are philosophers, biologists, poets, or whatever, is the way in which what used to be attributed to the independent God of the Judeo-Christian tradition must now be given over to what used to be considered his creation. This is to say, the thinker who regards Nature as the only explanatory principle is forced into the position of endowing it with all of the divine attributes needed to account for the advent of mankind. He has no other choice. That is, he has no other choice if he wants to avoid reductionism. It should not be surprising, then, that pantheism should be such a popular view in our time. It appears as the ideal way to have both "humanism" and science simultaneously. Evolution is good science, and humans are the best things evolved so far. And why are we the best? Because only we can know our own history. We are Nature experiencing Itself.

Unity

Another important point to be made about nonreductionistic materialism in contrast to both immaterialism and reductionism is the way it emphasizes the unity of human nature. It is typical of those in the new materialism to charge both those in the old spiritualism and in the old materialism with a failure to appreciate fully the unity of organisms. All the arguments against both dualism in the mind-body sense and the old-fashioned Greek atomism are meant to make this point.

Dewey, for example, mentions the way in which the chemical element iron selectively enters into combinations with other elements. Once the right conditions are present iron will react with other elements in a fixed pattern of change. Iron shows no strong bias to remain simply iron. This is true of both inanimate and animate reactions. Iron will change without resistance whether in or out of a living body.

The real question, though, is into what will it change? Herein lies the whole difference between living and nonliving things. In a living thing iron will react so as to maintain the overall organization and purpose of the living thing. In its reaction with water, however, it shows no such inclination. If it did, says Dewey, water "would have the marks of a living body, and would be called an organism. Iron as a genuine constituent of an *organized* body acts so as to tend to maintain the type of activity of the organism to which it belongs."[29] Such a body can be said to have a soul as long as this is not interpreted literally. The body has an adaptive unity. This unity, however, comes from a particular organization of nature in that particular locus where it is manifested. In conclusion, therefore, it may be asserted that the term "soul" is simply a shorthand way of talking about all our psychophysical activities insofar as they are organized into a unity. The higher the unity the more soul a body may be said to have. Just as some bodies have more fragrance, some have more soul. It's all entirely natural without the slightest need for any "mysterious non-natural entity or force."[30]

What emerges from the study of this position is the importance of explaining the integration of the human creature. The real problems for any serious account of human nature are: (1) What accounts for the unity of each human being? (2) What accounts for the origin of such unity? (3) What accounts for the unity of all human beings within the same species? The answer to the first question depends upon a particular level of organization. The answer to the second question depends upon the quantity-quality leap. As far as the third problem is concerned, though, the answer is not clear-cut.

Advocates of the new materialism are quick to affirm that species are not merely arbitrary names imposed by observers. To be meaningful and useful they must have some objective and nonarbitrary (nonsubjective) basis in fact. All those in the materialistic camp, whether old or new, appeal to similarities as a way of solving this problem. In contrast to the biologists, those in philosophy tend to emphasize morphology more. We must look at the creatures as physical wholes and group them together based upon observed similarities. As Sellars states, "Here we have, I think, the possibility of a new kind of nominalism which stresses similarity but has nothing in common with psychologism of the Berkeley-Hume type. Things can have similar natures. We can then think of these generically."[31] The subjectivism and skepticism of Berkeley and Hume must be avoided. They are not objective enough for modern science. However, neither must we project natural types into divine ideas or entities independent of nature. Again, a middle course is best, and this would be objective similarities as really found in nature.

For those in biology the usual explanation for biological types has been to appeal to something more hidden than outward appearances, namely, the nuclear gene structures of the organism's cells. All human beings are creatures of equal rank and dignity. Why? Because they all share in the same gene pool.

What this means in practice is that you look to see which creatures can interbreed with each other. Those which can do so must have a similar biological constitution. Based upon this similarity they can be grouped together in one species. This view has had several strong supporters in the past, but is now on the decline. There are many biological facts for which it cannot account, such as asexual reproduction, thus causing biologists to think twice about it. As Dobzhansky himself has said recently, "The recognition that species are reproductive communities was a step forward, but it raised more problems than it solved."[32]

All in all, then, the case for the nonreductionistic materialistic position rests upon the possibility of a series of quantity-quality leaps occurring by natural means and also upon the existence of inherent natural, active powers and forces of organization acting in just the right way to bring the human species to its present condition as observed in modern science.

Some Variations

On the outskirts of nonreductionistic materialism is the interesting case of Jean-Paul Sartre. From one viewpoint he is a disciple of Hegel; from another, of Lucretius. This duality shows up in his famous work *Being and Nothingness*. His aim in this work is to state a "general theory of being."[33] His answer to the question of "being" is to take the reader through a series of steps which end (like Hegel's beginning) in the identification of being and nonbeing. First being is equated with doing, which is equated with possessing an "original freedom," which is equated with nonbeing.[34]

What, then, is the essence of the human person? The closest Sartre can come to answering this question is to talk in terms of freedom, an original and generic mode of existence which characterizes all humans. Freedom *is* the being of man, the essence of *human* existence, what we all share with each other as our distinctively human trait.[35]

Now this is fine as far as it goes, but what explains freedom? At this point Sartre appeals to nonbeing or nothingness. But is "nothingness" intelligible? Sartre twists himself in every possible psychological direction in order to convince us it is. In doing so he shows his Greek atomism.

What is the "in-itself"? It is that which is completed, rounded off, finished, closed, determined, and predictable. In a word, it is the material world. It is "being." It is what we become at death. The "for-itself," though, in contrast to the "in-itself" or "being" or matter, is what is open to the future, undetermined, and free. These are radically contradictory and mutually exclusive types of existence for Sartre, just as "being" (eternal matter) and "nonbeing" (the void or empty space) were for the atomists.

Sartre identifies being with matter. The material world is like the solid part of a donut. He has no choice, then, but to identify freedom with nonbeing, because the only possible contrary for "what is" is "what is not." Freedom is the hole in the donut. An unconscious, completely material thing cannot be free. Only its complete opposite can be free. And what is the only possible complete opposite for being if not nonbeing or nothingness?

The main consequence of this is that the fundamental and absolute contradiction between being and nothingness must be eternal and constant everywhere it is found. Hence, human beings are "condemned" to be free. It is a case of all or nothing at all. By definition, every Sartrean donut must have a hole in it. We are forever and always free or we are not free even in the least degree. There can be no "degrees," only an either-or situation with respect to human freedom. Upon this foundation Sartre builds his amoral ethics of individual self-realization.[36]

What one sees in Sartre, then, is a well-camouflaged attempt to be both a reductionistic and a nonreductionistic materialist simultaneously. But this combination is impossible. On the one hand, Sartre wants to identify being and nonbeing deep down in the bowels of reality hidden from the vivid view of concrete things, just as Hegel did. On the other hand, though, he wants to keep nothingness up front, out in the open, and on the level of individual self-consciousness. In the tradition of Lucretius, Sartre must keep "what is not" on the same level of reality here and now as "what is" if he is going to account for human freedom. As Gabriel Marcel has said of Sartre's position, "The truth is that Sartre unites the idealism of which I have spoken with a materialism which derives from the eighteenth-century tradition of French thought."[37] The idealism is that of Hegel, and the French thought of two centuries ago is that of atomistic materialism.

Sartre's view, which he claimed to be a kind of phenomenological existentialism, was a strange hybrid species which could not possibly survive the first cold snap. As we know from history, of course, it did not last long. It suffered an early death in the 1940s, or rather a transmutation into an odd form of Marxism. This greatly reduced its inner tensions, but at the same time it also put upon it all the shortcomings of the original Hegelian basis of Marxism. Sartre could no longer claim to be an existentialist. Neither could he claim neutrality in the political sphere. Like it or not, there was no escaping the inner necessities of the material and social worlds of existence. In the end, therefore, it would seem that Hegel's approach to "being" turned out to be more reasonable for Sartre than that of the reductionists.[38]

Other problems as well, inherent in Sartre's position, have not escaped notice. In his own country Sartre found an able and powerful critic in the person of Maurice Merleau-Ponty, who at one time served as co-editor with Sartre of *Les Temps Modernes*. To Merleau-Ponty's way of thinking Sartre's phenomenological existentialism was neither existential nor phenomenological. Instead, Sartre was a pure and simple ontologist who consistently ignored the way in which the world ''appears'' within consciousness. As a result he got himself into a position so extreme that it could in no way be regarded as corresponding to the facts of consciousness as revealed in immediate subjective experience.[39]

At the same time that he found it necessary to reject Sartre, Merleau-Ponty also found it necessary to modify the ''materialism'' of his other early love, Marxism. Marxism attributes much too much influence to the material world. This is a great mistake. We are no more mere victims of a dialectical materialism, thought Merleau-Ponty, than we are the completely free masters of the *pour-soi* ''nothingness'' proposed by Sartre. What Merleau-Ponty wanted was a happy medium between the materialistic model of man and all those mentalistic models which make man into some sort of conquering angel subduing a totally external and alien material world of *partes extra partes.*[40]

Superficially, Merleau-Ponty wrote as a phenomenologist, often using the language of Edmund Husserl. It was within this context that he hoped to find, and indeed claimed to have found, the happy medium he sought. Nevertheless, a reading of what he actually said on the subject of the human person leads to a different opinion. What he offered as a solution to the problem of explicating man-in-the-world and the all-important problem of the human ability to know the world would indicate that he is in basically the same camp as John Dewey. In truth, it would not be far off the mark to look upon Merleau-Ponty as a John Dewey *en français,* but with a bent for the social sciences rather than the physical sciences.[41]

Early in his mature intellectual history, under the combined influence of Gestalt psychology and Husserl's phenomenology, Merleau-Ponty learned that any explanation of how the mind and the world achieve intercourse, which depended upon any kind of physiological transmission of material images from the world to the mind, must be wrong. The mind, or soul, is not an empty sponge soaking up images. Regardless of how detailed the medical analysis of nerves and brain tissue may become, there always remains that unbridged gap between what the biological instruments record and what people actually experience. There is no way in which actually experienced sensations and thoughts can be reduced to meter readings. Any attempt to fill in the gap with more and more minute chemical processes and refined "little pictures" is bound to fail. All we will get is an infinite regress which explains nothing. The old "spectator" view of human knowledge must go. Yet scientists keep multiplying the very factors which make a physiological explanation of body-mind penetration impossible. "Little images," whether immediately given or collected from the memory, are not what we actually experience.[42]

But how, then, can this problem be overcome while preserving both the facts of our own experience and the existence of an external world which is not wholly dependent upon our own minds for its being? Merleau-Ponty's answer is to regard all knowledge as an internal re-creation or re-cognition of an "appearing" world. He is convinced that any solution to the problem of how the mind relates to the world can come only from an internal analysis of the mind itself through its own consciousness. This is the very definition of a true phenomenology: A direct inventory of consciousness.[43]

When we actually carry out this process, what we discover is that the subjective and objective worlds are inseparable. The world appears to us "in person" as both mentally internal to us and yet as distinct from us. There is, in fact, no wall between the *en-soi* and the *pour-soi*. Even my own body, that aspect of the material world which is most *for me,* is something "constituted" within my own consciousness. By our concentrating upon the conscious activity which produces our ideas of things, rather than upon the differences between sense knowledge and intellectual knowledge, the body-mind problem disappears.[44]

But just what is this process? It must be a "dialectical" process of interaction, answers Merleau-Ponty. Matter, life, and mind are not three different sorts of reality. They are rather three levels of interaction producing different "significations" or meanings-for-man-in-the-world. They can also be looked upon as three forms of unity within nature. Life, for instance, is not a force *added* to physiochemical processes. It is instead a set of special dialectical connections which cannot be reduced to physics, and which require a special language to express. The life principle must be as "naturized" as body.

By the same token, the mental aspect of the human person is only a different "region" of experience within nature. It is a part of a dialectical process in which each partial action is adjusted to fit the whole organism. In relation to the body, which is a collection of functions showing varying degrees of integration within its environment, the mind is a locus of activity showing varying degrees of integration within *its* environment.

It can be said that the soul "acts" upon the body when our physical conduct has a meaning for us which cannot be reduced to physical vectors. On the other hand, the body "acts" upon the soul or mind when there is no language to express what is going on in purely rational or mentalistic terms. This view eliminates the need to think of two substances interacting. Instead, there is only a set of reciprocal relationships, a dialectical movement, within a certain locus of nature. The physical, vital, and mental are but varying degrees of integration in a localized and circumscribed region of the world. The body and soul, in direct dialectical contact with the world, know together and die together. There is no physical-psychic parallelism, only a localized natural dialectic.[45]

We see, therefore, that there is a truth to be derived from materialism, namely, that the body or matter proper, that is, matter *for me,* may be considered as the base or condition for the higher dialectical processes. At the upper levels of integration and interaction, though, matter cannot be considered as a controlling force over mind. It is consciousness which gives to itself its own set of meanings, its own history, and its own sociological status. Both matter other than my own body and matter proper are "ambiguous." It is largely plastic in the hands of the mind which is constantly structuring and restructuring its own world in an ever ongoing fashion. For the soul there is no *before,* no detached history, no "out there" or "back there" somewhere. For Merleau-Ponty the "thing" and the "idea" become indiscernible. The body is just a locus for a continuing organization of meanings into some personal order. The body is not an out-there machine. But then neither is it merely an "idea" of the mind.

True, there is a conservation of one's past as the dialectic continues. But it is not an overpowering conservation. True again, the retention is often only subconscious. But there is no need to explain this by means of the reductionistic theories offered by, say, Sigmund Freud. Such theories deny freedom and make it impossible to explicate the inner consciousness of choice. Instead of opting for determinism we must view each conscious event as a replacement of the preceding one. Yet there is continuity due to the assumption into the whole of its own self-structured history from moment to moment.[46]

For Merleau-Ponty, consequently, reality or "being" is not basically body or mind. There are only seeming dualities. In reality the only fundamental thing is "structure." Depending upon how the dialectic is structured from moment to moment, we have either a mental or a material aspect of reality. Depending upon the degree of integration and interaction of "body" with its environment we have different "degrees" of life and mind. The more complex the organization, the more soul. Body and soul are not absolutes, but relatives. There are layers of organization. There is the level of chemical interaction, the level of biological interaction, and the level of mental and social dialectic. "Each of these degrees," says Merleau-Ponty, "is soul with respect to the preceding one, body with respect to the following one."[47]

So we see that there are no separate spiritual substances in nature. There are only zones of "perspective." There is only the "lived" and the "known." Thus dualism is banished, and the problem of man-in-the-world is transformed. According to Merleau-Ponty consciousness both constitutes the universe and grasps objects in themselves. Only with regard to conscious centers of dialectical interaction do body and soul have any meaning. There is no detached *en-soi,* and there is no purely ideal world built up by the confluence of forms and ideas. The truth is in the middle course. What we call perception of the outside world is really the termination of a dialectical uplifting involving a perpetual flux process which *must* contact the "real" world because it *is* the real world. Therefore, Malebranche, with his appeal to God in order to unite human and worldly action and reaction, and Leibniz, with his divinely preestablished harmony to do the same job, along with Descartes and Sartre, are rendered irrelevant. Within lived consciousness all "antinomies" are finally resolved and harmonized.[48]

Although not as popular in North America as John Dewey, most likely because he used a great deal of "scholastic" terminology in his works, Merleau-Ponty seemed to be attempting to say much the same thing. It may be true, as A. L. Fisher points out,[49] that he was becoming more and more Hegelian in outlook as he got older, but, as shown in his view of the human person, it was a Hegelianism without Geist.[50] True enough, as with John Dewey before him, what he says about people may be interpreted spiritualistically as well as materialistically. Nonetheless, in view of what he *could* have said, as we will shortly see in the following chapters, his right to be placed in the nonreductionistic materialism position seems settled.

BACKGROUND

Evolution

Professor Stephen Jay Gould of Harvard University, writing as a nonreductionistic materialist, says that Darwin's theory of common descent by natural selection was too radical for the English Victorian mind to accept, because it

> explodes any concept of inherent progress, denies to life an ontological status separate from inanimate matter, and attributes the properties of mind to the highly complex workings of a material brain. The 19th century was not ready for this brand of materialism. Today, all scientists accept materialism (at least in their workplace), and the philosophically astute realize that it poses no threat to our love for music, subjective insight, and love itself.[51]

This may have been basically true for many people living in 1859. However, there is at least one Victorian who would have to disagree with Gould if he were to read his remarks today, and that is Charles Darwin himself. In at least two places in his *Origin of Species* Darwin affirms the existence of inherent progress in the world. In the early part of chapter 7 he assures us that,

> Although we have no good evidence of the existence in organic beings of an innate tendency towards progressive development, yet this necessarily follows, as I have attempted to show in the fourth chapter, through the continued action of natural selection. For the best definition which has ever been given of a high standard of organisation, is the degree to which the parts have been specialised or differentiated; and natural selection tends to-

wards this end, inasmuch as the parts are thus enabled to perform their functions more efficiently.[52]

While at the very end of the work we read: ''Hence we may look with some confidence to a secure future of great length. And as natural selection works solely by and for the good of each being, all corporeal and mental endowments will tend to progress towards perfection.''[53] Note that progress is not simply a possibility but a necessity.

Such views were not peculiar to Darwin. They were in fact very much the spirit of the age. People living at the end of the twentieth century, after world wars, germ and gas warfare, atom bombs, and the large-scale spread of dictatorships made possible only by modern technology, find such sentiments hard to believe. But things were very different in 1859. It was an age of optimism concerning world affairs. It was the age of Karl Marx and his dream of human perfectibility through politics, as well as of Darwin and biological perfectibility. It was the age of August Comte, the father of sociology, who saw the day when a new scientific religion would save the world. It was, most of all, the age of Hegel, the German intellectual who supplied the philosophical presuppositions for the whole theory of necessary progress. By and large these dreams have now gone by the board, except in certain areas of the philosophy of human nature where they still seem to serve a useful function.

Hegel and Parmenides

Hegel was beginning his philosophical synthesis about the time Immanuel Kant died. The whole thrust and intent of Hegel's philosophy may be rightly looked upon as an attempt to overcome the deep divisions he saw within human nature and between the moral nature of human beings and the material nature of the physical world. Some aspects of his original problem were derived from his study of the history of philosophy and science. Others came directly out of the problems left behind by Kant.

From the history of human thought he learned of the importance of the Parmenidean arguments proving by pure thought alone that all change and alteration are deceptions. From Kant he inherited the doctrine of the bifurcation between the intellect and the senses, as well as between human nature as possessed of freedom for moral choice and the absolutely determined and predictable material world inhabited by those very same human beings. Hegel found that he could not live with such divisions and bifurcations. Is not human nature one and united? Are you not one person? Are not the senses, which take the world in pieces and fragments, forever changing from one moment to the next, and the intellect, which is always striving for the common, unifying elements in the universe through rational laws and formulas, both aspects of *one* creature? How can this be? How can the human species be free in a world composed entirely of totally unfree matter? How could such a thing have come about? It seems impossible. It is an affront to the rational powers of the human thinker to have to live in such an irrational universe.

If Hegel had been a Plato, he could have accepted such fundamental divisions and simply gone on from there to glorify one part of man at the expense of another part. Hegel, however, could not ever bring himself to contemplate such a thing seriously. Some source of unity must be found, something rational and complete that would satisfy the human desire for integrity. Such a happy situation could not be obtained by use of the senses, for the senses are constantly tending towards fragmentation and dissolution. Any unity to be found in anything, including the information gleaned from the senses, must have its source in the intellect. The mind, therefore, is the only possible place to begin the search for the much-needed solution.

To Parmenides's credit he was the first thinker that we know of in history to have fully realized this primary point. As Hegel himself tells us near the beginning of his masterwork, *The Encyclopaedia of the Philosophical Sciences:*

> It is sufficient to mention here, that logic begins where the proper history of philosophy begins. Philosophy began in the Eleatic school, especially with Parmenides. Parmenides, who conceives the absolute as Being, says that "Being alone is and Nothing is not." Such was the true starting-point of philosophy, which is always knowledge by thought: and here for the first time we find pure thought seized and made an object to itself.[54]

But what did Parmenides say that was so important? It was his argument that showed the need for "nothingness" in order to have change. Somehow or another "what is not" must exist in order to have change. But Parmenides stoutly refused to admit any such thing as the existence of nonexistence. Consequently there could be no change for him. Nothing accounts for nothing, and something that is already in existence has no need to change into something. Hegel tells his readers to take Parmenides seriously. Only by so doing can the rational necessities laid upon Hegel's own shoulders be appreciated. He writes that the ancients saw plainly how Parmenides' argument destroyed all change in the world. A thing cannot become what it already is. Any thinking person can see that! How is it, then, that so many supposedly intelligent people so calmly go around saying that something can only come from something? Don't they know that such thinking must necessarily form the "basis of Pantheism" and that the ancients had already "exhausted" all that can be said on the subject?⁵⁵

By "Pantheism" Hegel understands a strictly materialistic doctrine. According to Parmenides' "Way of Truth" the really real Being is one unchanging, eternal material sphere. Although denied by some later followers of Parmenides, Hegel takes this materialism to be the very definition of pantheism. Such a view rules out any possibility for change in the world. But such a view is obviously wrong. Things do change. Consequently, his own doctrine must overthrow pantheism by attacking it at its very roots.

Hegel realized that in order to have a scientific system worthy of the name it must be coherent throughout. To Hegel this meant answering Parmenides first. What's the point of deliberately building a whole system on a faulty foundation? Hegel, as pointed out above, had little sympathy for those who failed to appreciate this problem. On this score he was basically correct.

As a historian of science has pointed out while speaking of Zeno of Elea, Parmenides' loyal disciple, it may seem at first that the more intelligent class of people should have fewer problems to contend with. In fact, though, the members of the more foolish class of people are the less troubled in their minds. This is because they think they understand something perfectly when in fact they do not. They lack the philosopher's ability to imagine difficulties. Only the brighter people see the problems clearly. "Practical"-minded people can get away with their lack of interest in "airy" problems only because some "airy"-minded thinkers have set the stage for them. This was the difference between the "down-to-earth" Babylonian mathematicians, for instance, and the theoretically minded Greek mathematicians. "We have many evidences of Greek genius," reports Sarton, "but none is stronger and more startling than the mathematical thinking of this time, incited by logical difficulties that the average man of today (twenty-five centuries later) would hardly notice."[56] The people who did the inciting were those of the Parmenidean school.

Hegel's method for overcoming the Parmenidean problem was to make nonexistence exist. This could only be done, he thought, by placing nothingness at the very foundation of reality. Reality could not be considered as one and unchanging. It must rather be multiple and dynamic, surging back and forth in what has now become a familiar manner, namely, a "dialectical" manner. Reality is the Absolute, the First, Being, Pure Undetermined Thought, the Idea. It is the supreme genus, as broad and all-encompassing as it is empty of specific content.

But that is not all. It is also Nothing, the Absolute Negative. The Absolute is simultaneously the supreme Positivity and Negativity. Any distinction between the two is purely conceptual. It is like combining the God of the Judeo-Christian tradition with the Supreme Nothing of the Buddhist tradition. Both are mere abstractions in which there is only an intellectual contradiction. In the real world of natural change and motion the contradiction is overcome in the fact of real changes and becoming. Hence Parmenides is overcome. And in the same way the dichotomies of Kant are overcome. Reality is not all broken up and fractured. It is unified on the level of pure thought. Change is possible, and more, it is real because nonbeing is as real as being. Nothing, if it be the same as something, will give rise to such a dynamic upheaval that the existence of becoming or constant change in the world is assured.

Hegel is fully aware of the new problems such a scheme of things gives rise to. "The proposition," he states, "that Being and Nothing is the same seems so paradoxical to the imagination or understanding that it is perhaps taken for a joke."[57] A little further on he returns to the same point: "No great expenditure of wit is needed to make fun of the maxim that Being and Nothing are the same, or rather to adduce absurdities which, it is erroneously asserted, are the consequences and illustrations of that maxim."[58]

What Hegel means by this last statement is that as long as the two opposites remain on the level of pure abstraction there can be no real conflicts. It is only on a different level, when the two opposites give rise to a surging back and forth which we call change, that concrete oppositions come into play. But then you are no longer on the level of pure abstraction. You are then in the world of ordinary experiences where it does make sense to worry about whether the sun, the law, the air, your home, God, and so on, are or are not. On the level of becoming it makes sense to talk about the contradictions of an "either-or" situation. As an explanation of how such a thing is possible, however, Hegel must postulate a "both-and" situation on the level of fundamental reality. After all, he insists, don't people realize that otherwise Parmenides would be right?

The Quantity-Quality Leap

Based upon the importance of mind Hegel could easily argue that if any kind of unification was to take place in our understanding of the world, it must be of a mental sort. Observing millions and millions of bodies falling to earth will never produce a scientific understanding of the phenomenon. If unification is to be brought into the picture, it must be the result of the unifying influence of mind. Not until we have a formula uniting in one insight all the diverse occurrences witnessed in this phenomenon can we really begin to understand the universe. Such work is obviously done by the mind rather than by the senses. So it is with all the sciences, including the master science of philosophy which is responsible for understanding all the rest.

But how far can such a process of unification continue? The greater the comprehension and universality of one's formulas unifying the diverse phenomena of nature, the greater the science. It can even be said that the formulas are more real than the phenomena which they unify because of the greater importance and dignity of thought, especially pure thought. As the thinker proceeds away from thought mixed up with the fragmenting influence of the senses he finds himself approaching closer and closer to pure mind or Geist. When this point is reached, the unification is complete. All the diversities we observe around us can be accounted for as deviations and modifications of the Pure Spirit or the all-encompassing One, Absolute, or God. This is an objective Spirit, the really real foundation for everything in the universe.

Hegel's explanation, however, is not yet complete. For although he has satisfied himself that he has solved the problem of bifurcation in nature by pure thought, he has now to account for this very fact of observation. Such an account must be based upon the nature and activity of the Absolute. The foundation for that activity has already been seen in the inner dynamism of the Being-Nothingness conflict. Within the totally complete Being-For-Itself or Absolute, which is the Pure Spirit or Immaterial Quality, there has occurred from all eternity a surging back and forth, or dialectic, which resulted in the alienation of the Itself from Itself. This alienation is pure quantity or extension, the material manifestation of the Pure Idea or Mind. Through a series of successive dialectical steps the matter of the universe, or Nature, proceeds to acquire further determinations. These are magnitude (determinate quantity), continuous and discrete quantity (the fact of being there and then), and measure, or the limiting of quantity into a form that can be captured by a mathematical formula.

The measurable, though, is not the final stage. The measurable can and has given rise to the measureless, which is another way of talking about a return to quality. In this fashion Hegel is justified in regarding nature as containing real hierarchies. In fact, there are in nature essential differences among many and various species. Consequently, even though ultimately everything is to be identified with everything else in the one reality of pure Mind, Hegel did not consider himself to be a reductionist. Neither did he think of himself as being a pantheist which, from the Judeo-Christian viewpoint at least, would have been the same thing as being an atheist, because pantheism was a materialistic doctrine, while his own position was radically spiritualistic. The ultimate One, the ground for all more determinate being, was pure Mind or Idea and so, according to his own definition, could not be made a part of a pantheistic doctrine.

The existence of material nature is a later development, logically considered, than the fundamental reality of Spirit. And even within nature it is quality which counts for more than quantity. The different levels of being which we observe in nature are all part of the dialectical movement. If higher and higher realities appear in nature, it is because this movement is a movement towards more perfect manifestations of quality in nature. Quantity is only the preparation for the natural leaps into higher levels of quality, as are found in minerals, plants, animals, and human beings. As Hegel states towards the end of chapter 7, ''Thus quantity by means of the Dialectical movement so far studied through its several stages, turns out to be a return to quality."[59]

A short time later he again emphasizes the importance of quality as the true outcome of all significant quantitative changes:

> The identity between quantity and quality which is found in Measure is at first only implicit, and not yet explicitly realised. In other words these two categories which unite in Measure each claim an independent authority. On the one hand, the quantitative features of existence may be altered, without affecting its quality. On the other hand, this increase and diminution, immaterial though it is, has its limit, by exceeding which the quality suffers change.[60]

And again, "This process of measure, which appears alternately as a mere change in quantity, and then as a sudden revulsion of quantity into quality, may be envisaged under the figure of a knotted line."[61]

The knot or node represents the change that occurs in an otherwise uniform chain of events in nature. The quantitative line of nature, in its necessary dialectical tendency always to exceed itself will, sooner or later, reach a point where a leap is inevitable, a point where a leap is indeed dictated by the material circumstances of that particular locus in nature. This is the nodal point. Here the revulsion of quantity into quality takes place. The new essence is implicitly present in the given pattern of the material parts of nature which are subject to measurement. Like a snare set in matter, the line of nature seizes and retains the new essence once the sudden change has taken place in the course of nature. When everything is just right, the loop closes into a knot, thus tying down the now explicitly expressed essential quality.

In support of his explanation of how nature operates Hegel gave his readers seven examples of what he believed to be quantity-quality leaps. The illustrations were meant to be familiar cases to most people in keeping with his desire to be as clear and open as possible in his exposition of some very difficult problems. The seven examples are the following:

1. The conversion of liquid water into ice or steam by adding or subtracting heat.
2. The conversion of numerous grains of wheat into a heap of wheat.

3. The conversion of a bushy tail of hairs into a bald tail by the removal of single hairs.
4. The conversion of a well-balanced economic state of a nation into avarice or prodigality by the increase in wealth.
5. The conversion of one type of government into another by the change in population density.
6. The conversion of one musical note into another by alterations in the vibration of a string.
7. The conversion of a metal into an oxide of that metal by a change in its material structure.

Hegel and Marxism

What are we to make of Hegel's examples today? In his own day they were apparently quite convincing. This was certainly the case with respect to the young Karl Marx and the cofounder of modern communism, Friedrich Engels. If terms such as "alienation" and "dialectic" are a part of the average person's vocabulary today, it is not due to Hegel but to the influence of people like Marx, Engels, Lenin, and Stalin. Whether or not someone is a Communist in the political sense, there can be no doubt that the need for every nation in the world to deal with the existence of communism in one way or another has necessitated that everyone at least speak the language of communism to a certain extent. As it happens the language of communism is in fact the language of Hegel.

Also, as it happens, it was not Marx himself who attempted to work out a complete account of how human beings fit in with the rest of nature. This task was taken up by Engels in his *Dialectics of Nature*. This work was left unfinished in 1883 due to the need to complete Marx's more important economic work *Das Kapital* following Marx's death in that same year. However, there can be no doubt about his basic position on man as a species. Except for the translation of Spirit into Matter, his entire program for explaining mankind follows the outline established by the German genius.

In opposition to the crass materialism of the ancient atomists and more recent reductionists Marxist materialism must be of a new and more sophisticated sort. What this means is that it must possess the basic characteristics of Hegel's Spirit. It must be internally dynamic, manifesting itself in the external creation of really new entities. Qualitative differences must be seen as emerging from quantitative organization. As before, the quantity-quality leap must occur. What Marx does in effect is to chop off the first stage of Hegel's dialectic (Immaterial Quality) and begin his own dialectic with the second stage (Externalized Quantity).

All the traits needed for internal evolution, though, are retained, simultaneously making Marxism into a materialism and saving it from reductionism. Only the doctrine of the quantity-quality leap allows for the existence of *true* hierarchies in nature. Once activated there is bound to be that necessary progress upwards in the biosphere that biologists call evolution. The human mind is truly and really something superior in nature, just as the existence of living things marks a true superiority over the inorganic world. By the same token, the rise of a new society would mark a true advance in the dialectical movement of the world. It would constitute one more radical change in the natural processes of matter.

Indeed, because dialectical materialism has so well explained every other scientific development in the past and present, says Engels, we can be certain that it will not fail us when we predict the advent of a new scientific utopia based upon our scientific materialism. In nature everything owes its origin to active matter. From the humblest cell to the most advanced civilization the inner dynamism of matter can be seen at work. No other explanation is required. As Engels states, "All qualitative differences in Nature rest on differences of chemical composition or on different quantities or forms of motion (energy) or, as is almost always the case, on both."[62]

Towards the end of the last century, when Engels wrote, the science of chemistry was well on its way to being a rival to physics in terms of the significance of its results for human beings. It had made major leaps forward in comparison to its state at the beginning of the nineteenth century, when Hegel wrote. It is not surprising, then, that whereas Hegel mentions the wonders of chemistry only in passing, Engels places a great emphasis upon the findings of chemistry as a major support for the quantity-quality leap theory. Although some of the original Hegelian examples remained in use and were later to be augmented by such things as the origin of biological species by natural selection and the conversion of a worker into a capitalist as soon as his wealth exceeded a certain limit, the field of chemical change now became the central theme for those Marxists seeking convincing examples of the nonreductionistic materialism view at work here and now.

After all, the origins of the different levels of reality were events that occurred in the past. Like the Bible story of creation, they were not events which could be directly investigated by the scientist. Why should one have more faith in the quantity-quality leap position than in the biblical account of human genesis? It was to reduce this faith element in a scientific theory which prompted the interest in chemical changes. Why accept the biblical story of creation when the non-reductionistic materialism view can be verified here and now in the chemistry laboratory? What need is there for fanciful pictures of God creating man when the interested investigator need only glance up at the periodic table of the elements hanging on the laboratory wall in order to discover the true picture of things?

What is the difference between laughing gas and the solid crystal, nitrogen anhydride? inquires Engels. It is nothing but the quantity of oxygen. Laughing gas has one atom of oxygen while nitrogen anhydride has five. And between the two there are three more oxides of nitrogen, each with characteristics quite different from all the others. These are truly amazing facts of nature. Yet, what accounts for the vast differences among the five oxides of nitrogen is nothing other than the quantity of oxygen. Here surely is a series of cases in which quantitative differences make quite radical qualitative changes. Judging by the traits and properties of the higher order oxides of nitrogen essentially different chemical compositions have certainly come into existence. The foundation for the leap, though, is nothing other than the pattern and organization of the material substratum of nature. This is truly an amazing thing to behold.[63]

SOME CONSEQUENCES

Causes and Effects

The nonreductionistic materialistic position lays claim to being scientific, not because it insists upon ostensive definitions and no others, but because it rejects any reference to the supernatural, God, or the spiritual in its explanation of the human person. Phrases such as "the spiritual aspirations of man" or "the divine spark in human nature" may be used, but if so they must be carefully redefined so as to leave out any reference to anything outside or above material nature in any literal sense. This being the case, and yet at the same time human beings also being truly unique and superior to the higher primates, it must follow that material nature alone is capable of providing the driving force behind this phenomenon. And indeed this is exactly the kind of nature that is postulated by the advocates of this position. The materialized version of Hegelianism sees nature as capable of indefinite progress even though lacking any superior spiritual force behind it. Inherent in matter itself are the native capacities and potentialities for greater and greater levels of organization and interaction. For example, Jacob Bronowski, the mathematician turned philosopher, finds this fact to be an essential ingredient in any naturalistic explanation of evolution. He tells us that, due to the vast potential for stable complexity hidden in matter, it is possible for higher and higher levels of evolutionary development to come about by "chance." Random encounters among the elements of a previously established layer of stability in nature will provide the basis for yet higher layers. It is as if nature were shuffling a "sticky pack of cards" and they held together in longer and longer runs.[64]

If nature is not outwardly directed by God and if progress is still to be made, then nature must be inner-directed. This inner direction cannot come from some mind or soul or "World Soul" because that would be to fall back into the superstitious ways of prescientific times. Consequently, the production of superior things such as human beings must be the work of inner-directed matter, dynamically self-moved so as to give rise to superior beings by a series of quantity-quality leaps. In other words, from something inferior in quality there comes something superior in quality. A particular human being might not be able to do it, but it would seem that it is possible for nature to make a silk purse out of a sow's ear.

Those advocates of the nonreductionistic materialism position who stop to think about it are fully aware of this consequence of their position. In the case of John Dewey, for instance, what the investigator of the human person finds is that he is very much opposed to what he calls the "dogma" of the superior reality of causes over their effects.[65] This dogma is held by both the reductionists and the spiritualists. The former talk about matter as the efficient cause of life and mind; the latter about some primal spirit as the efficient cause. In both cases it is maintained that the river of events cannot rise above its source. Yet effects, says Dewey, are only indicators of the potentialities inherent in nature. They tell us what nature is really like, much more so than the traditional causes of either one extreme or the other.[66] Both extremes fail to recognize the importance of evolution. In that sense they are both nonhistorical in their supposed explanations.[67]

Indeed, the behaviorists even have their causes and effects mixed up. What is the stimulus and what is the response to an accurate scientific observer? In an S-R situation the behaviorists assume that they are first observing the stimulus and next the response. But this puts the cart before the horse. What we actually see is what *has* happened. We see the results first. Only then can we go back and infer that a certain element in the situation was the stimulus. True enough, there are stimuli at work in man's mental life. However, argues Dewey, "I am pointing out that we are aware of the stimuli only in terms of our response to them and of the consequences of this response."[68]

If the reductionists were not so bound to the dogma that causes must always either exceed or equal their effects in terms of essential quality, such misunderstandings would not occur. The same is true for the supernaturalists who refuse even to consider materialism as a possible mode of explanation for human nature. By assuming that no matter how far back one goes in a chain of events the product can never rise above its source in dignity, they automatically cut themselves off from any real understanding of how nature really works.

Perpetual Motion

One of the chief critics of the old-fashioned reductionism has been Henri Bergson. His main objection rests upon the way such a theory denies any real novelty in nature. The language of that school of thought may include many references to evolution, but how can evolution really be taken seriously when everything is predetermined beforehand? Like a magician pulling rabbits out of a hat, the best the reductionists can do is to pretend that something new has arrived on the scene. In reality, though, the new form or creature has been there all the time. To use Bergson's own words:

It may perhaps be said that the form could be foreseen if we could know, in all their details, the conditions under which it will be produced. But these conditions are built up into it and are part and parcel of its being; they are peculiar to that phase of its history in which life finds itself at the moment of producing the form: how could we know beforehand a situation that is unique of its kind, that has never yet occurred and will never occur again?[69]

If this be true, some interesting questions immediately arise. Granting that effects can exceed their causes and that the new effects of evolution are intrinsically unpredictable, what justification does anyone have for claiming that the arrow of nature must necessarily stop here or there? In modern times the Communist philosophers were the first group of theoreticians to have to face this problem in a practical way. Josef Stalin had to justify stopping the revolution after it had succeeded so well in Russia. At the end of 1929 Stalin began his attack on those Marxist thinkers whose "theory had not kept pace with the practical and economic development of the Soviet Union."[70] What he had in mind was the way in which *too much* consistency in applying the basic philosophical principles of Marxism would destroy the stability so needed in Russia at the time. Confronted with Stalin's political power and his readiness to employ violent means to silence "revisionists" of all stripes, it was useless for the consistent Marxist ideologists to quote Marx and Engels against him. Within two years after Stalin opened his attack, Abram Deborin, the leader of the orthodox dialectical materialists, capitulated completely. Instead of theory dictating practice, practice must dictate to theory. German Hegelianism must bow to Russian nationalism. A more reductionistic approach, in the sense of a more pragmatic, matter-of-fact approach, was what Stalin required for the good of Mother Russia, and all good party members must obey.

Stalin himself, however, continued to be concerned with the problem. If Marx and Engels were the champions of true science, and if they thought that more quantity-quality leaps were demanded by the necessary dialectic, how could Stalin disagree with them and still be scientific? By the late 1940s Stalin had arrived at his own solution to the difficulty. He distinguished between two types of leaps. Some leaps are "explosions." These require opposites, such as space-time, matter-motion, and mass-energy, in order to eventuate in a new entity. When applied to political matters, a leap can occur when there are two antagonistic classes, as was the case in Russia in 1917.

Other leaps, though, are gradual. These do not require obvious and sudden changes in the quality of the situation. Examples of this type of leap are changes in language and in the social conditions of the U.S.S.R.[71]

Needless to say, such a facile solution was not very convincing. However, a pattern had been set, so that by the 1960s policies such as peaceful coexistence could be regarded as more necessary than the Hegelian dialectic. Instead of violent inner conflicts resulting in the creation of new entities, things must proceed in a fashion more consistent with the old-fashioned reductionism. According to this vulgar, mechanistic view of matter, everything is on a par. Everything changes slowly by degrees. Everything is continuous with everything else in terms of pushes and pulls. As unbecoming as such a shift may be to those orthodox Marxists looking for quick revolutionary changes, as found in chemical reactions, it was regarded as necessary by the political leaders. At least in Russia, therefore, the problem had been resolved.

Scientists in the so-called Free World would be the first to condemn the conditions under which the Communist-country scientists must labor. Yet right in our own midst there is an equally pressing difficulty which most scientists are not facing up to squarely. This is the whole issue of pollution and what to do about it. Assuming that the nonreductionistic materialism position is true, who can justly say what constitutes pollution in the universe and what does not? To talk about something as a pollutant is to use derogatory language. Pollution is supposed to be something bad. The language is parallel to that used in moral or ethical contexts wherein some action is referred to as being bad or evil or a sin. Pollution is often referred to as a crime against nature. It is as if someone were attacking his mother with a knife.

In fact, though, is it really very consistent to worry about strip-mining, the ozone layer, offshore oil drilling, and the like? This concern is based upon the argument that nature cannot absorb and recycle various man-made materials. But what is overlooked by the argument is that it presupposes that nature is somehow fixed and constant within very strict limits. Is not such a view at variance with the evolutionary approach? Does it make sense to teach classes in ecology that nature is an unbalanced, amorphous, shifting mass producing new forms by evolutionary leaps while simultaneously telling them that modern industry is upsetting the balance of nature? How can somebody say, on the one hand, that our present world came about by way of unpredictable, chance transformations and also say, on the other hand, that nature is a closed circle in which everything is finely balanced within narrow limits?

If in reality nature is all fluent and shifting, any kind of "balance" in nature must be very short-lived and temporary. Is not the biosphere composed of a graded series of organisms which are capable of indefinitely gaining and losing many different characteristics? Are not trial and error, "dead ends," and much wastefulness the order of the day? Why cannot the natural world take its nitrous oxides, microspheres of plastic, atomic wastes, old nylon shirts, DDT, phosphates, and so on and so forth and so reorganize the material parts of everything that some new and better forms of life emerge? After all, is this not what has happened all along in the past? How did present-day humans come about if not by way of struggle, upheaval, catastrophe, and unexpected mutation? Why try to stop the process now?

To be consistent, therefore, worry about pollution must cease within the nonreductionistic materialistic camp. In the minds of at least a few reputable scientists it has ceased. They no more worry about oil spills now than about the existence of dinosaurs a long time ago. Dinosaurs were a pollution in the ancient jungles. Old beer cans are a pollution now. However, in the future, after new quantity-quality leaps, the pollution of today may very well end up hanging in an honored position in some museum.

Species and Subspecies

Another consequence of the nonreductionistic materialism position of some importance is the existence of different races within the same species. Indeed the problem is even more fundamental than that. The issue is the unity of the whole human race once again. What are we to say to someone who seriously challenges the unity of the human species? Perhaps only certain races of mankind should be considered fully and truly human beings. Perhaps it is a mistake to talk about the brotherhood of man. Could it be that some members of the family are stepchildren, or even illegitimate? Could it be the case that some of those creatures called human beings in the past should now, after our scientific enlightenment, be regarded as being only on their way to being humans? Maybe they have not yet made the final leap?

This possibility certainly exists as a necessary consequence of the theory. According to the Bible the entire human species issued forth from one set of parents specially created by God. But this is wrong. Who really knows exactly when and where human beings originated? Was it necessarily in one place at one time? There is certainly no guarantee of such a thing. How many partial successes of nature are still with us today walking the face of the earth? Why is it not possible for nature to have produced retarded and crippled children, so to speak? Darwin himself was aware of this consequence. We read in his *Descent of Man*, "In a series of forms graduating insensibly from some ape-like creature to man as he now exists, it would be impossible to fix on any definite point when the term 'man' ought to be used."[72]

Surprisingly, though, he seems to have completely missed the social and political significance of this point. He even calls it a matter of little importance. He is sure, however, that once evolution, rather than special creation, is widely accepted the whole debate between monogenists and polygenists will quietly die out. What he means is that the polygenetic view will become so clear and obvious that no one, at least no scientist of any reputation, would ever again entertain the monogenetic view.

In another place in the same work he hints that there may even be some kind of species-subspecies relationship between the male and female genders. Darwin finds parallels between human beings and animals everywhere. People are like animals, especially the monkeys and great apes, in social and cultural habits as well as in physical considerations. As far as he could tell, for instance, some primates at least require a long time with their parents before they are capable of making it in the world on their own. He also finds that with respect to human beings, "Man differs from woman in size, bodily strength, hairiness, etc., *as well as in mind*, in the same manner as do the two sexes in many mammals."[73]

It would seem that somehow or another the male and female genders of the human species had to arrive on the earthly scene together if sexual reproduction of human beings is to be explained.

But can anyone be sure even of this? Could the male have somehow come first, perhaps by thousands and thousands of years, thus accounting for the fact that males are superior to women in mental capacity? Darwin does not say. Today, due to the predominantly female hormonal constitution of the fetus for the first few weeks after conception, we would be more likely to say that the female evolved first! But who can say for sure?

Apes and monkeys are usually thought of as being close to people on the scale of development. It is even possible to imagine a progression within the human species. From the monkey there developed the Negro race, then the Mongolian race, and finally the Caucasian race.

However, viewed biologically, there does not seem to be much reason for one race to lord it over any other race. Biologically all races are close to the ape in various ways. In terms of hair, for instance, Caucasians are the hairiest race. Considering how hairy apes are, Caucasians should be considered the most primitive. This is precisely how some members of the Mongolian race looked upon them. The only Caucasians known to the Japanese, Koreans, and some Chinese were the Hairy Ainu inhabiting the most northern region of Japan and some islands north of Japan. These hairy men were very primitive when the cultures surrounding them were relatively advanced. As a result they were looked down upon and considered an inferior type.

Then again, Caucasians possess large frontal skull projections relative to the other races. This characteristic strongly marks off Caucasians as being closest to the ape. As can be seen from the structure of ape skulls, the bumps over the eye sockets are an obvious feature. Certainly those creatures which today exhibit the same feature relative to the other races must be the more primitive.

But then again, in terms of body color, Negroes seem to approximate their monkey ancestors most nearly, while in terms of body size the Mongolian race would appear to be the first group to have broken loose from its ancient ties. If other traits are used, such as ear size, the Negro race would seem to be more advanced.

The Chinese tell the story that when God took clay to make man, he first left it in the oven too short a time, thus producing Caucasians. Next, he left it in too long a time, thus making Negroes. But finally he got it just right, thereby creating the Chinese. Every people could easily think up such stories about themselves. The point is, who is there to say, according to the nonreductionistic materialistic position, that any of them is wrong? In its own way this position is as much at sea as the reductionistic view when it comes to talking about the unity of the human species. Such a thing may be asserted, but there would be nothing scientific about such an assertion.

Behavior Modification

Although widely used by all members of the nonreductionistic materialistic group, whether Marxists or not, Darwin's works themselves do not really seem to be in that camp. For Darwin, changes took place in fine gradations. Nowhere does he emphasize the importance of major leaps. Rather than quantity-quality steps, alterations in nature take place along smooth curves. It is even doubtful whether he recognized the existence of truly qualitative differences in the hierarchy of natural types. Instead, his usual manner for presenting his position was constantly to play down any talk of "true" species. What are called species, he pointed out, are really only strongly marked and relatively permanent varieties. In fact there are no lines of demarcation among species. In the past, everyone admitted that varieties did not require special acts of creation by God. In the future, when homogeneity is widely recognized and emphasized, people will come to realize that species do not require special creations either.[74]

All in all, Darwin himself seems to have been much closer to the reductionism of Lucretius and David Hume than to the antireductionism of Hegel. Nevertheless, this did not prevent him from participating in the spirit of infinite progress so typical of the times.

The gap between Darwinian evolution and what was required for Marxist revolutions was recognized by Marx and Engels themselves. Darwin could not be fully accepted exactly as presented by himself or by his loyal followers, especially Herbert Spencer. He was, nevertheless, very compatible with Marxism. At a later date, after the Russian Revolution, any attempt to return to a more "gradualism" approach to social change would be branded as a "right-wing" deviation from orthodoxy. Such a slide back into reductionism would play down the need for actively creating revolutions here and now in those countries where antagonistic classes still exist. It would be a great boon to capitalism if people could be convinced that they must wait hundreds of years for the gradual changes to occur. By the same token, though, any attempt to depend too heavily upon the inner necessities of the materialistic dialectic must also be condemned. This "left-wing" deviation, which is in effect a movement back to Hegel, would also discourage people from actively revolting here and now. Instead, they would wait around expecting that nature would somehow automatically do the job for them.

What is interesting about these intellectual wars within communism is the way orthodoxy tries to ride the fence between Hegel and Darwin. This is important when trying to understand the nonreductionistic materialism approach to behavior modification. When Darwin spoke about the emergence of mankind, he was thinking in terms of a "straight-line" type of development. The ancestors of human beings were many (polygenesis), but they were all arranged in a straight-line course of development behind the first humans. All the races, he thought, descended from the same primitive stock of humans. This view is now largely defunct among modern biologists. As was said earlier, it is the *modern* Darwin who can be used to defend racism, even though the old Darwin may have appeared to have relegated such a thing to oblivion. In this way the original Darwin was much closer to the Bible than many realize.

In his day Darwin was still very much under the influence of the Bible story of human genesis. In the Bible there is no sophisticated attempt to solve the problem of universal predication (that is, the problem of species) as found in Plato or in many later philosophers and scientists. Instead there is simply the assertion that the whole human race is one because we all come from the same set of parents. This notion is preserved in Darwin's theory as originally stated. Today, however, we realize that it is in no way an essential aspect of evolutionary theory.

This at least is true among non-Marxist scientists. At the University of Moscow, however, things appear differently, at least officially. There the straight-line approach is still the order of the day. The emergence of one human species is still thought of as being the result of one leap after gradual quantitative changes. And more importantly, the advent of the new society is still thought of as following along in a straight-line progression from the quantity-quality leap that is to produce the true Communist society. What in the world could have led Marx and Engels to believe that once the revolution took place humanitarianism, altruism, and selfless love of neighbor would prevail forever in the new order? Why would the new proletarian society, as opposed to the old bourgeois society, be so superior in actually getting into practice almost all the virtues that eighteen hundred years of Christianity failed to get into universal practice? The only explanation for such an attitude is that they possessed a sincere faith in the power of the quantity-quality leap.

Such a faith is still preserved today in various Marxist handbooks. Unlike the utopian societies of More, Campanella, Saint-Simon, Fourier, Owen, Herzen, Belinsky, and others, Marxism knows what nature is really like. It fully understands the laws of natural development and the inner necessities of matter. It took Marxism to turn utopianism into science. What this science tells us is that there is a parallelism between leaps in nature, best exemplified in chemistry, and leaps in the social order, best exemplified in communism. From Hegel there is derived the conviction that such leaps are possible. From Darwin there is derived the need for a gradual quantitative build-up. From Marx and Engels there is derived the social consequences of the combination of Hegel and Darwin.

According to the nonreductionistic materialism view, then, it is possible to create a new type of human being. Unlike behavior modification within reductionism, though, there is no scientific need to work on the individual through operant conditioning. Those in Russia who advocated this sort of thing, such as Pavlov, though officially honored, were always regarded as unorthodox. Rather than individual conditioning, what is required is economic (material) change for the masses. By altering the material conditions of society (food production, ownership of the means of production, the circulation of money, and so forth) a new quality will emerge in society. If the changes are radical enough, a qualitative leap will occur which will produce a new human nature.

The task of the Marxist leader, therefore, is to work on the quantitative basis of society and leave the rest to Nature. Once the quantitative foundations have been gradually altered by human intervention the automatic inner dynamics of matter will take over and produce the qualitatively superior human being. In this way behavior will be modified in a manner that no reductionist ever dreamed of. It is only the sophisticated materialism of the antireductionist, consequently, and not the naive materialism of the reductionist, that will finally bring about the ideal society of the future. Without any appeal to God or spiritual reality it is possible for human beings to establish a new Garden of Eden on earth.[75]

As far as the non-Marxist thinker is concerned, the road to peace and happiness, although divided and taking more diverse routes, is paved with the same bricks. Whereas the Marxist suffers from tunnel vision in that he sees everything in terms of economics and two radically different economic classes in a war to the death with each other, the non-Marxist, nonreductionistic materialist sees life and its problems as much more complicated. There are many different kinds of problems to be solved, and perhaps many problems which will arise only in the future and about which we have no inkling in the present. The practical effects of this difference are, of course, quite great. Nevertheless, one should not be blind to their underlying theoretical similarity. Although the Marxist sees the rays of Hegel's genius moving in a bundle in one direction and the non-Marxist sees the rays as diversified in many different directions, the source is the same.[76] Yet even in the case of the non-Marxist the rays are somehow to be gathered together and brought to a focus in the future with the ultimate betterment of mankind.

In this sense the aims of both subgroups are essentially the same. For the Marxist, regardless of what he must do in the meantime, the ultimate aim of the final Communist leap is the happiness and well-being of each and every human being living on earth at that time. "The supreme goal of communism," declares a twentieth-century Marxist handbook, "is to ensure *full freedom of development of the human personality,* to create conditions for the boundless development of the individual, for the physical and spiritual perfection of man."[77] And furthermore, "Even its general contours show that the communist system from its very first steps realises the most cherished aspirations of mankind, its dream of general sufficiency and abundance, freedom and equality, peace, brotherhood, and co-operation of people."[78]

Lofty ideals—but not peculiar to Marxism. Dewey, for instance, would maintain that these are also the ideals of a democratic state, being careful to add that the freedom to challenge and criticize must also be part of the package. The last thing the world needs, Dewey would say, are dictatorships prattling on about freedom. If freedom is to mean anything at all, it must include the freedom to be scientific, to follow the evidence wherever it may lead. The existence of ideological roadblocks is the very antithesis of intellectual freedom. In the end, though, the goal is the same. Whether through Marxist guidance or the relentless pursuit of the truth via the true scientific method the ultimate aim is to give mankind peace and happiness *on earth*.

The two subgroups also share the same means for achieving their ultimate goal. In a universe of matter there is nothing else to do except manipulate matter if you want to accomplish anything at all. The restructuring of matter is the only means available. Dewey is very stong in his condemnation of those who are forever talking about the glorious ends to be achieved but who neglect the means to those ends. Science teaches us the importance of means. Every time some new discovery is made concerning the dependence of the mind on the body the world benefits because there is now something concrete to work on. What other alternative is there? "If life and mind had no mechanism," says Dewey, "education, deliberate modification, rectification, prevention and constructive control would be impossible."[79] Those who would damn matter because of some supposedly greater interest in spirit must themselves be damned. It is just another version of the old and bad habit of eulogizing ends while disparaging the means on which they depend.

Hence, he places great importance on education, something which must be a prime concern of anyone interested in changing the world. It follows quite directly from Dewey's position that it is useless to give students any sort of fixed content in their courses. The inner forces of matter are constantly changing the world. There are no eternal truths to be learned. Therefore, do not teach content. Teach technique. By technique he means the scientific technique. In this way the student will master the tools of research instead of some so-called body of knowledge which is out-dated even before the student finishes memorizing it. If there is anything of relative permanence, it can be stored away in handbooks or in some sort of electronic device. Using these storage devices would then become one of the tools to be mastered.

No doubt Dewey's views on education went through various stages as he matured. Early in his career he emphasized the "socialization" of the child as the primary aim of education. The community at large and its needs were to control the school, not the experts in certain subjects. Later he had to make room for the fact that the various subjects to be learned possessed inner necessities of their own, of which the teacher was supposed to be the conveyer. "Child-centeredness" had to be balanced with subject matter. Throughout his long career, though, regardless of what modifications had to be made, his basic outlook remained the same. It could not really be otherwise. His basic position of nonreductionistic materialism had inner necessities of its own which he could not deny.[80]

Remaking the world is not an easy task. First education must be remade. Then the new products of education can begin the cycles of progressively bringing theory and practice closer and closer together. The new world that would result would then be a fully scientific world. People would solve their problems in rational ways. To get to such a world, though, is going to take a great deal of effort and repentance in the sense of changing our ways of behavior. Both the Marxist and non-Marxist agree that the path to a new heaven and a new earth is a hard road to follow. Indeed it requires a kind of devotion unheard of in the past. The toil, sweat, tears, and self-sacrifices that must be made along the way cannot be motivated by expectations of immediate benefits to oneself. Only future generations will see and taste the sweet fruits of success. For the time being people must be prepared to suffer and perhaps even die for a future perfection in which they themselves can never hope to share.

In the doctrine of Christianity people are expected to suffer in the hope of a personal eternal life in heaven. No such promise can be made by nonreductionistic materialism. Instead, in the present there must be a much purer form of self-sacrifice and commitment than Christianity ever demanded of anyone if the happiness of future generations is to be realized. How can such a thing be? The Marxist says it will be whether you want it or not due to the inexorable march of Nature. Dewey says it will be if human beings use the powers of mind that evolution has so far granted to them. In the universe of scientific materialism these would seem to be the only two alternatives.

Does any of this sound familiar? It should. This sort of thing is precisely what has gone under the name of "liberal" politics for many years. The central doctrine of liberal politics is that the government has the right and duty to step into private affairs in order to manipulate material goods and services. Land, the products of the land, material commodities, and money are all to be controlled. One of the primary aims of this control is to assure the continuous circulation and redistribution of the goods and services. By this method, it is thought, human happiness on earth will be achieved. Poverty, crime, frustration, and discontent will vanish from civilization. Exclusively by material means a new Garden of Eden on earth will be reached in the long run.

And what is the basis for this view? Back in the 1930s Will Rogers is supposed to have remarked, "I remember the time when bein' a liberal meant bein' free-spendin' with *your own* money." This issue of who really owns what is the key point. It is what ties Marx and Dewey together. Both in Marx's dialectic of nature and in Dewey's overriding contextualism *Nature* really owns everything. We are only parts of this "God" of nonreductionistic materialism. To the extent that the rulers over men represent the Divine at work in society, they have the *right* to manipulate material goods, including educational institutions, in order to achieve "progress" in the world. Since everything you are and have *already* belongs to Nature anyhow, the custodians of matter are not really taking anything away from you when they force you onto collective farms or force upon you graduated income taxes in their effort to perfect society. Whether in the ancient world or the modern world, if someone were ever to take seriously the order to give back to Caesar the things that are Caesar's (or at least are *claimed* by Caesar to be his), he would soon discover that he must give up much more than he might think. Actually, once the process is begun there is no reason to stop it until everything has been repossessed. Philosophy may not bake any bread, but it does decide who owns the bakery![81]

No doubt this sort of political philosophy, which forces the redistribution of wealth, may do some good, such as holding down the crime rate. At all times, however, it must be remembered that massive government interference in your financial affairs is based upon the supposition that it works. But what is the basis for this pragmatic outlook? A certain view of the human person. But, we must now ask, are there not other possible paradigms?

CHAPTER 4

Psychosomaticism Without Immortality

THE POSITION

The Transition

Soren Kierkegaard had little respect for Hegel. In his opinion the German genius wanted both being and nonbeing and ended up with an abstract world capable of no concrete resolution whatsoever. Abstractions are the mortal enemies of real, living people. Hegel begins with a bit of drawing-room sophistry and ends up with an abstraction so vast that it is capable of swallowing up all real-life, either-or situations. Such a meal made Kierkegaard sick to his stomach. As he tells his readers,

> The dialectic of the beginning must be made clear. This, its almost amusing character, that the beginning is, and again is not, just because it is the beginning—this true dialectical remark has long enough served as a sort of game played in good Hegelian society.[1]

Not only did Hegel fail to come to terms with the needs of ordinary life situations demanding existential either-or decisions, he never even succeeded in achieving his primary goal, namely, escaping the Parmenidean trap. According to Kierkegaard, Hegel's followers were misled by his constant reference to process, becoming, and higher unities. Instead, "everything said in Hegel's philosophy about process and becoming is illusory."[2] For this reason Hegel's philosophy is of no use in understanding the human condition. People are constantly open to the future. They are unfinished. At every stage of its development, however, the dialectic is finished. Every birth of a higher unity is a stillbirth. Hegel, despite what he is supposed to have said over and over again, is a philosopher of the dead.

What kind of future does the "scientific" Hegelian abstraction really support? The answer is all kinds, or no kind at all. "Just as the assertion that everything is true means that nothing is true," says Kierkegaard, "so the assertion that everything is changing means that there is no change."[3] In a word, Hegel says too much, and in so doing says nothing. He is a completely plastic individual whose features can be twisted into any form one desires. Hegel is in the middle of a self-generated, pantheistic fog. As a real, living human being he is a fake. And not only does he drag himself down into insignificance, but everything else in the universe of any real force, emotion, and passion as well. Any system which sacrifices the future and the present to an abstract understanding of the past is bound to end sooner or later in lunacy. Before that happens, thought Kierkegaard in 1846, we had better smash the system.

As we now know through hindsight, the system was not smashed but went on to become the foundation for a social and political system which still, theoretically at least, dominates much of the world. Instead of undergoing a destruction, it underwent a materialistic transformation. But Kierkegaard may yet have his wish, long delayed though it be. It is quite possible that the transformation is not yet completed. It may continue until the whole intellectual atmosphere of the world is once again changed. Such a change, however, would not eventuate in something radically new, but in something radically old instead. This may or may not be true. Nevertheless, this is how Gustav Wetter has seen the situation.

Wetter foresees the day when the inherent press of the dialectical movement will bring about a genuine renaissance of philosophical thought in the socialist countries, especially Russia. All that is required for this to occur is a relaxation of the external forces which suppress real freedom and research.[4] If and when such a relaxation actually takes place, what kind of revamping of the intellectual understanding of nature can be expected? Wetter has no doubts that such a redirecting of Marxist thought would inevitably move in the direction of Aristotle's paradigm. If from time to time the Marxist philosophers sound rather more like Aristotle than Hegel in some of their pronouncements, there is good reason. In the process of putting Hegel back on his feet, as Marx claimed credit for doing,[5] the Hegelian doctrine was forced into a more commonsense mode of thinking. When Geist became Nature and Nature became the starting point for all future explanations of the human person, Marxism was *already* back on the road to classical Greek thinking. According to Wetter, this state of affairs is like a "curse" put upon Marxism. There is no escape from it. Like it or not, a "materialism," once freed from Hegel's mentalistic model of dialectic, must move in the direction of potency and act.[6]

Quality versus Quantity

If asked about Aristotle's anthropology in a direct way, any member of the antireductionistic materialism camp would feel bound in principle to reject it as an example of an out-dated mode of explanation. In many ways, of course, Aristotle's world—a world in which the earth stood still and in which the stars and planets were divine—is now long dead. Yet, in other respects, the wall between nonreductionistic materialism and psychosomaticism without immortality is not as thick or high as some may suppose. It is in fact quite easy to slide back and forth between one position and the other. There is a door in the wall (or is it more like an intellectual space warp so familiar these days from the science fiction movies?) through which the unwary mind can slip quite easily. Like an Alice waking up in Wonderland, the philosopher or scientist, who has already become accustomed to the "Charms," "Quarks," "Anti-Quarks," and "Strangenesses" of the contemporary physicist, can very easily find himself in a whole new world which is superficially the same and yet strangely very different from the one he has just left.[7]

What is it that renders such a transition so easy? The key lies in the relationship between quantity and quality. Simply stated, the nonreductionistic materialism view regards the quantity-quality leap as necessary; the psychosomaticism-without-immortality view regards it as impossible. We have already seen what the former position maintains. We must now endeavor to see what the latter position maintains.

When dealing with the extramental, real world of human experience, Aristotle found that he could analyze human experiences into a maximum of ten basic categories or classifications with respect to the things actually existing in the world.[8] These categories or classes, in parallel fashion, are also discovered to be part and parcel of ordinary language. When someone enunciates a proposition, he or she is in fact categorizing the world in one of the ten ways. In a way, the ten categories are a means whereby people question nature, and then proceed to provide answers to these questions based upon observations.

Aristotle's ten questions are as follows: (1) What is it? What kind of substance is it? (2) How much of it is there? (3) What qualities does it have other than its essential quality inquired after in question number one? (4) How is it related to other things? (5) Where is it? (6) When is it? (7) In what posture is it? (8) How is it externally equipped, dressed, etc.? (9) Is it acting on something else, and if so, how? (10) Is it being acted upon by something else, and if so, how?

Aristotle found examples of the ten categories in operation everywhere, especially with respect to what does and what does not make sense verbally. The only way, for instance, to make sense when talking about a substance is to refer to it as a singular, concrete thing. You can say "This is Socrates" or "Socrates is a human being." You cannot, however, say "Plato is Socrates" or "Human nature is Socrates." When referring to the terms of a proposition, a substance would normally function as the subject. It is that about which something is said. Everything else is said about it. Consequently, categories (2) through (10) would normally always function as predicates.

Aristotle thought in terms of the normal situation even though he did recognize the possibility that something properly belonging to one of the other nine categories might be made into a subject. Normally people would say that "Socrates is ugly." However, it is possible to make sense out of something like "Ugly is the predicate in the sentence" or "Ugliness is not prized by society." In this way one of the nonsubstance categories may be universalized just as Socrates, in a way, may be universalized when we consider the species (human being) to which he belongs. In the real world, though, as opposed to what is possible in the mental world, there are only particular substances with particular accidental qualifications. The individual substance, therefore, is truly the only subject of change. And the primary example of this is the individual human being observing himself.[9]

However, what is important in explaining what a singular, concrete human being actually is turns out to depend much more upon the categories of quantity and quality than upon the observation of any given member of the human species. After all, both previous views of human nature begin with the same commonsense observations on the superficial unity of each individual human subject. This is the fact to be explained, not the explanation. Aristotle was in the same situation. If he is to offer a possible alternative to the previous view of Marx and Dewey (just as they would differ with respect to Lucretius and Watson), the reason must be some different explanatory factor concerned with what the world is really like. From the Aristotelian viewpoint this means giving up any notion of jumping categories. The categories of experience are irreducible. This is taken for granted in his *Categories,* and is used as a principle in his work on the general nature of mutable things, the *Physics.*

In book 7 of the *Physics,* for instance, Aristotle raises a possible objection against his view that there are basically different kinds of changes which cannot be reduced to one another. How then, someone might ask, can the different sorts of changes be compared to each other? The answer is that they really cannot be. In his own time and in his own way Aristotle both raised and rejected what many centuries later was to become one of the central accomplishments of the scientific revolution, namely, the use of various mathematical devices for treating qualities quantitatively. As we have already indicated, the whole point of Descartes's philosophy of nature was to quantify qualities. The whole universe must be so conceived that matter, quantity, and space become identified with each other. The mathematician is then free to analyze nature as if nothing else existed.

Aristotle, however, would not hear of it. If such a thing were possible, qualitative changes could somehow be equated with quantitative changes. This would happen if someone were to try to treat becoming suntanned as equivalent to so many units of running at so many feet per second, or if a certain "degree" of prejudice were to be equated with so many units on a scale from one to ten. As Aristotle says, "If one thing alters and another accomplishes a locomotion in an equal time, we might have an alteration and a locomotion equal to each other, thus a qualitative change would be equal to a length, which is impossible."[10]

A little further on in the same chapter he raises the issue again within the context of trying to determine in what way one qualitative change in one subject, such as becoming whiter or sweeter or healthier, can be the same as in another subject. His answer is that there can be no literal identification of such particular qualitative changes. The best anyone can do is to generalize about all such changes and perhaps make some superficial comparisons with quantity by analogy. "We cannot," thinks Aristotle, "speak here of an equal alteration, for what corresponds to equality in the category of quantity is called likeness in the category of quality."[11] On a universalized level, in other words, the qualitative changes may be regarded as the same *sort* of thing, but not on the level of particular things. The same applies to universalized and particularized quantitative changes, except that in these cases they must be referred to as either equal or unequal.

In general, therefore, it is foolish to look for some common denominator for both quantity and quality by which one can be compared with the other. There is no common term capable of measuring both the quantified and the qualified either simultaneously or in succession. Try as we might we are forever bound to treat them separately. So concludes Aristotle.[12]

The division of change into several irreducible kinds, depending upon the sort of substance and circumstances in which they occur, is a natural outcome of the characteristics of quantity and quality noted in the *Categories*. Quantity, according to Aristotle, is the first accidental modification of a substance. That is to say, if all the qualities of a changeable substance were to be removed except for its essential quality or "form," the only thing left would be its quantity. Because of its quantity a body can be treated mathematically. Mathematics is the science of the *order* among *quantified* parts. There must be something quantifiable, and it must have parts ordered in certain ways.

But, since there are no quality-less entities in the real universe, the only way to get at the mathematical in nature is through the imagination. The thinker must imagine a body stripped of all qualities. A body in such a condition is called an example of "intelligible matter" by Aristotle. It would still be a subject or substance ultimately analyzable into potency and act, but it would not be something perceptible to the senses. By definition it lacks all sensible qualities. Consequently, if a mathematician is to work with this or that quantity, rather than with purely intellectual definitions of things like threeness or circularity, it must be via his imagination. In this way a smooth stretch of sand, a blackboard, or even space can be treated as pure quantity.[13]

If the parts of the substance to be considered solely from the quantitative viewpoint are separate the quantities are said to be discrete. Such quantity can be numbered and is studied in arithmetic. The numbers themselves, though, are not quantities but qualities. If the parts are only potentially divided up, that is, if they are in fact coterminus, we have continuous quantity. This is the subject matter of geometry. Furthermore, in the realm of quantity it makes no sense to talk about intensifying or diminishing the degree of a quantity. Within its subdivision of discrete or continuous, quantity is homogeneous in nature. Things may be many or few, large or small, but these terms are all relative to some arbitrarily chosen standard or starting point. One of the characteristics of a divided quantity is that each subdivision is as much a quantity as the whole. For example, Tom Thumb would be as much a quantified unit as the average professional basketball player.

Once in the realm of quantity there is no getting out of it by mere addition. A small number of parts is still a number; a short line is still a line; a small area is still an area. By the same token, the many, the long, and the large will always remain quantities. When comparing quantities, it cannot be said that one is better than another but only that they are either equal or unequal in quantity. This last point, affirms Aristotle, is the most distinctive trait of the quantified.[14]

Contrast this series of observations with those observations concerning quality. The most distinctive feature of a thing as qualified is the way in which it can be either like or unlike something else. This sameness or non-sameness can be of an essential nature, as when someone says that Socrates and Plato are both human beings, or of an accidental nature, as when someone says that both men are suntanned. In neither case can contrary qualities coexist in the same subject at the same time. Consequently, qualities cannot be added together. It makes no sense to try adding apples and oranges together, or even sickness and sickness, roundness and roundness, and so on. What discloses the category of essential quality is this "either-or" character. As a result mythical creatures such as a centaur (half man, half horse) cannot be taken seriously. Moreover, even hybrids are not really half and half of anything. As in a chemical change, in which two or more qualitatively different things come together to form a new essential quality, so in the case of hybrids: A new unified nature has been actualized.

Accidental qualities, on the other hand, do admit of "degrees." They can be intensified and diminished, as when someone is more or less sick, suntanned, speedy, and so forth.

No sort of quality, however, can be directly quantified in the sense of regarding it as equal or unequal to others. The best we can do is to systematize information indirectly about them for intersubjective purposes. What is measured by a thermometer, for instance, even though useful in weather reports, is not really heat *as felt* by a sentient creature. Neither is weight *as experienced* open to quantification. Likewise for time. Time is only a measure of motion, and some reflection will show that clocks do not measure time but distance.

Along the same lines it can be seen that qualities can be only indirectly divided. Although I can divide your complexion by cutting you in half, no one would think that such an operation will produce two human beings. Even the phenomenon of natural regeneration of lost parts requires that the creature go through some process of regrowth in order to achieve once again its complete essential type.

The same situation holds in the case of mathematical entities. A square is either a square or it is not. If it is cut in half, it may end up as two triangles, but then it is no longer a square. That is to say, it is homogeneous, intelligible matter that is in the process of being divided and not the *type* of figure. In the case of discrete quantities, a divided number is not really a divided number. All numbers in essence are already eternally separate and qualitatively different. This would be true of fractions as well as of whole numbers. The application of numbers to bodies may change but there can be no actual division of the numbers in use. In this sense each number (including each fraction) is a separate species.

All in all, therefore, according to Aristotle, all common sense and all science tell us that quantity and quality cannot be transmuted into each other.[15]

The Hierarchy of Beings

How would someone in the psychosomaticism-without-immortality camp look upon the several examples of quantity-quality leaps put forward by Hegel? As already pointed out, qualitative or specific differences are of two types. There are those which can be intensified (for example, sick, smooth, black, hot, hairy, dense, fast, and so on) and those of an essential type which can only be either-or (a stone, an orange, a man, a specific chemical compound, and so forth). Based upon this approach, the first six of the examples used by Hegel would fall into the class of accidental-type qualities. Only the seventh example could be classified as an essential either-or type of quality. But at precisely this juncture the investigator runs into the crucial question, namely, how are such chemical changes to be explained?

No one doubts that what occurs during a chemical change is a wonderful and amazing thing even though commonplace. Two poisons with respect to human beings, such as sodium and chlorine, can combine into a new entity which is essential to human life, namely, common table salt. Such examples can be multiplied a thousand times over. Aristotle himself, although he lived long before the age of modern chemistry, also shared in this wonder and amazement. Just see what happens when letters of the alphabet are joined together. Mere sounds, previously meaningless and empty, become words. These words, which are full of meaning and the foundation for fruitful scientific communication, are not merely conglomerations of empty sounds. They are something new and different in the universe. He observed the same thing in the case of fire and earth coming together to form flesh. Is flesh merely a conglomeration of fire and earth? No. It is something really new and different in the world. The word and the flesh are new somethings. "The flesh," announced Aristotle, "is not only fire and earth or the hot and the cold, but also something else.... And similarly in all other cases" where a new substance is formed.[16]

How would a modern philosophical follower of Aristotle go about accounting for such amazing occurrences? What alternative is there to the quantity-quality leap? For answers to these questions we can do no better than to look at how William R. Thompson, a contemporary Canadian biologist and disciple of Aristotle in philosophy, handles these troublesome issues. In his work *Science and Common Sense* he sets out to give a contemporary account of biological facts in terms of potency and act. First of all, the investigator must not be put off by mere differences in terminology. Both the modern biologist and the modern Aristotelian philosopher are looking at the same world. What the biologist calls "adaptation" the philosopher calls "immanent movement" or natural change, that is, adaptation which originates from some cause or causes within the organism. Ordinary people would refer to such activity as simply "life."

All this is on the relatively superficial level of observation. No one would think to explain the facts by simply postulating "life" as the cause of living things and leaving it at that. In agreement with those in the antireductionistic materialism camp, Thompson goes on to note that the primary trait to be explained in any living thing is the fact that it is a genuine unit. Although composed of many different parts, the organism is yet one thing. This is the very meaning of adaptation. The living thing is constantly readjusting itself internally to maintain a certain type of organization peculiar to its particular species. Death is the result of not being able to carry on such readjustments within the limits which define that particular species. Thompson sees nothing at all scientifically wrong or remiss in calling the internal force or quality which unifies the organism its "soul."

In this sense a living thing may be compared to a mere machine. The difference is that in the organism the unifying principle is within the creature whereas with a machine the unifying principle is outside it. "The soul is to the living thing," says Thompson, "what the inventor's idea is to the machine."[17] The soul is "in" the living thing; the idea of the machine is "in" the mind of the inventor.

Furthermore, what is said of living things can also be applied to nonliving things, such as molecules of matter. In general, wherever there is unity, there is a soul. This soul is not some sort of interior demon pulling strings or some kind of strange diaphanous haze filling the spaces between the particles of solid matter, but the principle whereby the parts are made into a unit. If the unit is a dynamic adaptive unit, it is a living thing. If not, it is inanimate.

In this way the person engaged in the study of nature, regardless of what special field he or she may be in, is constantly kept in touch with the fact that there are in nature real qualitative differences which must somehow be explained. Regardless of how refined the scientist becomes at picking apart a living thing, he or she must never forget what the thing was like before the process of analysis.

Life is essentially a principle of order directing the whole aggregate of parts. This principle is not like a pilot in a plane or a ghost in a house but is immanent in the component parts of the living system. If a physiologist cannot detect the real existence of "form" or soul, the reason is that he or she insists upon collecting facts in isolation from the whole. When viewed as a whole in operation, it is not hard to witness the greater whole directing and controlling its parts and subordinate systems in such a way as to produce the greatest degree of development for a creature of its specific type. Consequently, any attempt to view a living system, especially a man, as merely a conglomeration of hormonal, reflex, and instinctive reactions should be repudiated by the biologist as extremely incomplete. To complete it requires something more.

The new organizing energy needed to complete the new unity is a "form" or soul. Whereas some would say that there cannot be a soul in humans because there is hydrogen in water, the Aristotelian would counter by insisting that a body can have a soul because there is no hydrogen actually present in the new entity. The soul of the creature has recreated the parts into a new type of thing. Both the nonreductionistic materialists and the psychosomaticists without immortality are aware of the manipulation of material things and are amazed at what transpires. Explaining the change, though, is quite another thing. The former theorists appeal to a quantity-quality leap taking place after a certain period of time. To the latter group this is merely a restatement of the fact that a change has occurred. They would argue that this is not enough. Well-written enunciations of one's amazement concerning the wonders of nature may suffice to place the author in the class of outstanding poets (for example, Shakespeare's famous description of man in *Hamlet,* act 2, scene 2), but it is not enough to add his name to the roll of philosophers and scientists. An exclamation point is not an explanation!

But does the statement that a molecule of matter must have a "soul" insofar as it is a unity mean that everything in the universe is alive? The Aristotelian would say no. His reasoning would be as follows.[18]

Everyone begins with some vague and general notion of what it means to be alive. As children we have observed the vast difference between the rabbit and the log over which the rabbit jumps, or something similar. At times we may have been frightened by some clothes draped over the back of a chair in front of a breezy window, especially at night. In the imagination of a child the moving clothes could well be the outline of an intruder. When wondering whether or not some tiny speck on your arm is indeed an insect, how often do you wait and watch to see whether or not it seems to move under its own power. We all begin with the overwhelming assurance that life is a kind of activity, an activity which can be contrasted with a lack of such activity in nonliving things. Both those who go on to become biologists and those who do not begin with such knowledge.

Upon closer examination the first thing we notice about living creatures is their ability to operate under their own power. Regardless of the extent to which the thing is analyzed, this is the one feature to which our experience keeps returning us. Regardless of the amount of detail the biologist may discover, he or she cannot forget the beginning. No biologist would confuse the rabbit jumping over a log with the effects of the rabbit's knocking over a stick, which knocks over another stick, which pushes a stone, and so forth. In the latter set of activities the cause of the change always remains external to the change it produces. A stick hitting a stone, or a bat hitting a ball, will set the stone or ball in motion so as to change its position from one place to another, but at no time does the stick, stone, bat, or ball act upon itself so as to bring about its own change.

Contrast this with the activity of the lowest living things. With plants we find that a creature maintaining a certain close physical integration of its many parts can act upon itself. From the point of view of its *parts* it might appear to be merely a complex arrangement of mineral elements. However, from the viewpoint of its *activities* there is much more to a plant than sticking onto itself more and more chemicals as might happen in the "growth" of some inorganic crystals. Functionally, plants can assimilate water, salts, and carbon dioxide via a self-regulatory process which heaps of minerals cannot do. Unlike the external electrical input needed to run a computer, a plant can supply itself with what it needs to maintain itself out of unprocessed raw material. That is to say, the plant is both the manufacturer and the user of its own products. In this enterprise the plant is very efficient. By constant activity the plant not only maintains itself but produces surplus materials which go into an increase in the size of the plant. This working on itself from inside so as literally to build itself up is true growth.

In many instances plants actually manage to reproduce themselves. Some people, especially those working with computers, have said that if they could make a self-replicating machine, they would have made a living thing. The fact is, though, that biological reproduction and machine replication are not the same thing. There is more to being alive than simply reproducing. Many living creatures never do reproduce. And in some cases, as with certain hybrids, they seem incapable of reproduction. Where reproduction does take place, though, it is a case of the plant acting upon itself from within, given the proper raw materials. The result is a new plant of the same type.

Animals are also alive. Insofar as they are alive they do all that plants do with respect to self-acting and self-regulation. In addition, however, animals can do something that plants cannot do. They can sense. An eagle, while far away, can "take in" a rabbit leaping over a log and dive in to acquire it for food. A plant cannot do this. For a plant to take in anything, that thing must be in direct physical contact with the plant. Moreover, in the process of being taken in, the material object is broken down and reorganized. It is then either assimilated or given out as waste. Sense knowledge, in contrast, does not destroy its object. The eagle that sees a rabbit does not thereby change the rabbit any more than a billboard is changed when viewed by a million people.

In the case of animals we have a new level of self-acting. A dog is capable of undergoing internal activities called sensations whereby something, with a unity of its own independent of the dog, can become a part of the dog without being altered. Sense knowledge, therefore, can in no way be compared with digestion which must destroy and transform its objects. If sensing the pain of a wound, for instance, destroyed the pain and the wound, we would be put in the very awkward position of having to say that the only time an animal could feel pain was when it was unconscious. We find, therefore, that animals can engage in at least one kind of activity which is quite different from anything plants can do.

Now then, what is to explain this "being alive"? The Aristotelians argue that the nonreductionists cannot both eat their cake and have it too. They cannot claim special benefits for living things, especially people, while also claiming that we are just so much hydrogen and carbon. Instead, they must cease being simply amazed and start admitting explanatory principles ("forms" or "souls") which are distinct *(but not separate*—like your weight and height) aspects of each unified being. In this way we can have a hierarchy of essentially different things in the universe.

Matter and Form

The key to understanding the psychosomaticism-without-immortality position, once the quantity-quality transformation is ruled out, is to be found in the way two factors can be distinct without being physically separate. To the Aristotelian, to regard the body and soul as really separated would be to return to the position of Plato and Descartes. Rather than a real, extramental separation there is a real distinction, that is, one factor, independently of the knowing operation of our own mind, cannot be identified with the other factor. The soul is a new principle of organization in each new unified entity in the universe. It is irreducible to matter. Yet it is not like a person in his or her clothes or a pilot in an airplane.

Thompson takes great pains to emphasize this point. Over and over again those who would separate the body (matter) and the soul (form) in a living thing speak of the soul as if it were some kind of immaterial or material power or energy which directs and deflects the course of physiochemical events. Such a view, however, quickly leads to insurmountable problems. No such vital force can be discovered in nature. As a whole the living thing acts differently from a nonliving one. Yet from the point of view of its parts there is no one part which can be isolated as being the vital energy. As far as the scientific observer is concerned the elements that go into a living thing are the same as those which go into a nonliving thing. From the viewpoint of their individual functions and effects they operate according to the same properties they would exercise outside of the living body. The pigmentation of the skin, for instance, serves to reduce the ultraviolet rays of the sun in the same way that a suntan lotion or a sunscreen would do. Also, as far as the body is concerned, whether a mechanical device or a hand of the same body is used to produce heat by friction makes no difference whatsoever to the effect on the body.

As far as Thompson can tell, there can be no vital force really separate from the body. If a body acts on another body, it is via its material properties, not via its psychic powers. To heat a body requires heat. If a separate vital force were responsible for the heat of a living body it would be possible to have the effects of heat without heat. In addition, such a force could move bodies without itself having any mass or momentum, and so on and so forth. This is completely contrary to the ordinary course of natural events. As separated from the material parts of the body such a vital force could roam freely from one part of matter to another, or even from one body to another, performing any or all of the material functions of a body. "So far as we can see," says Thompson, "such a 'principle' could do anything with anything."[19]

Denying the existence of a separate vital force, however, does not entail a return to a materialistic position. Just as the scientist observes that the parts of the animate thing are the same whether in or out of the creature, he also observes that the living thing as a whole differs radically from a nonliving lump compounded of the same substances. All bodies possess certain inherent qualities which govern their interactions with other things. Carbon monoxide has, for instance, a much greater affinity for hemoglobin than does oxygen. Zinc will combine with sulfur but not with gold. Certain woods can last for years under water. Others rot quickly. The list can be extended indefinitely.

Such peculiar ways of behaving are called the "ends" or "goals" of the substances. Since all substances possess inherent properties, and acting in accordance with such properties in very predictable ways is what is meant by acting for an end or "teleological activity," all bodies act for an end.

But there is more to it than that. What the scientist observes in the hierarchy of forms is that the "end" or "goal" of a body will change when incorporated into another body higher up in the scale of bodies. A substance such as carbon, when left alone, will follow its own course and achieve its own ends, but when it becomes an integral part of a living body, it no longer pursues its own ends. Its goal now becomes the goal of the organism of which it is a part.

This much, as you will recall, was recognized by John Dewey. The difference between the nonreductionistic materialists and the Aristotelians resides in the way the interacting parts are understood to exist while in combination. Does iron in fact remain iron when in use by the body? Both parties would agree that it acts so as to maintain the identity of the body of which it forms a part. The former party, however, would want to say that it remains really iron with all the properties of iron. The Aristotelian, however, would say that properties, "physico-chemical or otherwise, have in themselves no independent existence and *derive all their reality,* and, consequently, all their significance, from the being of which they are properties."[20]

It is the substance, with its special essential quality, which determines everything. The accidents of the substance—its quantity, accidental qualities, relations, and so on—have no reality of their own. They are entirely dependent for their existence upon the unified substance. When it goes, they go. As Aristotle himself pointed out, does not a dead human body *look* the same as a living one? Yet it is not a man, that is, a unified substance. To call a corpse a real human being would be comparable to calling a doctor in a painting a real doctor. Try as you might, though, you will never be cured by him. "Precisely in the same way no part of a dead body, by which I mean its eye or its hand, is *really* an eye or a hand."[21]

As an analogy with what he is talking about Thompson uses the example of a cyborg. Imagine a machine and a man combined into one unit. Is the machine part alive? As far as Thompson can see, in a way it is. Those theorists who attack the Aristotelian doctrine of souls are constantly bringing up the fact that someday a machine will come alive and thus destroy the Aristotelian position forever. But in fact no such thing can happen. The hope that someday such a thing will happen "is derived, we suspect, from a dim perception of the fact that the machine *in use* does, in a certain strange but not entirely mythical sense 'come alive'."[22] A machine composed of metal, plastic, and whatever is in itself merely an aggregate of parts. However, *in use* it partakes of the *idea* of the organism which is using it. Every machine, whether in use or lying idle, is teleological in the sense of having a designed purpose. In use, though, it comes closer to being a part of the human substance. If this line of thinking can be extended to the point where the substance and the mechanism become one, you would have a living substance.

The soul does not use the body. This is what a vitalist like Plato or Descartes would say. Neither is the soul a mere function, somehow or other, of the body. This is what the materialist, whether or not he is a reductionist, would say. Instead it is the case that the form or soul working within matter makes the particular type of organized complex body to be the type of organism which it is. Even though the soul cannot be without a body, it yet is not a body. It is the first actuality of a body which is ready to be unified. A living body is a besouled body. No longer is it a conglomeration of separate parts each pursuing its own goal. Due to its soul or form the matter of the body is now a qualitatively different type of thing, a part of a hierarchy of types, which, in a somewhat Darwinian fashion, passes through insensibly fine grades from the minerals to the vegetables to the animals and to the human race.[23]

Although there is a similarity to Darwin in a certain way, it would be a mistake to press the comparison with Darwin too far. On Darwin's theory the present array of species among living things is in reality made up of only the survivors, the leftovers, the residues, of the struggle for survival. What we call organic species are the wave peaks, so to speak, of the great continuous ocean of organic matter. In reality, according to the theory at least, there were innumerable intermediate types which died out. Even now this is supposed to be true in the sense that the innumerable gradations are constantly being formed and eliminated in the process of trying to adapt to an ever changing environment. The upshot of this view is that in reality there are no species, only apparent species made up of relatively short-lived collections of individuals. What we see is one thing, but what the theory says is true behind the appearances is something else.

This is true up and down the whole line of organic beings. "Higher" types are only higher in the sense of being more complex and better adapted. This is what Darwin meant by progress. Aristotle, however, would strongly disagree. Certainly some things are more complex than others, but their superiority is due to their form or soul, not their material components. When Aristotle speaks about the fine gradations among organic types, he is referring to what is actually observed, not to what was supposed to have existed at one time. He finds specimens which seem to be on the borderline between minerals and plants, and plants and animals. Even within the major classes there are, of course, gradations from the simpler to the more complex. But these facts do not contradict his view that each species is separated from every other one as one number is separated from another.

In the past some thinkers, such as Alfred Russel Wallace, the codiscoverer of the theory of natural selection, wanted to compromise with Darwin. Why not have the main classes (mineral, plant, animal, man) specially created by God, while within the classes things can evolve according to natural selection? Darwin would have none of it. From time to time, though, the idea comes up again. Often this approach is thought of as a way of reconciling Darwin and Aristotle on the hierarchy of souls. Unfortunately it never works. To think of the main classes, for instance, as the true Aristotelian species (that is, abruptly separated and eternal), while all within them proceed in, say, "fractional" stages, is to miss Aristotle's main point completely. According to Aristotle, the whole array of hierarchical types is to be regarded as abruptly separated. In this view there can be no reality behind the appearances in the Darwinian sense. On the contrary, observation tells us that species do not transmute from one to another. We shall see more about this a little later. For the time being suffice it to say that there are true hierarchical types in nature.

Now, since there are true qualitative differences in nature and since there is no quantity-quality leap, both reductionism and nonreductionistic materialism must give way to another position. This new view explains the existence of a qualitatively superior human being by means of a qualitatively superior incorporeal form or soul. Does such a view contradict the sciences of nature? "Certainly not; on the contrary," insists Thompson, "they are *used*."[24] Truly, then, the whole is greater than its parts; not, however, in any quantitative sense but in the sense of dominating its parts.

BACKGROUND

The Happy Medium

When Thompson writes as an Aristotelian in philosophy, he sees himself as the well-balanced medium between the vitalists on the one hand and the materialists who put their faith in complexity on the other hand.[25] This same opinion was shared by Aristotle himself, although he does not seem to have been aware of the possible differences between the reductionists and the nonreductionists. In his work *On Generation and Corruption* he has occasion to criticize both the Platonists with their separated Forms and the materialists who want to explain everything by matter alone.[26]

Aristotle saw himself in the same light near the beginning of his work *On the Soul.* How would Plato define anger, for instance? He would say something like that it was an appetite for returning pain for pain. The materialist, however, would say something like that it was a boiling of the blood around the heart. The same would be true when talking about a house, for example. One person, the Platonic "dialectician," would define it in terms of its purposes relative to human needs. The other would talk about it simply in terms of the materials that would go into its construction. "Which then," Aristotle wanted to know, "among these is entitled to be regarded as the genuine physicist? The one who confines himself to the material, or the one who restricts himself to the formal essence alone? Is it not rather the one who combines both in a single definition?"[27] Aristotle himself, of course, is the third way.

But how is it, Aristotle wants to know, that this intermediate position was not discovered earlier? It is true that all good scientists seek out the causes of things. Merely stating the data is hardly sufficient. In addition to knowing the facts we must also know the reasons behind the facts. Beginning with what is most obvious to us the scientist works backwards towards what is most clear and reasonable in itself. The investigator, in fact, does not really have science until he achieves this level of thinking in his reasoning. "For it is not enough for a definition to express (as most do now) the mere fact. It must also express the reasons for the fact."[28]

Another way of saying the same thing is to say that the mind of the scientist, in opposition to the mind of the ordinary person, is always seeking unity behind the great mass of individual facts and observations. Such an undertaking is the hardest thing to do, intellectually speaking. Yet it must at least be attempted if a thinker is to be a true scientist. Science is not really concerned with individual cases. They are only examples useful for exhibiting the universal laws of nature.

Unorganized and unexplained heaps of data produce nothing of any value for the scientist. Until the hidden unities of nature are uncovered the mind remains in darkness and ignorance. "For all things that we come to know we come to know insofar as they possess unity and identity, and insofar as some attribute belongs to them universally."[29] Science is always of the universal.

An early leader in this process of scientific reasoning, although he abused it to the point of arriving at outlandish conclusions, was Parmenides. Parmenides, it seems, went too far in his search for unity. "The first among those who studied science," relates Aristotle, "were misled in their search for truth and the nature of things by their inexperience."[30] Right at the beginning they got off on the wrong foot. How can anything new come into existence? From what already is? Of course not. Things cannot change into what they already are. From what is not, that is, nonbeing or pure nothingness? This also is impossible. As a result, Parmenides and his followers "went so far as to deny even the existence of a plurality of things and maintained that only Being itself is."[31]

Following in the wake of Parmenides' dilemma came the Platonists and the atomists. As far as Aristotle is concerned, among those who spoke of the universe as if it were one, and only one, unchanging entity Parmenides spoke with the greater insight.[32] In addition to the Eleatics there was also the "Italian School," that is, the Pythagoreans. This school attempted to make number into the essence of everything that existed. This was a great mistake, but at least they began the process of discussing the essence of individual things. Finally, though, and just before Aristotle himself, came Plato. "After the systems we have named came the philosophy of Plato, which in most ways followed these thinkers."[33]

Aristotle also credits Parmenides with giving rise to the atomistic doctrine. Leucippus, the founder of atomism along with Democritus, wanted a theory that was logically cogent but which would allow for the fact of change. The evidence of the senses regarding generation and corruption and the multiplicity of things must be preserved. "He made these concessions," reports Aristotle, "to the facts of perception. But on the other hand he conceded to the monists that there could be no change without the void."[34] In this way the atomists decided that all reality must be made up of both little "beings," which possessed the traits of Parmenides' one Being, and Parmenides' nonbeing or nothingness in order to give the atoms some place in which to move about.

Aristotle is not greatly impressed by these reasons behind reductionism. In fact he finds them rather easy to dismiss as being the result of putting the problem of change in an "obsolete form." All those who came before himself, thinks Aristotle, made the mistake of not looking over the whole field of possibilities before framing their own theories. The atomists, for instance, took Parmenides at his word and thought that they had to accept his statement about the necessity of the existence of that which does not exist in order to have change. Consequently, "They thought it necessary to prove that 'that which is not' is."[35] But what if there are other meanings for "being" and "nonbeing"? Perhaps there is no need for extremism if some third way can be found. Being scientific need not mean being either a materialist or a vitalist. There is indeed unity in the world. Such unity, however, is not of the Platonic type or the atomistic type. It lies instead in the middle course between the two extremes.

The Physics

Aristotle divided the sciences into the practical (for example, political science), the productive (for example, how to make something useful in daily life), and the speculative. This latter group included the study of nature, mathematics, and the study of the perfect heavens above the sphere of the moon. The investigator of nature has for an object of study things which are extramental and which constantly change. The mathematician studies objects which do not have extramental existence (for example, the perfect circle) and which do not change. His metaphysics or theology, though, takes the best of the other two and deals with the movers of the celestial spheres which are *both* extramental and immobile.[36]

In the study of human nature the only place to begin is in the changeable world. Obviously human beings are part of the natural world of birth and decay. Consequently, whatever explains other things in the changeable world will also explain human nature. The only fly in the ointment might be some sort of very special power possessed by human beings which cannot be explained as part of the changeable world. If there should be something of this sort, for instance the peculiarities of intellectual knowledge, the general system may have to be modified in order to accommodate it. In effect, Aristotle realized that he had to come to terms with Plato on the human person. However, this problem was of secondary interest to Aristotle. He in fact died before giving any extensive treatment of it, thus leaving it largely unresolved, because his main interest was in the ordinary course of changeable events. To explain such events in a general way he taught his students the *Physics,* the main point of which for our purposes is the doctrine of matter and form.

Aristotle begins his *Physics* by attacking Parmenides on both logical and factual grounds. Logically speaking, there is no need to accept Parmenides' starting point concerning the definition of being as that which fully and actually exists. Once the student realizes this, everything else that follows can be dismissed as well. Factually speaking, it is obvious to the investigator of nature that there is change, motion, alteration, birth and decay, and so on in the world. To deny the facts of experience is possible but of little value to the true scientist. Such an approach can only make one's arguments contentious without making them enlightening.[37]

After this opening, he goes on to analyze other views on the true status of nature. Although each one is rejected as a final conclusion on what nature is really like, he does attempt to salvage something from each and also to find whatever common elements he can among the different views. From this "history" he concludes that the basic explanatory principles of nature must be contraries and must be few in number. He now feels free to state his own position.

Everyone recognizes the vast difference between the death of a human being (a radical change) and the moving of the same person from one location to another (place change), his gaining weight or becoming suntanned (accidental qualitative changes), or his growing taller or losing an arm (quantitative changes). In these latter accidental changes one quality replaces another in the substance man. It is always a substance which is the subject of change on the level of macrocosmic observation. A modern Aristotelian would have to say the same thing of a molecule of matter, the smallest unit of a given substance. It is always a substance which is in potency to change, which is the subject of one accidental form and then another. All reality belongs to the substance. "Substance alone is independent."[38] In the sense that a given substance, such as this human, is in potency to receive contrary forms, such as going from being white to being suntanned, it may be considered the "matter" of change.

But what about radical changes? For this Aristotle, reasoning by analogy, postulates a "primary" matter to serve as the substratum of change. The substratum is literally the *hypokeimenon,* that which underlies the radical change. When Aristotle talks about "matter," he usually means this primary matter. When he wants to talk of the combination of matter and form into a kind of "secondary" matter, which is the substratum of accidental changes, he does not say "matter" but "substance." "For my definition of matter," says Aristotle, "is precisely this: It is the primary substratum from which each thing comes to be without qualification and which persists in the result."[39] In other words, matter is the purely indeterminate; it is pure potency. Obviously it can never be directly observed. It must be reasoned to. In this respect Aristotle is no different from the advocates of the previous two positions. No one ever observes their basic principles directly. They must all be reasoned to.

Based upon its function in the process of change, Aristotle found that other properties must also be applied to matter. It must be incorruptible, since there is nothing more fundamental into which it can be analyzed. It is also one and undivided. Only quantity can be divided. But matter alone (if it could exist as such) is not yet anything. It must first be informed by its essential quality in order to become a substance. Only then can the accident of quantity apply to it. A single matter, therefore, can account for all actual and possible substances.[40] In addition, of course, it must be regarded as incomplete. Without the form or soul it is no particular thing at all.

The other essential factor in a radical change is the form or soul. Form is the first actualization of prime matter. It is what gives to a substance its essential quality. In the fission of uranium into barium, in the changing of iron and oxygen into rust, and in the fuming of potassium and water into potassium hydroxide the identities of the initial substances are lost and new essential qualities are produced. Form is what makes each of the new unities what it is. Similarly, vegetables and animals have forms or souls which decide their essential natures. The same is true of the human person.

The number of principles involved in change is now almost complete. A principle is that from which anything comes in any way whatsoever. The principles of change correspond to the factors responsible for the origins and end results of the change. First there is a subject of change (matter), then the arrival of something really new in the world of flux (form), and finally, Aristotle notes, the subject's previous lack of the new state of being must also be taken into account. This third principle is called "privation" by Aristotle. To speak of a privation is to speak of the form which a subject could possess but which in fact it does not. It is matter regarded from the viewpoint of what it lacks. In most contexts the principle of privation, being really only a secondary and an accidental principle, can be ignored, and in fact Aristotle does so.

In summary then, matter and form are the explanatory principles for all the different changes that occur in the world. These various changes can occur within four different categories of being: Substance, place, quantity, and quality. Substance is the relatively independent subject of accidents or attributes. It is the answer to the question about what a natural being is; an accident is what the being has. A substance is not to be compared to the core of an apple or onion. It has sometimes been argued that a substance can either be defined in terms of its attributes or it cannot be so defined. If the former, then there is no need for the notion of substance as a substratum; if the latter, it cannot be defined at all. Hence, the notion of substance is either unnecessary or meaningless.

Such a dilemma, however, is not valid. The alternatives are not exhaustive, and neither consequence follows as stated. A substance can best be understood by example. Water, sulfuric acid, a cow, a man are substances. The sky, a television set, a ship, a corsage (even though they can be used as the subject of a sentence) are not. A substance is an individually existing thing within its kind. It is a nature that is no longer considered as universal but as a thing concretely existing. Substantial change means the generation of a new substance and the destruction of the old. It is primarily from their changes that substances are known.

The Metaphysics

Aristotle must have been aware of the fact that he had not really defeated Parmenides at the beginning of his *Physics* because he came back to him again towards the end of book 1. Not only must the three principles of matter, soul, and privation be right for Aristotle, they also must, so to speak, be right for everyone else who ever worked on the problems of change and life. Aristotle's opinion is that his solution is the *only* one that can fulfill such a tall order. But it must be realized, Aristotle himself admits, that everything he has said so far in support of his theory was only an analogy. How do we know about matter? Only "by an analogy" with things such as the bronze which underlies differently shaped statues or the wood which underlies the different products made of the wood.[41] In order to show the true power and force of his theory he must do more than this. He must show how it *rationally* and *intellectually* answers Parmenides. This approach, after all, was the only approach that Parmenides himself would have accepted.

To do this, though, he must change his terminology in order to conform better to the language of being which his predecessors (who had failed to answer Parmenides) had used. The language developed by Aristotle is the language of potency and act; *dynamis* and *energeia*. In order to upset Parmenides' position Aristotle must redefine being. This he does by breaking down the univocal usage of the term "being." Being cannot mean only one thing, namely, what actually is, if we are to account for the fact of change in the world. It must also mean "what *can* be." This "what can be" would correspond to matter, while "what actually is" would correspond to the form or soul of some definite thing. A new and different thing, therefore, does not come from "what is not" in the sense of pure nothingness but only from a relative nothingness, that is, a relative nonbeing. With these few remarks Aristotle ends his treatment of the subject in the *Physics*, telling his hearers to go to metaphysics (the philosophy of being) for a more complete treatment.[42]

When commenting on the difference between Aristotle's treatment of change in the *Physics* and in the *Metaphysics* Saint Thomas Aquinas states:

Yet the Philosopher does not use change to prove that matter differs from all forms (for this proof belongs to the philosophy of nature); but he uses the method of predication which is proper to dialectics and is closely allied with this science as he says in Book IV.[43]

What Aquinas is referring to is the way in which Aristotle finds it necessary to defend the basic principles of reasoning against rational skeptics. A dialectical approach, in this case, is one based upon pure reasoning. It involves the framing of definitions and making deductions from them. It is largely an intramental method of problem solving. Obviously, if the principle of noncontradiction is denied, no such process can be carried out. Therefore, Aristotle must make a point of showing that there is a highest or first science which deals with being *qua* being rather than with some one subdivision of whatever exists. Next he must make a point of showing that it is possible to carry on a reasoning process about the things of the world. This would be impossible if people were allowed to go around saying that everything is equally true or false. In that case all reasoning must stop and the human investigator would be forever plunged into the darkness of utter ignorance.

In this context, those who try to identify all reality or being with what is recorded by the senses are as much to be rejected as those who base everything on reason and who end by denying all becoming or change. Parmenides, therefore, must be rejected for reasoning his way into the Immobile One Being. But then so must be someone such as Cratylus, the disciple of Heraclitus, who went to the opposite extreme and declared that being was so changeable that it was impossible for anyone to say anything about anything.

As a rebuttal to this form of extremism Aristotle points out that it contradicts the very fact of knowledge. Knowledge depends upon knowing the essential nature of a thing. But, if Cratylus were right, there would be no essence left to anything. This everyone knows not to be true. There *is* a difference between a true physician and a quack. People might argue about whether or not a wine is too sweet, but they all know wine when they experience it. In other words, there are definite types of things in the world. The universe is not an amorphous mush in which everything is everything else. When all is said and done, quantity and quality cannot be transmuted into each other. The quantity of a substance may constantly change, but not its quality. As Aristotle says, "Let us insist on this: That it is not the same thing to change in quantity and in quality. Even if we grant that a thing is not constant in quantity, it is nevertheless due to its form that we know each thing."[44]

Once the value of reason itself is established, it can be used to reason one's way out of Parmenides' extreme position without going to the opposite extreme of saying that *everything* is in constant and eternal flux. Neither extreme can be taken seriously as an accurate explanation of nature. But neither can the modified versions of these two extremes be taken as true, although they might appear to be much more plausible. These last two modifications, as we have already seen, are materialism (atomism) and Platonism. In the face of Aristotle's dialectic, however, all positions converge and finally disappear into Aristotle's happy medium. Aristotle, unaware of positions two and four, regards himself as happily situated between paradigms one and five.

When analyzed dialectically, there is no need to appeal to sense experience except for purposes of illustration. In the rational process of explaining change and the existence of qualitative hierarchies in nature it is sufficient to begin with a given problem and then to seek out the solution to the problem within the parameters of reason and experience. The problem in this case was given by Parmenides. What does it mean to be real? Parmenides himself had made the mistake of staying within one parameter (reason) but violating another (experience). The atomists had tried to make amends by affirming the void, but this was a violation of the parameter of reason. To affirm that what is not, or does not exist, really is or does exist is nonsense.

No, if nature is going to be explained it must be in terms of what *is* rather than in terms of what does not exist. New entities must always arise out of what is.[45] Consequently, by pure reasoning alone it can be seen that Democritus must be wrong in his attempted solution.

By the same token Plato went too far in separating the forms from the visible aspect of things. He went too far in his attempt to find the permanent amid the constant flux of sense knowledge. There is no need to "double" reality by having the real man in the world of forms and also somehow having a real man on earth. Neither is there any reason to have a separate form for each of the predicates applicable to man, such as animality, whiteness, tallness, and so forth. But, "Above

all we might ask what in the world the forms are supposed to contribute to sensible things, either to those which are eternal [stars and
planets] or to those that come and go.''[46] Aristotle can find no convincing reason for postulating an intelligible world of pure abstractions (forms) separate from the visible world. Such abstractions can do
nothing for science, especially biology.

True, there is a divine world composed of the planets, sun, and
stars. But this is not an abstract world. It is a world of real, visible
things. And even the separated forms which are not seen but which
accompany each celestial body are not abstractions but real immaterial
substances. The same is true of the First Cause or Prime Mover that resides at the edge of the universe. It is a pure mind, a real being; in fact
the really real being, the purest essence of Thought. Whereas Plato
merely thought about the World of Ideas, Aristotle can call upon
thousands of years of human sense experience to show that there has
never been any sign of disorder or alteration in the heavens above the
moon. His metaphysics, consequently, is well founded while that of
his teacher is not.[47]

The significance of Aristotle's reasoning for our purposes is that it
gave him great confidence in determining the true nature of human
beings. As parts of the changeable world human beings must be composed of the same principles that go into the composition of every
other changeable thing. To answer Parmenides, while simultaneously
avoiding the extremes of materialism and abstractionism, it *must* be
the case, dialectically speaking, that "is" has two senses. What is
potentially is as real as that which is in full *actuality*. Meth-
odologically, this means that the highway to hylomorphism runs
through metaphysics rather than physics. Truly, only with this metaphysical distinction can change be properly defined as the actualization of what exists potentially.[48] "Therefore not only can *a* thing come
to be out of what is not in a relative way, but also *all* things come to be
out of that which is, but that which is potentially rather than
actually."[49] Among "all" things are human beings. To explain
human nature, consequently, it is not necessary to be a reductionist,
nor is it necessary to deny the principle of noncontradiction and try
mixing up being and nonbeing as Hegel did later.

Instead of these irrational approaches Aristotle offers the world his
own solution. Man has a form or soul of a special high quality. And it

did not come about by some sort of evolutionary accident or by means of a quantity-quality jump. It is the soul which determines the matter so as to form one being. The soul *is* the actualization of the matter. The body and soul make up the one substance of one human being. Once constituted as a substance, which is a condition that is never lost as long as the person is alive, the person can exercise the vital functions of growth and external action through his or her quantitative organs.

The comparisons used by Aristotle in an effort to make his view more picturable are those between the matter of an axe and its essential quality of axeness, and between the matter of an eye and its power of sight. The axeness of an axe corresponds to the humanness of a human being; it is its essential quality, that which makes it what it is. Likewise the power of sight is, by analogy, the soul of the eye. These are features which are not lost even when not in full use. An unused axe is still an axe. An eye with its eyelid closed is still an eye. Similarly, a man or woman asleep is still a human being. Like an impression made in wax, the two (wax and impression, body and soul) are inseparable as long as the person is alive. Whether or not the soul is in full use makes no difference to its function as the essential quality of its body. With its soul the body is alive, and the whole can adapt itself to its ideal healthy state. Without its soul the body is dead, never to rise again.[50]

SOME CONSEQUENCES

The Effect Cannot Exceed the Cause

Where does the form or soul come from? Put this way the inquiry can easily become a loaded question. It might give the impression that in one way or another there are forms somewhere suspended from sky hooks just ready and waiting to be picked up and placed into matter. Aristotle never tires of saying that such a view is totally false. The potencies of matter are activated by the form in one definite way. The result, in the case of human beings, is a member of the human species. By its form he or she is placed in a qualitatively superior level of material being. But the matter and form are not two different things in their own right. Instead, they are two factors of *one* substance. This is the importance of *beginning* with substance and working backwards to its constituent factors.

We can define a human being. But can we define his causes? Apparently not. We can know about them as a result of our reasoning to them, but in themselves they are the undefined causes of the substance. Such a situation will trouble no one except the "definition mongers"[51] who foolishly try to deny that they know something simply because they don't have a ready definition of it. Such an approach is only for "uneducated" people.[52] The more sophisticated thinker realizes that when he gets down to the very roots of something, he may have to be content with factors which define but which cannot themselves be defined. Such are matter and form arrived at dialectically. The best the scientist can do is to define one in terms of the other and vice versa. It is potency and act which define the substance man. Seek no further. There is no third thing gluing them together. Together they exhaust the *substance* of the human person as they do of any particular substance. They are not parts but principles or sources which give rise to the new unified whole.

It makes no sense, therefore, to ask about the origin of the form or soul as if it were a separate part of the whole thing or person. The actuality of a substance can come neither from the matter, as if it somehow preexisted in the matter, nor from outside of the matter, as if it somehow preexisted in the heavens. Matter may be one and eternal, yet alone it is insufficient to produce a substance. It must be actualized in a certain definite way. But how is such a thing possible? Matter is pure potency and cannot act of and by itself. Neither can the form act because, obviously, it is not yet there.

The consequence of this situation is clear and obvious to Aristotle. Since the combination of matter and form is what constitutes the new being and neither part can bring itself into existence, the whole cannot bring itself into existence either. Hence the need for an agent cause or an efficient cause in order to bring the new thing into existence. This cause of change cannot be the thing itself that is being changed. No being as a whole can move itself into existence. To be produced requires the operation of an already existing agent (not necessarily human). A form or soul is not a physical object that can be moved from place to place. It is an organizing principle making the object as a whole to be what it is.

When an artist, for instance, makes a brass sphere, he does not produce the form any more than he produces the matter. What he makes is a brazen sphere. The advent of the informed matter is a unified operation. The informing of the matter and the appearance of the new form, which together constitute the new substance, are simultaneously brought into existence by the activity of the agent.[53] That the body and soul of any unified thing *cannot* be complete things in their own right cannot be emphasized too much. It must be said again "that no one makes or begets the form, but it is the individual that is made, that is, it is the complex of matter and form that is generated."[54]

The need for an efficient cause, then, is clear. In order to produce a change there must be something else, already in existence, capable of bringing about the complex of matter and form. In the case of human beings, for instance, only other, already existing, humans can do it. There can be no other alternative for Aristotle.

> But we may learn from these cases a special feature of substance, namely, that there must exist beforehand in full actuality another substance which produces it, for instance, an animal if a [new] animal is produced.[55]

> For from what is existing potentially what exists actually is always produced by an actually existing thing, for example, a man from a man, a musician by a musician. There is always a first mover, and the mover already exists actually.[56]

> Note next that neither the matter nor the form is generated—I mean the final matter and form [of a particular thing]. For everything that changes is already something and is changed by something into something. That by which it is changed is the proximate mover. That which is changed is the matter. That into which it is changed is the form.[57]

We see here, then, the difference between psychosomaticism without immortality and nonreductionistic materialism concerning causes and the reason for the difference. What was a "dogma" to John Dewey was to Aristotle a necessary deduction from the way nature really is. To Aristotle's way of thinking, to say that the effect cannot exceed its cause could not possibly be a dogma in the sense of something dictated by an authority with the right to speak definitively on a subject. The only authority at work in Aristotle's case was his own reasoning power. He had a problem to solve: How to account for the fact of change within being, that is, within "what is" as opposed to "what is not." He solved the problem dialectically in his *Metaphysics*. To solve a problem in such a fashion means to do and say something like this: "Look, here's my solution to the given problem. It fits all the available data. It's internally consistent. Furthermore, it doesn't violate any rational parameters. If you can come up with something better on all three counts, fine. If not, accept mine as true. What more can anyone ask of a scientific theory? In all, it very nicely explains what is to be explained by means of the most proximate causes possible. Given the boundary conditions, my explanation sets forth the facts in such a way that both the causes and their effects cannot be other than what they are. But please don't be so naive as to ask me to go on and on giving definitions and causes of the causes."

Ultimately, Aristotle's need for efficient causes led him to the real existence of the Purest Substance of the highest essential quality. This was the "Prime Mover" or "First Cause of Change" which resides at the outer limits of the finite, spherical universe. The Prime Mover was a real immaterial substance, forever thinking its own thoughts. It moved other things to action, not by some direct outward activity of its own, but by the way the lesser separated substances desired to be like it. From the modern viewpoint this collection of cosmic traffic cops is just so much nonsense. But before the telescope it was not.

Just *look* at the heavens! When compared to the decay of our world they are surely divine. Even a small amount of knowledge concerning the eternal heavens is better than all the knowledge of the world down here. Who would dare say that such perfection could come about by chance? Certainly not Aristotle. "If then there is a constant cycle [of recurring species of changeable things, as well as of the motions of the heavens] something must always remain constantly acting in the same way."[58] The observed eternal and uniform changes require an eternal and constant motor. This ultimately is the Prime Mover, the summit of a qualitatively arranged hierarchy which, without any nonbeing, rises up out of the world of decay through the eternally revolving heavens to the Self-Thinking Thought. "On such a principle, therefore, depend the heavens and the world of change."[59]

No True Novelty in Species

Does this theory of matter and form, potency and act, allow for evolution? This, of course, will depend upon what you mean by evolution. Taken as meaning common descent through natural selection, there does not seem to be any room in such a theory for the evolution of anything, especially humans. After all, what is a human being when considered as one species among many? A human is a besouled body capable of vegetative, animalistic, and intellectual activity as befits a creature occupying such a high level in the hierarchy of souls. In the sense that human beings eat, grow, sense things with their five senses, will, move about, reproduce, and think, they sum up the whole universe from the lowest mineral to the highest entities possible below the perfect heavens. Despite all this, though, human nature does have its limitations. These limitations are a direct consequence of Aristotle's theory of matter and form and can be taken as a sign of its inferiority by the theories on either side of it.

When compared with the previous view of human nature the theory of body and soul would seem to be rather restrictive, as indeed it is in many ways. According to the previous theory new entities can emerge from material nature due to the constant inner workings of matter. Quantity-quality transformations can, and indeed must, occur, producing higher and higher levels of perfection in nature. No such thing can happen within the universe as conceived by Aristotle. In his world everything occurs in constantly recurring cycles, carefully regulated by the eternally perfect and fixed (except for their eternal revolutions) celestial intelligences. Whatever species there are must be forever fixed. Like can only reproduce like. There is no true creation of anything new. New examples of the species must come from previously existing substances of the same species. Human beings come from human beings, dogs from dogs, cats from cats, and so on throughout the whole biosphere.

This is a result of the denial of the quantity-quality leap and the ensuing need to offer some alternative explanation of substantial change. In a fashion reminiscent of Socrates, as Aristotle matured as a thinker, he moved from trying to explain things by inductions from nature (physics) to trying to explain them by deductions from being.[60] It is just as well for the intellectual history of the world that he did; otherwise we would have been denied a possible option on human nature. On the natural level of data collecting alone he would have had little to offer that could not have been just as well explained by reductionism or antireductionistic materialism. Both of these latter theories can call upon the same types of analogies used by Aristotle. Once their theories are enunciated it can be seen that all sorts of illustrations can be used to support them.

Lucretius, for example, called upon the way in which living worms spring from dead dung, organisms with sensations come from insensitive atoms, and laughing, eloquent, thinking human beings arise from nonlaughing, noneloquent, and nonthinking minute factors of being (the atoms).

In a similar fashion, Dewey, Dobzhansky, and many others can refer to the wonders of chemical change and the way in which the elemental parts of the human body act to subserve the good of the whole organism once incorporated into it. For the nonreductionistic materialist any appeal to different levels of explanation, with the Aristotelian level being the most fundamental and all others being relatively superficial variations on it, simply will not do.[61] The whole point of their theory vis-à-vis Aristotle is to do away with immaterial energies or souls. Life is the result of material complexity and internal organization. When a biologist observes a living thing, he is looking at an amazingly intricate complexity of material parts which, in act, operate as a unit. By "material" one simply means what can be handled, has weight, occupies space, and in general is open to human sense experience. It can even be called "potential" if by this one does not mean some sort of quantity-less, magnitude-less substratum. The advocates of this view can even claim to be avoiding any appeal to nonbeing in material nature as much as Aristotle ever did, that is, once they manage to get over Hegel's original starting point.

Aristotelians old and new would certainly allow for evolution in the sense of a creature developing toward its end as a mature member of the species to which it belongs. A tiny acorn will grow into a great sprawling oak—quite a transformation! Nevertheless it is controlled from the beginning by the form of oakness determining the matter of the acorn and all other elements which are incorporated into the developing tree. As everyone will admit, however, this is not really the sort of thing that a modern evolutionist means by the word. Certainly things within their own species will develop from fertilized egg to mature adult. This is their end or goal, biologically speaking. Some may even reproduce themselves. But that is not the issue. The question is whether or not, after many generations, something really new in the way of species can possibly emerge from such reproductions. The answer to this must be in the negative.

Aristotle is well aware of the strange phenomenon of regeneration. Some plants and insects will go on living even after being cut in half. This means that the soul *has not* been cut in half. Each half possesses the whole soul of the species, even though it might not be able to function as well as before due to the lack of some material organs. A soul, therefore, has potential parts just as quantity does. Whenever it is one, it is actually one and whole. However, in some cases the soul can be divided in an accidental way by dividing the body. It would seem, though, that this can happen only in lower organisms.[62]

We see here Aristotle's great emphasis upon the function of the soul in the body. If a lower organism is cut up and if it continues to live and develop according to its specific type, then it must be due to its form or soul. It is the soul which guides the matter to its goal. In fact, as far as the developing creature is concerned, it *is* its goal. The fully actualized creature within its species is the goal of the energy or soul of the body. This is just one more example of the immutability of the soul. When it is there, it is all there doing just what it is supposed to be doing. There is no room for it to transform itself into the act of a different type of creature.

In other places Aristotle seems to hint at certain things which may appear to be evolutionary in content. In none of them, however, do we find any real inkling of a common descent. He notes, for instance, how fish produce many, many more eggs than could possibly survive and develop.[63] Elsewhere he notes the existence of "intermediate" types of creatures between the lifeless and the living, and plants and animals.[64]

In all the various cases he mentions, though, his problem is to determine not their origins but their place in a hierarchy of souls. For one thing, the lower down in the scale of forms the specific type happens to be the more expendable are its members. For another, if we can determine the functions of which the species is capable, we would know how it ranks relative to other species. There is never any talk of changing species but only of determining species. The species are all eternal.

For a mature creature, "the most natural act is the reproduction of another like itself, an animal an animal, a plant a plant, in order that it may partake of the eternal and divine as far as its nature allows. This is the goal towards which all things aim, that for the sake of which they do whatever their nature makes possible."[65]

What is it that is eternal and divine? The species. How then does a thing become immortal? By continuing the race. In such a scheme of things there may certainly be new creatures coming into existence all the time, but no one of them is really a new species. It is easy enough to understand how such a view can elicit criticism from both the left and the right. The materialists who emphasize creative evolution will object to its lack of creative power. Those on the other side who are very much interested in personal immortality will not be at all happy with its reliance upon a merely biological sort of afterlife.

The true Aristotelian, of course, would not be fazed in the least by such criticisms. If the materialists want an evolutionary universe, let them first show that such a thing is possible by giving a rational answer to the question of what it means to be. If someone wants personal immortality, let him also first of all figure out an answer to the Parmenidean problem which fits both sense experience and reason. Plato had an immortal soul as a necessary part of his view of human nature—but at what cost! Plato, extremist that he was, thought everything was just fine. Aristotle, however, cannot see it.

No Personal Immortality

The issue of personal immortality in Aristotle's version of psychosomaticism has been debated over and over since the reintroduction into Europe, starting about 1150, of Aristotle's main scientific works. Along with the Aristotelian texts came various commentaries by Arabian scholars, the vast majority of whom were in the Islamic tradition. The new texts caused a resurgence of learning in medieval Europe and contributed in large part to the development of universities.

The best known intellectual of the thirteenth century is Saint Thomas Aquinas. Relatively late in his lifetime he sat down to compose his own commentaries on Aristotle's main works. His objective was twofold. One was to take Aristotle away from the followers of Islam as an authority that they could use against Christians. The other was to deny Aristotle's authority to those within Christendom who would use him to deny or alter the teachings of the Bible. With respect to the human person this meant, first and foremost, showing that Aristotle, even though a pagan, had arrived at the notion of an immortal soul on rational and scientific grounds alone.

It is hard today for us to imagine the importance of doing what Aquinas set out to do in his own time. Europe was surrounded by hostile forces on the verge of what appeared to be a military conquest of Christendom. Within, the church was riddled with corruption and heresy. What a victory it would be to get *the* scientist of the times to agree with a defender of the faith. The situation would be comparable to getting someone such as Albert Einstein in the twentieth century to support the religious tenets of some one contemporary religious group. Indeed, even this does not fully delineate the parallel. Aristotle was the master of *all* the physical sciences at the time. To imagine a comparable modern situation you would have to imagine all the leaders of *all* the main fields of modern science getting together and supporting the tenets of one religious group. Not surprisingly, therefore, Aquinas bent over backwards to have Aristotle say that each human soul is immortal.

Now the fact is, also, that Aquinas was no historian in any modern sense of the term. Consequently, for these two reasons (his prejudgment and his lack of historical scholarship), no one in the twentieth century should be surprised to learn that Aquinas was wrong. This in fact is the conclusion of most modern historians of the subject. To see this for ourselves we should begin with a consideration of what Aristotle had to say about the ancient notion of the transmigration and reincarnation of souls.

In a word, he found the whole idea absurd. How easy it is for people to talk about the soul without ever taking into account the body, thinks Aristotle. But don't they know that if the body and soul are to work together as a unit they must be fitted to each other? A human soul requires a human-type body in order to function as the form of the body. This cannot be overlooked. Yet this is exactly what is overlooked when the Pythagoreans and Platonists tell their followers about the ways in which souls come and go from one body to another. Even assuming, for the sake of argument, that the soul is like a carpenter who uses his saw (body) as a tool in order to achieve his material purposes, it must be remembered that the tool must be suited to the job. To talk about the indiscriminate redistribution of souls "is as absurd as saying that the art of carpentry embodies itself in flutes. Each craft must use its own tools, and each soul its own body."[66]

This same view is reiterated later in the same work. The soul is the actuality of the body, not vice versa. "Hence the rightness of the view that although the soul cannot exist without a body, it cannot be a body."[67] The body, though, cannot be just any sort of arrangement of parts. It must be an appropriate sort of matter. Hence, all those previous thinkers who wanted to fit the human-type form into the bodies of dogs, fish, and so on are to be regarded as grossly misled and naive in their thinking.

The question of personal immortality naturally follows from the question of the transmigration of souls. Granted that souls cannot move from one body to another (and indeed they cannot move at all as souls, since only the complex substance can change places), is it nevertheless possible for the individual soul of an individual human being to survive its body? From the contemporary religious point of view of some people it would be nice to be able to say yes. They could then have an unprejudiced pagan scientist coming to the support of a monotheistic religious doctrine. It might also serve to make Aquinas appear to be more of an honest historian than a rhetorician.

In recent years one of the best attempts to rehabilitate this interpretation of Aristotle has been an article by F. L. Peccorini.[68] In a nutshell his argument is this: Everyone admits that for Aristotle each human being has only one soul. Yet it is possible to distinguish various functions within it. One of these functions is thinking. Thought or reason, though, is said to be immortal by Aristotle. Now, since all the parts of the soul are only logically distinguishable, there is no reason to leave them out when immortality is considered. It is an all-or-none situation. And the evidence favors the "all" alternative. So, it is the whole personal soul that Aristotle is talking about when he mentions immortality.

The argument sounds good, but it does have its weaknesses. First of all, it is based upon only the *De Anima* and even there only upon certain passages. Secondly, it does not sufficiently take into account the wider context of Aristotle's hylomorphism. And thirdly, the conclusion is based upon indirect rather than direct statements. In other words, in order to arrive at the conclusion it is necessary to *interpret* Aristotle's words so as to get him to say something positive about personal immortality. Given the many contexts in which Aristotle had ample opportunity to state the conclusion directly himself but in which he did not, it seems highly unlikely that he really held such a view.

The main passages in Aristotle concerning his conclusions about immortality are the following:

For, as we said, the word substance has three meanings (form, matter, and the complex of both) and of these matter is the potential and form the actuality. Since, then, the complex is the living thing here, it cannot be that body is the actuality of the soul but rather that soul is the actuality of a certain kind of body. Hence the rightness of the view that the soul cannot exist without the body even though it cannot be a body. It is not a body but something relative to a body.[69]

Actual knowledge is identical with its object. In the individual potential knowledge is prior in time to actual knowledge, but in the universe as a whole it is not prior even in time. Mind is not at one time knowing and at another time not knowing. When mind is set free from its present conditions it appears as just what it is and nothing else. This alone is immortal and eternal (however, we do not remember its former activity because, while mind in this sense is impassible, mind as passive is destructible) and without it nothing thinks.[70]

It remains, then, that Reason alone enters in, as an additional factor, from outside, and that it alone is divine, because physical activity has nothing whatsoever to do with the activity of Reason.[71]

But such a life [constant rational contemplation] would be too high for man, for it is not insofar as he is a human being that he will live so, but insofar as there is something divine in him. And by so much as this is something superior to our composite nature is its activity superior to that which is the exercise of the other [practical] kind of virtue. If reason is divine then, in comparison with human nature the life according to reason is divine in comparison with human life. So we must not follow those who advise us to think only of human things because we are humans and only of mortal things because we are mortals. But we must, so far as we can, make ourselves immortal and strain every nerve to live in accordance with the best in us. For even if it is very little, it surpasses everything else in power and worth.[72]

What these passages tell us is that Aristotle was not prepared to say anything too definite on the subject. It seems clear that there is no personal immortality in any Christian or Islamic sense which would include the body as well as the soul. Neither is there any Pythagorean or Platonic type of preexistence and immortality of the subsistent soul, which would allow it to move from body to body. More than likely Aristotle is thinking in terms of a continuous hierarchy of *ousiai* reaching from the lowest mineral with unity to the highest Self-Thinking Thought. Somewhere in between comes the god Reason—perhaps!

Human beings obviously know things. Much of this knowledge is universal, necessary, and unchanging. Once someone grasps the sum of two and two, the definition of a circle, the principle that no part of a physical whole can be greater than the whole, or the nature of a dog or of a tree, he or she is taking part in the eternal truths of Reason. How is such a thing possible to an ever changing creature immersed in an ever changing world? Or rather, how is such a thing possible without becoming Platonic about it? Aristotle's answer is that something happens within the human soul. Within the one soul there is both the possibility and the actualization of such knowledge.

The actualization, however, cannot be due to the human soul alone. That would make it an eternal possessor of eternal truths. In effect, that sort of activity would make it into a little god, just what it was for Plato. Such a situation was precisely one of the things Aristotle was very much opposed to. No, it must be that in the very act of knowing, when the form of the thing known stripped of its matter becomes identified with the human soul, another power (Reason) is acting within the soul to bring about just such an identification as intellectual knowledge calls for. Just as a table (matter on the observable level) requires an agent (the carpenter) to bring it into existence, so the human mind requires an agent (Divine Reason) to bring into existence within the human mind the forms of the things that are known.

Obviously the form of a tree, when a tree is known by a human mind, does not literally leave the tree and enter the mind of the knower. No, the form of the tree comes to exist in the mind of the knower due to the work of the Universal Reason. And, as with all efficient causes, it must be a really existing independent substance. Its work, though, is *within* the rational faculty of individual humans as long as they are alive and thinking. All this, believes Aristotle, is a matter of common experience. A rational human being is a sign of the Divine Reason working within him or her. The age of the thinker makes no difference. A youngster can have an old head if favored by Reason; while an old person, although feeble in every physical way, can still be a great rational scientist as long as ageless Reason is with him.

Consequently, there are no solid grounds for imagining any kind of personal immortality in Aristotle. When all is said, he was a natural scientist living in a universe of fixed species rather than in an evolutionary universe. Give him enough to eat, good health, a well-equipped laboratory, some social standing, many colleagues to converse with, and a chance to contemplate the eternal truths discovered by his research and you will have given him the happiest life possible for a human being. This is as close to the immortal gods as a human being can get. A rational man making rational choices in life cannot ask for more. The desire to go on living forever is not a rational choice but a childish wish because only truly possible means to an end can in fact be chosen as means to a given goal. You may wish for something impossible, but no truly rational person would expect actually to get it. As Aristotle points out, "If a man were to say he picked something impossible he would be thought to be a fool. However, we can wish for impossible things, for example, immortality [ἀθανασίας]."[73]

Behavior Modification

Both reductionistic and nonreductionistic materialists regarded themselves and their doctrine as being highly scientific. For instance, anything less than a complete scientific revolution in all fields of human endeavor would not have satisfied Dewey. The influence of science must be extended to its limit. It must embrace all. Nothing is to be left outside the pale of the calm, intellectual scrutiny of science. Science must then, of course, be extended into ethics and politics. Retrogressing into prescientific times in order to obtain one's personal and social values was to Dewey the basic error at work in the modern world.

He felt with great intensity that such an approach to values was no longer tenable because people now possessed the scientific means for resolving the problems which were previously solved by such retrogression. In the twentieth century, going back to the past for goals, ideals, and values is completely unnecessary. The investigator of the new scientific age need not rely on black and white, preset, prejudged standards and values in making judgments upon present personal and social situations. The modern man or woman must work with the multitudinous factors and considerations present in modern life. This will constitute an ever changing, ever onward-moving process. There are no fixed ideals, only constant readaptations. "If such changes," declared Dewey, "do not constitute, in the depth and scope of their significance, a reversal comparable to a Copernican revolution, I am at a loss to know where such a change can be found or what it would be like."[74]

In his own way, though, Aristotle was also attempting to be scientific. He was as much interested in determining the true causes of things as was Lucretius or Hegel. He was also a revolutionary thinker for his times when one considers his emphasis upon the absolute need for a substantial efficient cause of change and the importance of considering the overall aim or goal of a substantial entity. And, as with thinkers like Skinner, Dewey, Marx, and others, his very definite view on how human beings fit in with all other kinds of things in the universe was bound to have very definite consequences in the realm of social and political affairs.

In this area Aristotle's thought was dominated by two elements. One was the way in which people differ in quality. The other was the way people are dominated by pulls from ahead rather than by "drives" or pushes from behind. Both reductionistic and antireductionistic materialists are forced into the position of emphasizing the material base of human existence in order to change human behavior. In psychosomaticism without immortality, on the other hand, there is no need to insist upon such an emphasis. To Aristotle the carrot counts, not the stick. To him intelligent people are motivated by their knowledge of things rather than by the hidden forces of matter which they do not know. This attitude naturally leads to an emphasis upon sitting down and reasoning together in order to settle problems rather than upon forcing some change in the material substructure of human life. The material aspect is certainly there. It is not, however, regarded as the determining factor.

Along with human knowledge goes the freedom of choice necessary to act upon what we know. The human mind is the "form of forms" in the sense that it can become all other forms (dogness, catness, oakness) with the help of the Divine Reason. This gives human beings a great advantage over irrational creatures. A dog or a cat is very much limited in its potentialities. No amount of training will turn a Fido or a Felix into a scientist. Their souls run in fixed grooves. Human beings, on the contrary, are open to the whole universe. By being able to hold before themselves, through the power of their minds, a whole variety of different objects, human beings can be guided by a variety of ends. The same is true of the means to the ends. Only under such conditions can there be rational choice. "For the nonrational potencies," states Aristotle, "are all productive of one effect each, but the rational powers can produce contrary effects."[75] Put otherwise, this means that people can go in more than one direction. Humans can change their modes of existence. Cows and deer, however, continue in the same ruts forever.

We see, then, that for Aristotle there is more to human freedom than simply being conscious or aware. Even in animals, willing, desiring, or appetite go along with consciousness. With animals the apprehending of something naturally good for the animal and the going out after it always go together. However, if consciousness alone, with its naturally ensuing tendency towards apprehended goods, is thought to be all there is to any kind of freedom, what is distinctly different about human freedom will be eliminated with the result that human and animal freedom will be regarded as being on the same level. In order to avoid this it is necessary to emphasize that an act may be voluntary but not free in the human sense. To be a human free act the act must not automatically intend a consciously apprehended good, but must also involve an intellectual deliberation upon the means to the end. To repeat, human freedom is not a blind intending of some object. To be free a man must be intellectually knowledgeable.

Where this is forgotten, overlooked, or not emphasized, great confusion can occur. When the role of the intellect is left out, it is easy to attempt substituting all sorts of other things for the kind of freedom distinctive to human beings. Some of these attempted substitutions would be the following.

Sometimes mere possibility is taken to exhaust the meaning of human freedom. We say that something is possible or *can* happen, as for instance when a dog is unleashed and is regarded as free to run, in the sense that it *can* run or has the physical capability for running. Mere possibility, though, would not make man any more free than his heart, which *can* expand and contract, or the tree in his back yard, which *can* grow. Only those who do not understand the true center of human freedom would want to be as free as a bird.

The unleashed dog can also be said to be free from another angle. Without a leash the dog is now missing an external restraint. The mere absence of external restraint has also been sometimes taken to exhaust the meaning of freedom. The dog is now free to run in the sense that there is nothing holding it back. The same situation, however, can obtain in most other parts of nature. The heavenly bodies are free to move in their orbits. Water, unrestrained by a dam, is free to flow or fall. When a prison door is unlocked, the prisoner is free to walk out.

A variation on the lack of external restraint view of freedom is the position that freedom means being exempt from a law. The law can be either a natural law or an arbitrary civil law. Some people think that being free means nothing more than being exceptional in some physical or legal way. An exceptionally large or strong man is in a way more free than a weaker man, but his freedom is that he can do physical feats which the other man cannot do. Also, in a way, the dictator who is above the law is more free than one of his poor subjects who must bear the full weight of the tyrant's coercion and oppression. These uses of the term freedom, though, say nothing distinctive about man. An ox or elephant is more free than the strongest man according to this approach to freedom. And a colony of insects in the heart of Africa, which need obey no human law whatsoever, would be the most free creatures of all.

There are, of course, limits on human freedom. These limits come from nature and from society. Someone might not be favored by Divine Reason to the same extent as someone else. Then again, the good of someone's society as a whole may make it necessary that the leaders of that state not give to everyone every bit of information available on some topic or other. In any event, though, it is the lack of knowledge that limits free choice. Once knowledge is present, however, there is the possibility for voluntary or free action. "By voluntary," Aristotle tells us, "I mean...any of the things in a man's own control which he performs with knowledge, that is, without being in a state of ignorance concerning the person affected, the instrument used, and the results; and also without accident or force being involved."[76]

As we have already seen, a thing acts according to its nature. Some natures are closed in upon themselves. Once this type of nature is known by us we can anticipate its every act. Agents with no cognitive powers at all, such as stones, always react in the same way whenever acted upon. Corn does not complain when popped, and the boxer's punching bag never wins or loses. Animals, though, which can apprehend a multitude of objects on the sense level, are more unpredictable in their responses. People, who have an intellectual knowing power, can take into themselves natures other than their own and thereby possess a freedom of action far above that of their animal brothers. Anyone who has ever attempted to study individual human beings in the same way as one would study a stone or a rat soon gains a rudimentary appreciation of how different people are in this respect. As a nature, then, the intellect has the capability of becoming other natures, and this is highly important to an understanding of the basis of human freedom.

The nature of the will, though, cannot be isolated from the intellect. There is a reciprocating relationship between these two powers. To know is to know something and to will is to will something. The intellect must specify the good. This, however, is insufficient to make the human agent act upon what is judged the "right" thing to do. It is the will which must determine the action actually to be done. Since no means to an end is absolutely necessary in the vast majority of our decision-making situations, the intellect cannot make a necessary judgment with respect to action. Another factor, the will, must come in to terminate deliberation and make the actual choice. Since it is the will which terminates the reasoning, and the will is a power of the human agent, it is the person determining himself. The result is freedom within necessity. Man is determined by all sorts of forces as well as his own naturally acting nature. However, there is still the possibility for man to be *self*-determined in certain ways.

Choice, then, and human freedom are acts of the intellect *and* the will. The intellect determines the will while the will determines the intellect. It is not that there is a lack of motivation as if to be free means to be acting in a totally uncaused way. It is not that you are undetermined when you act. Quite contrary to the lack of any causal factor, there is a motivation, namely, the specified object of desire. When people will, they always will something. Rather than being completely undetermined, in some cases we are undetermined by external forces.

There is still determination, however, but it is a determination of one's self. We determine for ourselves how the means to an end (that is, the possible choices) are to be specified and at which point deliberation will be a cut off. Therefore, human freedom is a complex act which cannot be explained by either a simple voluntarism or a simple intellectualism. All truly human decisions, both great and small, spring from the intellect and the will, knowledge and love, the head and the heart. "The origin of action," thinks Aristotle, "in terms of its efficient cause rather than in terms of its goal or purpose, is choice, and the origin of choice is desire and reasoning directed to some end.... Hence choice may be referred to as either thought related to desire or vice versa; and man, as an originator of action, is a union of desire and intellect."[77]

All this is well and good. Nevertheless, we must come to realize that Aristotle no more succeeded in unifying the human species than the previous two positions. What is it that guarantees, according to Aristotle's view of human nature, that all human beings are of equal quality? Actually, there can be no such guarantee. It may be the case that certain individuals are to be regarded as more or less equal, but there is simultaneously a great deal of room left over for all sorts of varying degrees of worth and dignity. That such degrees should exist is an essential part of Aristotle's doctrine of matter and form. In the vast hierarchy of forms there are bound to be many levels close, but not equal, to each other. Such would be true near the upper end of the scale as well as near the lower end. When all is said and done, Aristotle remains an aristocrat—one of nature's noblemen. He remains, in his own judgment, one of those people to whom nature has given the power of right judgment as a spontaneous gift. He lived and died as a person born to be a master—and, in his own opinion, rightly so.[78]

In the natural order of things various unions or associations are demanded of people. First there is the union of male and female in order to supply new members of the race. This much people have in common with animals. In addition to this union there is another one, that of natural ruler and natural follower. Far from being unjust, such an arrangement is positively beneficial. Those who possess reason, intelligence, foresight, and the physical means to exercise such powers are bound and destined by nature to be the rulers. Those who lack such traits are suited to be slaves or tools of the masters. Slaves, thinks Aristotle, should be grateful that they have masters, for without them they would not be able to make it in the world on their own.

There is, therefore, in nature a natural aristocracy. Such a hierarchy can be seen operating throughout nature. But, whereas in animals leadership might depend upon physical strength, in the case of humans it must depend upon Reason. This in no way involves "God." The Self-Thinking Thought sits in isolation from the rest of the universe, unconcerned with anything lesser than Itself. People's only direct contact with the divine world is through the Separated Intellect or Divine Reason, the lowest of the divine beings. Whatever the hierarchy of separated substances may be doing in the universe, it has little or nothing to do with human social, moral, and political life. For practical social purposes Aristotle was an atheist.

In the world of people, the first qualitative distinction is between the Hellenes and the barbarians. No one can question the general inferiority of the barbarians. However, even within the civilized races there are qualitative differences. First, within the family there is the hierarchy of father, wife, and child. In addition, every family has its slaves—beasts of burden in the case of poor families, and other humans in the case of better off families. From one viewpoint, given their inferior mental powers, even women and children can be regarded as "natural" slaves.

Outside the family the same situation obtains. Slaves of the state, as those of the family, come from two sources: Warfare and native births within society. In this regard, however, Aristotle was always willing to allow for social mobility, whether up *or down*. (Aristotle himself was "from the colonies.") The prizes of war, he had to admit, might be better masters than the victors. And merely being a free Greek in no way guaranteed that one's son would make a suitable master. Reason is what counts, not physical strength or the inherited shape of one's nose.

Yet, how does one get into practice the social, moral, and political consequences of these two facts of nature? A rich and free citizen is not about to let his low-IQ son become a slave, while the victors in battle are not about to allow the vanquished to rule them. Will the rich wait until they see whether or not their sons have been visited by Divine and Aristocratic Reason before passing on to them their fortunes? Not likely. Whether or not the free, the strong, and the rich allow for social mobility in individual cases, though, is of secondary importance. In any event the theoretical point has been made. There is no fundamental equality among human beings. In this sense, Aristotle's psychosomaticism without immortality and the two previous positions are the same.

Assuming now that one is a free person of high intellect, how can one best live out one's life? There is only one way. It is to be like the bodiless gods as much as possible. And this can only be accomplished through the activity of pure rational contemplation. Aristotle's ideal man, therefore, is a male of the race sitting atop a hierarchy of goods and services all of which enable him to engage in uninterrupted scientific thinking as long as he may live. Such a person is rare. The essential quality of his soul is not something that can be made through art or technology. It must have been born within him. Then and only then can training and teaching have any great effect. Assuming that such a mind is in a healthy body with good family connections and wealth enough for an economically free life, such a man can go far. By constant training and education from his earliest days he can, in his later years, practice that virtue which is its own reward: Rational scientific contemplation.

As far as the rest of the population is concerned, they are best kept in line by force. Since they either cannot or will not live their lives according to reason, they must be kept from doing any harm to the state by the state's own police power. While the virtuous man will be guided by reason, "the base, whose desires are fixed on pleasure, must be punished by pain, like a beast of burden.''[79] For this reason it is important to have strong laws, rigorously enforced. In such matters one would do well to look to the military state of Sparta for an example of how to do things correctly. This, then, is the ultimate practical conclusion of this possible position on the human person. There is science for the few; bread, circuses, and police dogs for the many. Aristotle's rational salvation, which in the end is based upon luck (being lucky in mind, wealth, and education) is indeed for the few—and for the very few.

CHAPTER 5

Psychosomaticism with Immortality

THE POSITION

Aristotle and Aquinas

At the beginning of his final chapter on Aquinas' view of the person Anton C. Pegis says that we must not question Aquinas on his points of agreement with Aristotle. We must rather question him about how he struggled to use Aristotle's *language* in order to express a view which could grow only in a "Christian soil" and which could live only in the "mind of a theologian."[1] The forum for his words was a lecture series devoted to Saint Augustine and the Augustinian tradition. This may seem a little strange at first sight. After all, some people may say, was not Saint Thomas Aquinas a devoted follower of Aristotle? Some commentators have gone so far as to identify completely the philosophical thinking of the two men. Bernard Suits, for instance, while discussing whether or not people have some final purpose within the Aristotelian scheme of things, asks himself why he should not completely ignore Aristotle's argument in favor of the thesis that human nature has a final purpose. One reason is that

> There is the Aristotle Fan Club to consider. Beginning with its founder, Thomas Aquinas, its membership has avowed a creed consisting of two articles of faith. The first is that Aristotle is

always assumed to be in the right on any issue unless he is proved beyond any unreasonable doubt to be in the wrong. The second is that such a thing has never happened in the history of thought.[2]

This sort of very bad history is all too common, even today. There are many thinkers today who would dismiss Aquinas with a hyphen (Aristotelian-Thomistic). Worse than being very inaccurate history, however, such an attitude is also very destructive of any sort of comprehensive contemporary understanding of the human person, because such an approach would rather gratuitously eliminate one of the six fundamental views on human nature. This deletion would be a disservice not only to good history but to good science as well. When discussing the possible positions on human beings as a species among others in the world, such an easy elimination cannot be allowed. The combination of psychosomaticism and human immortality is both possible and widespread and consequently deserving of serious consideration.

In a way Aristotle does represent a certain high-water mark in philosophy and science. He was able to give a credible account of change without having to involve himself with nonbeing or nothingness in any literal sense. Neither did he have to appeal to a world of mere abstractions. In the Aristotelian scheme of things only substances can have an effect upon other substances. Numbers and ideas alone cause nothing. In his own way, therefore, Aristotle was true to Parmenides. Parmenides had called upon his fellow intellectuals to explain how change was possible without an appeal to the nonsensical "what is not." The answers he elicited constitute the core of the best of Greek science and philosophy. His influence is still with us today. In this sense philosophy, as well as much of early science, may be considered as a series of footnotes to Parmenides.

However, while bending over backward to be down-to-earth and concrete in his explanations of the changing world, Aristotle could not avoid that other world—the world beyond the moon. Aristotle was a man devoted to experience, observation, and critical thinking. Try as he might, though, he could not withdraw his attention from the heavens. Had not the Egyptians, Babylonians, and Persians been observing the heavens for thousands of years? In all that time had any significant alteration been observed? No. How unlike the shifting world of sensations experienced on earth are the beautiful stars of heaven!

Such a world, substantial though it be, must be quite different from the world under his feet. Consequently it required a separate science—the science of the divine. So Aristotle wrote of his separated substances. It was not a matter of choice on his part, but a situation forced upon him by the scientific observations of the times. So he wrote, with his whole body hunched over towards the ground, but with one eye always on the stars.

This and only this view of Aristotle renders consistent the various things he attempted to do in his main philosophical works. On the theoretical side this great effort of Aristotle's is summed up in his *Metaphysics*. How is it possible for him to deal simultaneously with being *qua* being, substance, and theology all in the same work? It is precisely because of his great reverence for the heavens. If there were no separated and divine substances, thought Aristotle, the physical sciences would be the highest sort of knowledge to which human beings could aspire. But there are such substances. They are separated from matter and inhabit the celestial regions. Their number may be small (about fifty or so) but they exceed in worth and dignity everything else in the universe put together.

We speak of such substances when we ask about being *qua* being. For they, and especially the Prime Mover, are true being and reality. Overall, then, Aristotle is quite consistent. The true substance is the form and the true form is the distant and disinterested Self-Thinking Thought. Only in the heavens, consequently, do we find true substance, being, and divinity.[3]

A New Heaven and Earth

Physically speaking, the thirteenth-century world of Aquinas was very similar to that of the ancients. The quiescent earth was still at the center, and the unchanging stars still eternally moved in their courses. In another way, though, it was an entirely different universe. Aquinas' world was a created world, dominated by an infinite number of spiritual creatures, and ruled by a loving God who counted the very hairs on one's head. As a *moral* universe it was entirely different from

Aristotle's world, "moral" meaning the way in which Aquinas conceived of interpersonal relationships. Although the universe of the thirteenth century was as secure and compact as Aristotle's universe in physical terms, it had developed over the centuries a new sort of moral freedom and looseness which Aristotle would have completely rejected.

This new freedom and lack of neatness in the world was a direct result of the religious influence of Christianity. The world of the Bible is a created world. Moreover, and even more importantly, it is a *freely* created world. The ultimate reasons for its creation are unknown to us as human beings. The thoughts of God are not our thoughts, and his ways are not our ways. Once created the universe may be a solid, secure, and predictable place in which to live, but behind it all is the supremely free God of Abraham, Isaac, and Jacob. He is the one and only God, before whom no idols can be placed. He is the God who forgives sinners, even though they be unforgivable in the estimation of finite human minds. He is also the God who reads people's hearts and who justly condemns some to eternal punishment on account of their freely chosen evil ways. He is the God who recognizes no distinction among human beings from their earthly positions of power or wealth.

The only criterion for being a "superior" human being is that one is pleasing to God. Human opinions count for nothing. It was precisely to prove his love for human beings, and to encourage them to seek salvation from God rather than from earthly things and people, that God himself became man. The moral universe is a very fragile place. Whole worlds of eternal happiness and despair are won or lost by millions and millions of individual personal decisions and interactions. How easy it would be to despair of ever finding true peace and justice in the universal scheme of things.

No one saw this more plainly than Aquinas. Why did God become man? Why did he suffer with and by man? It was for no other reason than to give mankind hope. It was God's way to prove to human beings how much he valued each of them. It was to convince people in an incontestable way that they need not be eternally frustrated in their desire for happiness. "It was, therefore," states Aquinas, "most fitting that God should take on human nature in order to spur men on in their desire for happiness, so that, after the incarnation of Christ, men began to more ardently aspire to heavenly bliss."[4] But what is man that God should care for him and his offspring? And what is God that he should be in a position to care for human beings?

He Who Is

In the Old Testament (Exodus 3:13-14) God defines himself as the One Who Is. God is pure existence.

"But," said Moses to God, "when I go to the Israelites and say to them, 'The God of your fathers has sent me to you,' if they ask me, 'What is his name?' what am I to tell them?" God replied, *"I am who am."* Then he added, "This is what you shall tell the Israelites: *I Am* sent me to you."

In the New Testament (John 8:58), while discussing with the Israelites of a later age the possibility of immortality based upon belief in him, Jesus repeats the same words. "Jesus said to them, 'Amen, amen, I say to you, before Abraham came to be, I am.' " Those listening to him immediately understood this to mean that he was calling himself God. They therefore sought to stone him to death for the high crime of blasphemy, as prescribed in Leviticus 24:16.

As Aquinas realized, such an existential approach to God cannot be fitted into ordinary scientific discourse. It is very hard to speak of a situation in which existence precedes essence in all cases. God is "Is." Compared with the way we are used to defining things this is a rather strange statement. A Euclidean triangle, for instance, is a plane closed three-sided figure. What we are doing here is comparing triangleness to similar things and saying how it differs from them. Euclidean squares or circles, for example, are also two-dimensional (plane) closed figures, but they are not three-sided. But this kind of thing won't work for God. We have nothing with which to compare Pure Existence. Everything we are directly familiar with is always restricted and limited in many ways. To put it another way, God is not a "what" which can be defined in terms of our world of experience. In this sense, God is unknown. We cannot form an idea or concept of God.

Does this mean that God is unintelligible, that he cannot be spoken about at all? No. Even though we cannot get a nice, neat definition of "existence," we do in fact understand the meaning of "to be" or "being." The existence or nonexistence of something, even if it is just in our own minds, is highly significant to us. People recognize this in their own life experiences, but usually carry it no further in their thinking.

Here the philosopher comes into the picture. Everyone recognizes the significance of statements about whether or not something exists. "Your grandmother is no longer with us." "I have an idea for a new porch but it's not made yet." "I wish I still had that book I threw out last year." In more generalized terms we can talk about the being or nonbeing of something. "Your grandmother was a being." "The porch has being in my mind but not outside my mind." "The book is a being." "The being of the book is not present to me." Rarely, though, would the man in the street ever turn his attention to explaining the meaning of being. This, however, is the very thing which the great philosophic minds have been concerned with.

Some people worry about what kind of shirt they should wear. The philosopher asks "Why wear a shirt at all?" Some people are concerned about what's the right thing to do in a certain case. The philosopher asks "Why be moral at all?" Everyone understands someone who says that an orange is a being. Only the philosopher, however, makes a subject out of "being" and tries to complete the statement "Being is...." It's the philosopher who's the real radical in society.

Concerning creation, God gives what only God can give in any absolute sense, namely, existence. This existence is given freely. To understand Aquinas' view of the human person we must begin as Aquinas himself did, with God's love for the world and everything that is in it. God's creation and conservation of our world is absolutely free. As with God's giving of existence, the nature and destiny of each individual human being is not based upon any divine need to be filled but upon an existential fullness to be given away. If all human beings are fundamentally equal in some moral sense, it is not due to an accident of history but to the will of God. All men are *created* equal.

Fides Quaerens Intellectum

Aquinas lived and died primarily as a theologian. At the time he lived the theologian held a well-defined place in society. He was a thinker, but not merely a thinker in the Greek sense. His thinking, whether in the Jewish, Muslim, or Christian tradition, did not start from scratch. It started from Revelation. This is the main difference between the philosopher and the theologian. The theologian has Scripture; the philosopher does not. By design or accident their topics of interest may overlap, but they can never be regarded as two species of the same genus. Their starting points are entirely different. The philosopher proceeds by unaided reason, drawing the principles according to which he reaches his conclusions either from what is self-evident or from some other natural science. The theologian's starting point, however, is Revelation.

For Aquinas this included not only the words of Scripture passed down from the original writers but also the continuation of God's Revelation as contained in the universal teachings of the Church. The results of these two sources taken together are called the articles of faith. These constitute the principles of the theologian in the Christian tradition according to Aquinas. As he says, sacred doctrine "does not try to prove its principles, which are the articles of faith, but from them it proceeds to prove other things, as the Apostle in first Corinthians 15 from the resurrection of Christ argues to the resurrection of everyone."[5]

In true theological thinking, therefore, it is not just possible to reason from authority, it is essential. Someone who would speak of God and his creatures without first making an affirmation of faith in the articles of faith is not a theologian at all. The best such a person can hope for is to be a philosopher or scientist. In Aquinas' own words:

It is most proper in this doctrine to argue from authority, because the principles of this doctrine are obtained through revelation. And it follows that we must believe the authority to whom the revelation was made. Nor does this degrade the dignity of this doctrine, for though appeals to authority based upon human reason are the weakest, appeals to authority based upon divine revelation are the most effective. But sacred doctrine can use human reason, not indeed to prove faith (for that would destroy the merit of faith) but to set out other things which are contained in this doctrine. So, since grace does not destroy nature, but perfects it, natural reason should serve faith, just as the natural inclination of the will serves love.[6]

What this means is that no one, speaking as an individual thinker on his own, can put his authority above that of the articles of faith. At best, philosophers and scientists can give only probable arguments with respect to God and his creatures. Any definitive statements must come from the authority of Revelation or its guardians.[7]

It would be untrue to deduce from this arrangement of things that human reason is left with very little to do. On the contrary, Revelation causes an increase in the activity of the reasoning powers of human beings. Holy Writ gives the human thinker a great deal to think about. There is, first of all, the whole area of internal evaluation to contend with. Texts must be comprehended within themselves and in relationship to each other. Next there is the vast task of filling out the words of Scripture so as to understand their meaning for individuals and society in any given period of world history. Taken together, the dual tasks of internal evaluation and external applicability are worthy of a lifetime of labor.

Consequently, the intellectual Christian is worth his salt. Rather than suppressing his rational powers, such a person is under a religious obligation to develop them as far as he or she can. Even though teachers may rank as only third, after apostles and prophets, in the Church, they nevertheless come ahead of miracle workers, medical doctors, social workers, administrators, and translators (1 Cor. 12:27-28). Now, considering the fact that apostles and prophets are either dead or very rare, it would seem that practically speaking the Christian teacher is really in the first rank of importance within the Church. Aquinas himself made no bones about this. Can someone be both entirely dedicated to God and entirely engaged in contemplation, study, and teaching on a full-time basis? The answer can only be in the affirmative.[8]

The reason has already been given. Scripture is incomplete. It did not fall out of the sky one day written in perfectly clear and precise medieval Latin. It requires interpretation, which is just another way of saying that it requires the use of reason. Although the final word rests

with the teaching authority of the Church, one cannot expect that a
new and direct Revelation will be made to the pope on every little
point of interpretation. In major matters, and overall, God will not
allow the Church to go wrong. Under normal, everyday conditions,
though, one cannot expect grace to supplant reason. Reason is itself a
God-given power meant, like every other gift of God, to be used and
perfected. These two aspects of biblical interpretation always go together. Scripture is the word of God; but his words are often jumbled.
Consequently,

> In discussing these questions, as Augustine teaches, two things
> are to be observed. The first of which is to hold firmly to the
> truth of Scripture. Secondly, since divine Scripture is open to a
> multiplicity of interpretations, one should adhere to any particu-
> lar explanation only to the extent that one is ready to abandon it
> if it is proved to be certainly false, lest Scripture be exposed to
> the ridicule of infidels, and obstacles be placed in the way to
> their believing.[9]

By the same token, the human thinker must have recourse to his or
her own reasoning powers in matters which are not covered by Revelation at all. If all matters of human concern were outside or above the
reach of human reason, we would be entirely dependent upon
authority all the time. However, this is not the case. In many matters
we are forced to use our natural powers, which include our sense
powers, simply because we have nowhere else to turn. Aquinas asks
himself if children born to Adam and Eve before original sin would
have been born with complete knowledge of everything. He answers,

> As was said earlier, concerning things which are above reason we
> believe on authority alone. But where authority is lacking we
> must follow the usual condition of nature. As it happens it is
> natural for man to acquire knowledge via the senses, as was said
> before. And hence the soul is united to the body which it needs
> for its proper operation. This would not be the case if from the
> beginning it had knowledge not acquired via the powers of
> sense.[10]

Consequently, even in the Garden of Eden children would not have been born with innate knowledge. Instead, they would have had to acquire it through natural means. Undoubtedly such acquisition would have been much easier before the Fall of mankind through sin. Now, after the Fall, loaded down with a corruptible body as we are, the body more often than not hinders the soul in its acquisition of knowledge. This is true not only in childhood but in all the age periods of human life. Unfortunately, there is little we can do about it at this late date in history.[11]

We see, then, that faith must precede the use of reason where and when possible. This was not a new idea in the thirteenth century. It was part and parcel of the Christian tradition for many centuries before being adopted by Thomas Aquinas. Indeed, it goes right back to the Bible itself. In the Old Testament an act of faith on the part of Abraham allowed his offspring to come to know the true God. In the New Testament an act of faith on the part of Simon Peter, speaking for the Twelve Apostles (at least he thought he was speaking for all twelve), allowed him to recognize Jesus as the son of God. Jesus had just made the startling announcement that eternal life and salvation depended upon eating his flesh and drinking his blood. He did this in the synagogue at Capernaum. Many of his listeners could not believe their ears. Jesus continued,

Does this scandalize you? What if you saw the son of man ascending to where he was before? It is the spirit that gives life. The flesh [food from earthly sources] profits nothing. The words I have spoken to you are spirit and life. But there are some among you who do not believe. ...This is why I have said to you that no one can come to me unless he is enabled to do so by my Father. (John 6:63-66)

As a result, many of his followers left him. It is recorded that a short time later Jesus again raised the issue with his more faithful group of disciples. "Jesus therefore said to the twelve, 'Do you wish to depart also?' Simon Peter then answered, 'Lord, to whom shall we go? You have the words of everlasting life and we have come to believe and to know that you are the Christ, the son of God.' " (John 6:68-70)[12]

Aquinas took exactly this sort of thing most seriously. First there must be belief. After that comes knowledge. This is not merely an accidental temporal sequence. It is a cause and effect relationship. Faith sets up the necessary conditions for further penetration and development through knowledge. One leads to the other. To Aquinas' way of thinking, then, faith seeking understanding is a happy combination. Faith gives impetus to reason, and reason completes the course of faith. Faith is a great stimulus to reason, and reason is a great natural human response to faith. The *"quaerens"* of Aquinas is an active searching after wisdom, a chase, a hot pursuit. In no way is it a degrading pursuit as long as it is constantly fixed upon its ultimate and final goal, which is a closer association with God. God will in fact reward the honest intellectual. As Aquinas is fond of reminding us, "without faith it is impossible to please God. For whoever comes to God must believe that God exists and that he rewards those who seek him." (Hebrews 11:6) It came as no accident that universities devoted to liberal studies grew up in medieval Europe. That's where the seeds were.[13]

Personal Immortality

According to Marxist doctrine, the Marxist system will ultimately eventuate in the fulfillment of humankind's most cherished aspirations. These are the desire for material sufficiency and even abundance, freedom and equality, peace, brotherhood, and cooperation among all peoples. Conspicuously absent from this list is the desire for immortality of an everlasting and personal nature. However, what is not even mentioned in Marxist doctrine becomes something of central importance in Thomistic doctrine.

Aquinas takes it as an obvious fact of experience that all normal human beings of adult intellectual maturity desire their own personal immortality. The ways of overcoming the fear of death are many and various, but they all have the same motive at their root: The desire to live forever. Whether through biological offspring, physical works of a bodily or intellectual nature such as a building or a book, or continued personal existence after death, the need to feel that one's being does not end in the grave is a constant in human nature. Such a need cannot be suppressed. It is grounded in rational human nature itself.

As intellectual creatures humans can grasp existence absolutely *(sed intellectus apprehendit esse absolute)* and as extending for all time. Since the will naturally follows the intellect, humans naturally want to participate in timeless existence. Such a desire cannot be in vain. It is foolish to try to deny it. If it does not come out in one way, it will come out in another. Aquinas' approach, of course, is to take the desire for personal immortality seriously in a literal sense.[14]

Furthermore, in conformity with Revelation, human immortality is not merely something concerning just the spiritual soul. To be a real and complete immortality it must also include the body. A personal immortality must include the whole person. In the New Testament, for example, Jesus is debating with the Sadducees (a subgroup within Judaism which denied the resurrection of the body and accepted only the Pentateuch as authentic Scripture) about whether or not a woman legally married to a series of different men will have to be a wife to them all in heaven.

> But Jesus answered them by saying, "You err because you know neither the Scriptures nor the power of God. For at the resurrection they will not marry nor be given in marriage, but will be as the angels [who do not engage in biological reproduction] of God in heaven. As to the resurrection of the dead, have you not read what was said to you by God: 'I am the God of Abraham, Isaac, and Jacob.' He is not the God of the dead but of the living." (Matt. 22:29-33)

Later in the New Testament, in Saint Paul's first letter to the Christian community at Corinth, the doctrine of the resurrection of the body is discussed at greater length. There Aquinas could read in part, "For the trumpet will sound, and the dead will arise incorruptible and we will be changed. For this corruptible body must put on incorruptibility, and this mortal body must put on immortality." (1 Cor. 15:52-54) Consequently, the Christian theologian is bound to mean both the body and the soul when he searches for an understanding of immortality.

This is one of the two main points which modern Thomists are always sure to make. The other main point, in addition to the unity of body and soul in each individual human being, is the preeminent position of the soul in the compound of body and soul. The soul in its own right is necessarily immortal. It may indeed be the case that the body is naturally corruptible and was so even in the Garden of Eden. As a material thing it is inherently liable to coming apart. It is not sin, but the very nature of a material thing, which accounts for the destructibility of the body. Sin alone cannot be the cause of either mortality or immortality. This is confirmed by Scripture. If sin could cause a loss of immortality, the devil should have been the first to die. No, it must be that the soul is inherently indestructible while the body is not. If Adam and Eve did have immortal bodies, it was due to a special grace of God.[15] This inherent indestructibility of the soul is called the "subsistence" or substantiality of the soul. The soul is a substance, or subsists, in its own right.

A contemporary Thomist, such as Etienne Gilson, places this dual functioning of the soul (as both form and substance) at the very center of the Thomistic position on the human person. We are now, he states, at the very heart of the anthropology of Saint Thomas Aquinas. His whole interpretation of human nature rests upon the possibility that an intellectual substance can also be the form of its body.[16] How is such a thing possible? Gilson's main reference on this point is to book 2, chapter 68 of Aquinas' *Summa Contra Gentiles*. In order for the soul to be the substantial form of its body, explains Aquinas, two conditions must be met. In the first place, the form must be the cause of the thing's being a human being. Through the informing effect of the human soul the properly disposed body becomes a human body. Secondly, the two factors must make up one unity. As we have seen with all the other views on the human person so far, the unity of the human person is a prime concern. Likewise with Aquinas. The body and soul must be united by one act of being *(conveniant in uno esse)* if it is to be truly one thing.

This raises the further question of how there can be one existential act of being in a thing made up of two factors. The answer given by Aquinas is that the act of existing as a human being is given to the body by the soul. It does not belong to the body primarily but to the soul primarily. It is only through the soul, which subsumes the body into itself, that the body can receive the unifying act of existing. As a result, the soul, which can exist in its own right through its own act of existing, is the agent primarily responsible for the existence of one unified human being. In other words, although superior to the body, the soul is nevertheless the form of the one human being. "Thus can we consider the wonderful *[mirabilis]* connection of things."[17]

What Aquinas has done here is to provide a new basis for human unity. A person is one being because he or she has one act of existing. Ultimately unity is rooted in an act of existing, which is neither a substance, an accident, nor an essence. In a manner quite different from Aristotle's, for whom a material substance is unified because it has one substantial form, Aquinas says that unity is the result of one act of existing, belonging primarily to the soul and communicated to the body through the soul. Because of its act of existing the soul is indestructible in its own right. Thus it can be immortal and the form of the body.

Obviously, his argument is good or bad depending upon how much sense one can make out of the soul's "act of existing." That this is where Aquinas puts his emphasis, though, cannot be doubted. This is most clearly seen in his relatively late work known as *The Disputed Questions on the Soul.* It was written about 1270, after the first part of the *Summa Theologiae.* Article 14 is concerned with the immortality of the soul. Here he argues that only if a form *does not* possess an act of existing in itself can it be subject to corruption when the composite of body and soul is destroyed. But when a soul already exists in its own right, there is no way it can be destroyed. In that case the human soul is a necessary being. Once created by God it is bound to go on existing, unless deliberately annihilated by God himself. Some sample statements by Aquinas would be the following:

The soul has the power of existing forever, but it did not always have that power. Hence the soul need not always have existed, but it must never cease to exist in the future.[18]

Although the soul and the body of man have one and the same act of existing in common, nevertheless that act of existing is communicated to the body by the soul. Thus the human soul communicates to the body that very act of existing by which the soul itself subsists.[19]

Sin takes away grace totally, but it does not take anything away from the essence of a thing.[20]

When Aquinas argues rationally in support of the thesis that the soul is superior to the body, one runs across something that is a little strange. It would seem that the reasons he puts forward should not really conclude to anything more than what Aristotle himself could have concluded to. His main arguments, as with Aristotle, are drawn from the facts of intellectual knowledge. The mind can do things which no sense organ can do. The intellect can become all things. For the senses to try it would mean their destruction. If the mind were material, it could never survive the knowledge of knowing even one single thing. As soon as it knew a tree or a certain color, it would be prevented from knowing anything else. But this obviously does not happen.

Moreover, the mind conceives of things in a universal way. We possess universal ideas. This is strictly impossible for anything material. Every material thing is necessarily particularized. Yet, an idea such as "man" can apply to many individuals without any loss of being or meaning. What does this tell us? "The sole conclusion to be drawn from all this, then, is that the intellective principle, by which man understands, is a form having its act of existing in itself. Therefore this principle must be incorruptible."[21]

He then immediately goes on to appeal to the authority of Aristotle for added support. The unusual aspect of this situation is that there is nothing in Aristotle to justify the divisions which Aquinas wants to introduce. The body is one factor. The soul is another. But within the soul there is a further factor. Because the soul performs acts in which the body can in no way share, it must be separable, a form that can stand alone on its own. It is immaterial, certainly. But more, it is also immortal. This is not a necessary characteristic of something immaterial. To be subsistent, or immortal, requires that the soul possess its own act of existing. From what rational argument does Aquinas acquire the notion of the soul as encompassing two factors, its essence as a substantial form and its own act of existing? It does not derive from the facts of intellectual knowledge as opposed to sense knowledge. If it did, why didn't Aristotle see it?

The real historical reason why Aristotle never saw it is that he lacked Christian Revelation. Aquinas, on the other hand, could differentiate between the "what" of the soul and its "act of existing" because of what the Bible told him about God. As a theologian, he had no qualms whatsoever about appealing to Scripture. In his *Summa Contra Gentiles,* after arguing that the soul is an intellectual, immaterial substance, he goes on to show that the soul nevertheless contains a certain kind of composition. Its act of existing cannot be identical with its nature as a form. If it were, it would be God himself. Only in God are essence and existence identical.

> It was shown that God is his own subsisting act of existing. Therefore nothing else can be its own act of existing. Therefore it is necessary that in all substances which are not God the act of existing is other than the substance itself and vice versa.[22]

> It remains therefore that since God is Subsistent Being nothing else is its own act of existing.[23]

The circle is complete. The human soul is created by God to be an everlasting substance. Although the form of a body, to which it communicates its own existence, the soul remains superior to the body. Indeed it ranks only below the angels in dignity. As Gilson states, "Only an illusion of perspective can make us imagine that there is any difference between the case of the separate intellectual substances, or angels, and that of the nonseparate intellectual substances, human souls."[24] What is the human person? An incarnate angel!

The Happy Medium

Because the human soul is an incarnate angel is no reason to think that it must disdain the body. Quite the contrary, the human soul is incomplete without its body. The whole design of the human soul is such as to orient it toward working with a body. Near the beginning of his *Summa Theologiae* Aquinas asks himself about the definition of a person. Can the person be identified with his or her soul? No. Why not? Is not the separated soul an individual substance of a rational nature? Yes, but it is not designed to function in a manner that is independent of a body as is an angel. In the case of human beings the person is both the body and the soul. Just as the hand, or any other part of a human being, cannot be called the whole person, neither can the soul be looked upon as the real person.[25]

This is not to deny that angels and humans have the same ultimate destiny. Both angels and people are ordained to eternal happiness with God. Was not equality with the angels promised to humans by Jesus himself for those who persevered in the faith? The human soul, separated from the body, will immediately enter into the presence of God if it deserves such a reward. The same is true of the angels. The difference is that an angel can secure its beatitude immediately after one meritorious act while a human being must work at it for a long period of time through corporeal things. This is the way God ordained things. The body is not an unnecessary accident to human existence but a necessary part of human nature.[26]

We must never forget that Aquinas, as with other ordinary people, takes the flesh very seriously. The most powerful image of this fact for Aquinas was the Christ himself. Unlike most modern movies about Christ, the Christ of medieval times was a real, down-to-earth human figure. He was a hairy creature with dirty feet who smelled under the arms. The importance of the material world was everywhere present to the minds of the medieval thinkers. Salvation meant working through matter. There could be no salvation via a merely mental assent. Unless the worldly cup is drunk down to its dregs, the human person cannot share in the Resurrection. This means being faithful in marriage even if it kills you, helping your neighbor until it hurts, and even loving those who hate you. Hence it seemed perfectly fitting to Aquinas that God's relationship to his people should be expressed in the ''fleshy'' language of the Bible. Not only did God create a good world, but, as if that were not enough, the Second Person of the Trinity took on flesh to show God's love for it. Such a world must be good indeed.

Nevertheless, the body cannot be emphasized to the detriment of the soul. For Aquinas it is perfectly proper to protect people against themselves when they tend to run off in that direction. This is especially true in sexual matters. The sexual instincts in humans are very strong and, if not controlled, will push out thoughts of all else. People may kid themselves into thinking that they can walk around a beach nude and still be thinking of swimming, but the government at least should know better. Women parading around nude in a bar may think themselves quite clever and sophisticated, whereas in fact all they are doing is confirming the typically unbalanced male view of women as basically and primarily servants and sex objects.

In any event the main point is that even though the three-dimensional, extramental body is basically good, uncontrolled and unbalanced sex is not. In place of sex as fun without responsibility what the fourth paradigm sees as good is responsible sex; that is, sex between a man and a woman with a mutual commitment to each other and which is oriented toward cooperation with God in the creation of new persons. As it happens, this approach is also what is best for a healthy society.

Anything that tends to the contrary is to be discouraged by law and education. Such a tendency is especially strong in pagan males who regard an infinite amount of sex with a zero amount of responsibility as heaven on earth. If there happens to be a large number of pagan women around willing to go along, the society can very easily degenerate into a welter of unproductive mutual abuse. It should come as no surprise that even non-Christian rulers must often impose rather rigorous rules regarding sex upon their citizens.

When Aquinas speaks of the soul as an incarnate angelic thing, the carnal part is therefore to be taken most seriously. But, because the human person is one being with one act of existing, the only source for his one act of existing is the soul. "To be" belongs primarily to that aspect of the person which is most special to him or her and which differentiates him or her from the beasts, namely, the rational self rather than the psychosomatic composite. However, the nature of the soul is such that it depends upon the body to operate fully.

Many Christian thinkers previous to Aquinas' time favored Plato's view that the soul exhausted the entire meaning of the human person. This was because they feared that by viewing the soul as dependent upon the body for its operations, they would be forced to view it as also dependent upon the body for its existence. Aquinas had no such fears. Through its one act of existing the soul can be both an independent substance and the form of the body. Consequently, even though subsistent, the soul depends upon the body in order to operate in a truly human fashion. From the viewpoint of its existence the soul is a complete substance. But, because of the type of substance it is (that is, was *created* to be by God) it cannot act without the body.

Thus, all activities are performed by the psychosomatic whole, that is, by the person, rather than by either the soul or the body alone. From the point of view of its activity, therefore, the soul may be considered as incomplete. This is true even in the process of reasoning. It is not the mind or soul that understands but rather, more strictly speaking, the person that understands *through* the soul *(quod homo intelligat per animam).*[27]

As a result, the Thomist feels very much at home with all of the social and physical sciences which keep emphasizing the connections between human beings and their material conditions of existence. Surely each individual human being is the result of his or her interactions with the material and social world. But this is not all there is to say on the subject. Because of his or her unique act of existing every individual human person is unique and could never actually change places with any other creature. As given expression by Gilson, in this life "to be is to become." And matter, considered an obstacle by some other paradigms, is here considered a help. From conception to maturity the soul is progressively giving itself the body it needs. The physiological "paves the way" for the intellectual.[28] As a consequence phenomena as divergent as religious mysticism, ESP, and the marvels of yoga control can be reconciled with the effects of bodily injuries on mental powers, drugs on the mind, and hormonal changes on personality. Emotional, mental, and physical health always go together in humans. In a very real sense, therefore, as the old saying goes, you are what you eat.

Furthermore, the range of usable intellectual powers from retardates to geniuses comes as no surprise. Although once understood any given truth is known with equal understanding by everyone with a rational nature (for example, $2 + 2 = 4$), it is possible for one person to function better than another due to the disposition of his body. "This is because the act, and form, are received in matter according to the capacity of the matter, so that, because some people have a better disposed body, their souls are capable of greater power in understanding."[29] Faulty interaction between body and mind is due only to the body. Once known, all truths are equally true; yet it is possible for one person to sense and understand more easily and quickly than another because of their different material components.

From the Thomistic perspective this situation is regarded as the ideal happy medium. Human beings have the best of both the material and the spiritual worlds. Aquinas states this explicitly in the same place that he discusses how the soul can also be the form of its body. Human beings exist on the horizon or borderline between the corporeal and the spiritual. In human nature we are at that point in the hierarchy of nature where the highest thing in an inferior genus touches the lowest thing in a superior genus. As a body the human body is the best nature can offer. But as a spiritual substance the human soul is the lowest thing of its order that can be found in the overall scheme of things. Below man are all the inferior animals, plants, and minerals. Above man are the unnumbered ranks of angels. With a foot in each camp humankind is certainly the strangest species upon the face of the earth.[30]

This Thomistic attitude is confirmed in another way in the Supplement to the *Summa Theologiae*. There Aquinas asks whether or not human beings will have their same bodies after their resurrection to their new life. He answers in the affirmative. As a second rising of the *same* person, it is necessary that both the body and soul be united as before. If this were not the case, you would not have a resurrection of the body but a transmigration of the soul from one body to another.

Some of the ancient philosophers, for instance, explains Aquinas, thought that it was possible for a soul belonging to a given species to transmigrate into a body belonging to a different species. If a soul led a life contrary to reason, some thought, it might pass into the body of a dog, because of its lustfulness and the shameless way in which dogs have sexual intercourse in public. If the soul were given over to robbery and violence, it might end up in the body of a lion the next time around. These views are rejected by Aquinas because they are not in conformity with the correct position on human nature. The correct view allows for both mind and body, without denying the rights of either one. The false views on human nature, though, would go to one extreme or the other. So again, how is it that some thinkers asserted the transmigration of souls?

But this opinion comes from two false sources. First, they said that the soul is not conjoined to the body essentially, as matter and form, but only accidentally, as a mover to a moved, or as a man in his clothes. And so it was possible to affirm that the soul pre-existed, before being infused into a body produced by natural generation. And also that it is united to different bodies. Secondly, they affirmed that the intellect differs only accidentally from the senses. Hence it can be said that the human intellect surpasses that of the other animals because, due to his superior bodily constitution, man's sense powers are more acute. So it was possible to assert that human souls can transmigrate into animal bodies, especially when the human soul has become fixed in brutish ways.[31]

In agreement with Aristotle, therefore, Aquinas would say that the body and soul are made for each other and cannot be haphazardly separated and mixed up with other souls and bodies. This is the anti-Platonic aspect of his happy medium. In addition, though, he must also be opposed to any sort of materialistic view which would attempt to regard the soul as merely a function of the body, even if it be regarded as an excellent and superior function. The soul is a self-existing intellectual substance. It is something really different from matter.

Moreover still, Aquinas must pit himself against the true historical Aristotle in a certain way. Not only is the soul an incorporeal substance that cannot be identified with the body, but it is also immortal in each and every individual human being. And beyond Aristotle still further, there is the promise of the resurrection of the body. Everything positive said of man in the previous views would be accepted by Aquinas. Certainly man is material, the matter is arranged in a highly complex and organized fashion,[32] and there is a form or soul required to account for this observed organization. But there is more to be said. Human beings have an eternal destiny which can only be completed by the resurrection of the body. Even though the soul can exist alone, it would be a depreciated existence unsuitable to the unity of human nature.

In summary then, the position of psychosomaticism with immortality teaches that there are only three ways anything can go out of existence. First, by way of a decomposition or substantial change, as when water is decomposed into hydrogen and oxygen or paper is burned. Secondly, by way of an accidental or indirect change, as when the color of burning paper ceases to exist or the hunger pains of a dog are eliminated by killing the dog. Thirdly, by way of annihilation through the power of God. According to Aquinas, none of these ways will happen in the case of the soul. The first two are impossible given the nature of the soul, and the third is not likely given the nature of God.

Now, in light of the immaterial and essentially superior acts of intellection observed in human beings we know that the soul is an intellectual substance and that its immortality is very likely. At this point you can go on to affirm immortality by faith alone. But faith seeking understanding asks for more. Aquinas answers that "to be" belongs immediately to the soul and through the soul to the body. Upon separation its *esse* remains. Next, if we admit the unity of man in nature, then the immortality of the whole person, not just the soul, becomes a reasonable expectation.

Finally, in subrational organisms we have no evidence that they perform any acts which transcend the powers of matter, and hence their individual acts of existing belong primarily to the psychosomatic composite rather than to their forms. Their life principles are therefore not subsistent, and death for such creatures is truly the black veil of nothingness.[33]

BACKGROUND

The Need for Revelation

Aquinas did not look upon Revelation as a nice, but unnecessary, thing to have. Given the weakness of human nature due to original sin, it was at least a moral necessity for God to speak directly to the human species in order to provide the ordinary human being with the possibility for salvation. To appreciate this in modern times, a parallel between the ideal and the real-life political situations in human affairs on the one hand, and the role of Scripture in the lives of even the most intelligent human beings on the other hand, may be helpful.

Consider the typical "conservative" attitude in contrast with the typical "liberal" attitude in North American politics. The central doctrine of conservatism is that people should stand on their own two feet. Individuals and small groups of human beings should do things for themselves. "Don't let the government take over," is the motto. "Why let the government bureaucracy bribe you with your own money, which they collect from you through taxes?" is the key question. Fight government controls! Resist the government's attempt to keep trying to protect you against yourself. People should be as free as possible from government interference, especially in money matters. The government that governs least governs best!

Obviously in order for the conservatives to have their way, each human being in society must be a rather well-educated and responsible person. Hence the emphasis upon a "liberal arts" education, the education suitable to a free person. In such an educational process one learns to be "his or her own person." As its advocates are willing to admit, such a political approach does have its problems, the main one being the difficulty of really being consistent in the application to social affairs of the "freedom first" program.

For example, if the government has no right to protect you against yourself in money matters by forcing you to save money for your old age through social security taxes, how is it that they have the right to prevent sexual prostitution as a free-enterprise undertaking? Or again, if the government has no right to force up your taxes in order to pay welfare costs (without denying the possibility that you may wish to help support widows and orphans voluntarily), how can one justify the government's forbidding you to freely use hard drugs? In other words, there is such a thing as a pagan conservatism in politics and social ethics.

In contrast, the liberal view is that big government is good. Instead of fighting it, give in to the welfare state. "Relax and let the government decide things for you," is the underlying attitude at work. Don't fight higher taxes as long as you are getting more services for your money. Neither should you be afraid to "rob the rich," especially the middle-class rich because that's where most of the money is, in order to pay for government programs. In general, it is better to have somebody else take care of you than to worry about taking care of things yourself. As anyone can see, such an approach tends towards a dictatorship. But is that really such a bad thing, especially if the people in power are good people with your personal well-being in mind?

Although many people will theoretically object strongly to the liberal philosophy, in practice it is the one which always seems to win. What the conservatives consistently overlook is the weakness and frailty of human nature. The rugged individual, and the independence of groups of individuals, may be the better situation in the sense of the ideal, but it is not the *de facto* situation. The masses may not exactly be asses, but it often helps to act as if they were.

This can be seen very clearly during political campaigns. The politician who goes around saying that if elected he will see to it that people are forced to do more for themselves is rarely successful. When conservatives do win, they do it by promising people lower taxes and less government control without telling what the consequences are. By far, though, the best thing to do is to avoid the issues altogether and concentrate instead on personality appeal and Hegelian generalities which allow everything to coexist with everything else. This, in fact, is what usually happens in political campaigns.

Aquinas' approach to the need for Revelation follows the same pattern. Just as in the long run the "liberal" approach will always win out if put to the one-man-one-vote test over and over again, the scriptural approach to salvation will ultimately prevail over the strictly philosophical approach. The ideal human thinker and reasoner does not need to be told some of the things which Revelation in fact tells. But, if salvation were to rest upon such a basis, the salvation of the masses would be impossible, practically speaking. After all, how many perfect human philosophers and scientists are there in the world at any one time? Consequently, given the ignorance, laziness, sensuality, and so on of the average human being, Revelation is a necessity.

There is also another factor to take into account. What about all those facts in Scripture concerning the ultimate destiny of human persons and the means for reaching that goal which cannot be derived from natural reason regardless of how great the mind that is doing the reasoning? Here, too, Revelation is required. How can people direct themselves toward God if they are not aware of the means instituted by God for their doing so? And who besides God could possibly instruct people in such affairs? It is clear to Aquinas, then, that Revelation is required from both the viewpoint of what the average person actually is and from the viewpoint of what he or she could be and do, even ideally speaking.

Theology and Philosophy

Where, then, does natural human reason come into the picture? Is this fourth position on human nature purely theological or not? About 1958 one of the best-known contemporary Thomists, Etienne Gilson, began to write a history of his own intellectual development. It was published in English in 1962 under the title *The Philosopher and Theology*. As with anyone pursuing philosophy there is a whole series of questions and problems to be probed and discussed. With respect to his own particular career, though, he tells about one large, dominating issue of great concern: How the whole range of secular science and philosophy could be related to the religious area of theological studies. In other words, is there a place for the thinking religious person in modern times?

As a youth, before 1900, Gilson was taught to believe in God. Was this a bad thing? As he goes on to point out, the situation changed as he got older. It was not so much that *he* changed, but rather that the approach to God in Catholic schools had changed. By 1950 in France people were being left with the impression that a rational proof of God must necessarily precede any belief in God. First know and then believe. With respect to the subject matter, he comments, this is a queer way of doing things. Children were being asked to substitute something of great difficulty for an immediate assent of faith. What is worse, what was being substituted, that is, what was being offered as a rational proof (namely, in this case, I believe in God because the world could not have made itself) was terrible philosophy and worthless physical science. What the designers of such a religious studies program were attempting to do was to give an instant-pudding, rational proof for God in order to make religion look more modern. But there is no such thing, and they should have been the first to know it. The whole thing was a sham. Young people were being given a cheap watch that could not stand the test of time even though it might look good to the ignorant. What the instructors should have done instead was the same thing Vatican I (1869-1870) had done in order to counterbalance the extreme of traditionalism, namely, simply state that rational demonstrations of God are possible, but that nevertheless it is highly unlikely that more than one student in a million will ever get around to studying them.

As Gilson explains the history of the case, the French materialists of the eighteenth century, such as Denis Diderot, had set the stage for a Christian counterreaction. By emphasizing a hyper-individualism devoted to doing your own thing in your own way, the materialists drew Christian thinkers into a battle which pitted reason against faith. To many Christians reason became the enemy, and they in turn could think of no better rejoinder than "to pitch faith and revelation against reason."[34] This was the situation from about 1750 to 1870. As a result the Christian had to choose between Revelation on the one hand and science and reason on the other hand. The situation was similar to the one which often prevails within "fundamentalist" Christian groups even today.

In 1870, though, after Vatican I, things began to change. Due not only to the council's insistence upon the compatibility of faith and reason, but also to the obvious prestige of science and technology, Catholic thinkers began to move in the direction of out-rationalizing the rationalists. As Gilson notes, this was a very strange stance to take. It was the exact reversal of what had always worked so well in the past. Ironically, the people promoting such a stance really did not believe in it themselves. Most of them were zealous priests who wanted to attract nonbelievers to the faith by showing how very reasonable it was. Moreover, the Christianity which concerned them was not the watered-down version of someone such as Locke, but the full Catholic version. Things got so bad after a while that every priest and his brother was cranking out a series of textbooks in philosophy. Adopting the attitude of Descartes on the initial separation of faith and reason, their purpose was to show the perfect agreement between religion and philosophy by a reason that was "wholly independent of faith."[35]

But even with that things had not reached their nadir. In time it became a motto that if you *know* something, you cannot *believe* in it and vice versa. Students were taught that if you hold something on faith, then it cannot be rationally proven. Gilson reports that when he made bold to speak against such an arrangement of things, he could not make himself understood. Not only, he would be repeatedly told, *need* you not believe in God once his existence was rationally proven, but you *could* not.[36]

Since about 1962 the trend has again reversed itself. Catholic thought has gone back to a sentimental approach to God devoid of intellectual discipline. And morality has become liberally laced with a lot of relativistic neo-pagan ethics, especially in sexual matters. We are once again in an anti-intellectual era of *feelings*. No longer do priests write philosophy books for the masses; now they write folk songs for the mass.

Is there any way to stop this running back and forth between extremes? For Aquinas "theology" was the way out. Although rejected in many quarters, there is still a great deal of this approach in modern thought. Today it is still easy to slide back and forth in our estimation of man in the world as we go from philosophy to theology. In their own ways each gives an overview of the world. Philosophy might even be considered as a sort of nonauthoritative theology. Such an approach, though, would be somewhat off the mark. The tendency of the "overview" approach is once again to enforce the reason-faith separation thesis. Based upon such a dichotomy, philosophical conclusions derive entirely from nonreligious human experiences, while theological conclusions follow exclusively from "faith propositions." Theology then ends up having to do only with inner personal feelings about God, while philosophy and science deal with the outside world. This is one of the reasons why subjects such as metaphysics are so poorly understood today. To the secular mind, which outrightly rejects the very possibility of theology from the outset, and which regards the subject matter of metaphysics to be, if anything, about the mind or God, metaphysics should be shunned because it is too close to theology.

Such a position, however, is not necessarily the case. There is no necessary reason to assume beforehand that all conclusions in theology must be deduced from propositions held on faith. Although it is true to say that "All philosophical statements are based upon unaided reason," it does not follow that "All statements based upon unaided reason are philosophical." This would be like going from saying that "All human beings are individuals" to saying that "All individual things are human beings." In logic such a move is called the unjustified conversion of a universal affirmative proposition. When applied to theology this means that there is no reason why purely rational propositions and conclusions cannot belong to theology. If the object of theology is to obtain some insight into God and his view of his own creation, even if it be only a glimpse, there is no reason to suppose that anything at all should be left out. Free speculation, participation in the divine life of God, and theology all become blended together.

The theological point of view, then, does not exclude the rational; it includes it. Rather than there being an opposition of faith and reason, there can be a unity of the two in the life of one thinker. It is possible for someone to be a scientist, a philosopher, and a theologian simultaneously. The mental battles we often find surrounding the reason-faith controversy are not due to anything intrinsic to the subject matter of either philosophy or theology. The opposition is a pseudo-problem which can be explained by the course of historical events. As a result of these events, the main means by which human beings can get some insight into the way God sees himself and the world, namely, Scripture, was subjected to criticisms which put it across the border into the land of the irrational.

On the same basis it is possible to understand how the theologian can claim to be the leader in all fields of knowledge while not actually being a philosopher or a scientist in an explicit or professional fashion. In considering God one considers everything created by God as well. Explicitly, though, theology does not have a monopoly on knowledge. Graduating from some school of religious formation after studying theology does not bring with it infused knowledge of everything. Few today would fall into the extreme position of saying that it does. Many, however, do not hesitate to assume the opposite extreme, namely, that in order to know anything other than theology you must abandon theology altogether. Even though it need not be so, historically things have come to this point.[37]

Essence and Existence

Today all thinkers take for granted that the universe must be unified according to some one principle or cause. This was not the case among the ancients. Aristotle, for instance, saw no problem with having both a First Cause of Motion and uncreated prime matter. For him the universe ran along parallel fixed rails when considered in terms of the past and the future. Part of this arrangement was the existence of a series of separated substances responsible for maintaining the eternal revolutions of the heavens. Due to the influence of Christianity, which insists upon one and only one cause of everything in terms of existence, the ancient view of the universe is no longer acceptable today even to atheists.

I am not here speaking about what science has done to break down the physical world view of the ancients. I mean that even modern materialists are unhappy unless they can reduce everything to one cause, even if it is just the one material universe. Modern intellectuals, even though outside the realm of monotheistic religion, are still monists in philosophy. Their main struggle is with the unity of things.

The ancient Greeks, however, were quite content with having gods to explain one type of situation, mainly situations involving inter-personal relationships, and the material world of nature to explain purely natural events.

The advent of Christianity, however, could not allow the Greek universe to go on existing. Whereas the Greek world was full of gods, the Christian world was highly restricted in that regard. Hence, there was a problem for Christian intellectuals. If there is a hierarchy of beings in the universe, some of which are far superior to human beings, how is it that they are not gods? Indeed, how can it be that human beings, which possess substantial souls, are not just so many little gods in their own right?

Needless to say, that is not a hot issue in the twentieth century. Yet it was an issue of some importance for those pre-seventeenth-century thinkers who were simultaneously living in the moral universe of Christianity and the physical universe of the Greek pagans. This is pre-cisely the problem Aquinas faced up to in his early work *On Being and Essence*. This work, written when Aquinas was only thirty years old, like most world-changing works, is relatively short. Nevertheless, it contains the insight into the nonidentity of the "what" and the "to be" of everything other than God which became the cornerstone of his whole view on the human person.

In the chapter dealing with essence as found in separated substances Aquinas sets out to show two things. One is that the "intelligences," or intellectual substances, whether human or angelic, are not gods or God. The other is that they were created by God. Both conclusions are deduced from the same starting point, namely, that God is He Who Is. Once it is known that God is pure existence and that he and he alone is the creator of the whole universe, it becomes easy to see why there must be a lack of identity between the essence, "what," or definition of something and the very act whereby it exists. Is it not possible to know *what* something is and yet not know whether or not it actually exists? It is, says Aquinas. Intramentally, at least, then, every-one is aware that the definition and the existence of something cannot be the same.

Is this the situation, though, in every existing thing which has ever existed, exists now, or ever will exist in the universe? Again the answer is yes. This must be the case extramentally as well as intramentally because in one and only one being can essence and existence be identified. This being, of course, is God. "To be" is, in fact, the very definition of God, revealed by God himself to his chosen people. How, then, can any other being be so defined? The answer is that no other being can be so defined. We know, therefore, that human souls and angels are not gods, nor are they parts of God. There is God, and then there is everything else. To Aquinas' way of thinking he had found the hard and fast line of demarcation for which he was looking.

Next, it must be realized that if no creature possesses an act of existing in itself from all eternity, it must have been bestowed upon the creature by some being which is eternally in possession of existence. This being can only be God. Consequently, before existing, a creature lacks existence, while after coming into existence, it possesses a definite mode of existence. Could the nonexistent creature have given itself existence? Of course not. It had to be given existence. And what is creation if not precisely that? So it is that all creatures, including human souls and angels, require creation. God creates beings, that is, things which exist in certain ways. Aquinas has thus made his second point.[38]

With respect to each human being, therefore, God is the beginning and the goal of his or her existence. Each individual is as really different and yet as ultimately alike as the children of the same set of parents. Insofar as you have existence, you are made in the image of God. Because human beings exist they can act, "and they are because His name is *He Who Is.*"[39]

SOME CONSEQUENCES

Racial Unity

Is God perfect? And if so, what does it mean to be perfect? Unlike many thinkers both before and after him, Aquinas did not merely take existence for granted. To those who might object to his statement that God is perfect because God is mere existence, Aquinas answers that "to exist is the most perfect of all things. In comparison to all else it is act, for nothing has actuality except insofar as it is. So it is that to be is the actuality of all things, even of forms themselves."[40]

Is not a live worm better than a dead horse? Is it not obvious that in order to do anything at all, the creature must first exist? This is especially true of human beings. Their very mode of existing is their claim to dignity. Through their act of existing humans are empowered to act in the world while also rightfully belonging to another world. "Person," says Aquinas, "signifies what is most perfect in all of nature, namely, a subsistent individual of a rational nature."[41] But what is it that makes a person to be a person? It is nothing more or less than an incarnated soul with its own act of existing.

Only after being created to be the kind of soul that a human soul is can we speak about the operations and activities of the person. Because of the type of soul each human being possesses he or she is capable of performing acts which are not dependent upon matter.

Strangely enough, in modern times this arrangement is often exactly reversed. The investigator does exactly the opposite of what should be done. Instead of seeking out what is common to humans the emphasis is put upon what is different. Furthermore, instead of carefully examining how humans differ from animals and other things the emphasis is put upon the similarities. All too quickly the absolute gap between humans and nonhumans is forgotten. This does not mean that studying what humans have in common with other things is totally uninteresting or useless. It means that dropping a human being off a bridge and timing the fall at thirty-two feet per second squared, or extracting sugar from human urine and noting that it has the same chemical composition as sugar in the sugar bowl, will not allow us to note what is special about people.

When interest is upon differences, do not look at similarities. In fact, some thought will show that it is impossible to do so. To say that you are *like* a stone, or a carrot, or a monkey is to also say that you are *not exactly the same as* a stone, carrot, or monkey. Where similarities are present, there are also diverse factors to consider. If there were no diverse factors similarities would not be similarities; they would be identities.

But is not listing human powers as far as one can go in stating the difference of human beings? That is to say, maybe there is nothing essential behind the acts, no "what" that would set people off from other primates. Such an attitude leads to very peculiar consequences. Suppose someone attempted to identify mind with consciousness or thinking. To be mind is to be in the act of thought. What happens when a person is not actually thinking? Does that person cease to be human in the sense that the mind disappears leaving behind nothing but inanimate extension? This is the inevitable outcome. How can such consequences be avoided? If we say that to be an apple is to be red, what happens to a green apple? If to receive light stimuli is the essence of an eye, is an eye an eye when its eyelid is closed? The fact of experience is that people can perform many different kinds of functions, but that we are not performing each and every one all the time. If any one of these activities were the essence of humans, then, in order to remain a human being, one must be always performing that activity.

As a result, what it means to be human cannot be reasonably identified with any one of the powers which we discover people to have based upon the acts we discover people to perform. It should be clear then that any definition of the human person based upon any one of these abilities must be inadequate. Examples of such definitions, which one can still find in vogue among many modern scientists and philosophers, would be the following:

Man is a poor creature full of ignorance, suffering, and pain;
Man is an ethical animal;
Man is an animal capable of articulate speech;
Man is a symbolic, searching creature;
Man is an animal capable of using tools;
Man is an animal that can delight in beauty;
Man is a creature capable of changing his mode of existence;
Man is a progressive animal;
Man is an animal that takes great joy in his own accomplishments;
Man is an animal capable of acting spontaneously;
Man is an animal forever seeking to transcend himself;
Man is a creature able to deceive himself;
Man is a thing capable of responding to doubtful situations as
    problematic;
Man is a creature with legal rights and obligations;
Man is a being that can accept life;
Man is a self-conscious being.

With a firm grasp of these points in hand one is free to go on to something more than a relatively superficial appreciation of just what it means to be a human being.[42]

Those who do not see this never do come to immediate grips with the crucial and central problems and issues. Aquinas would suggest that the failure is the result of their investigating the relationship between people and animals in such a way that they systematically leave out of account what is really special about people. Comparisons, of course, are always made upon the basis of one factor at a time. As soon as someone suggests comparing human and beast, the question concerning what factor to use immediately arises. In order to have a controlled experiment, one must know what to control. Depending upon the factor selected, one will find that man as a species is the same as, or diverse from, the animal specimens. When one hits upon the lack of social deviation, for instance, as the factor which is to act as the basis of comparison, the human comes out inferior. When one chooses certain physical powers as the basis, the human sometimes comes out ahead (for example, man versus worm in strength) and sometimes behind (for example, man versus elephant in strength). When intelligence is selected as the basis, however, the human always comes out ahead.

Intelligence here must mean a distinctively human intelligence. Intelligence is generally recognized as the distinctively human characteristic. But what is so distinctive about it? Various conclusions will follow upon various different definitions. When giving such definitions, though, one must be careful not to do an injustice to humans. An unjust definition will still allow for the possibility for a controlled experiment, but the results will not disprove the unique status of humans. A just definition will give the possibility for *both* a controlled experiment *and* for a definitive answer to the question of whether or not the human is truly a unique species. But how does the investigator do justice to humans? He or she begins by examining human acts in order to discover what it is people are doing when they reason. This leads to a realization of the immateriality of the human mind. The experimenter is then in a position to run controlled experiments to see if animals exhibit the same action traits. Any other approach may yield very interesting, but also very inconclusive, results.

According to Aquinas, intelligence means the ability to recognize a means as a means to an end. As a power, intelligence is the ability to understand the "nature" or "essence" or "what" of a thing or situation so that we can come to know how it is related to other "whats."[43] This ability allows for the possibility of scientific knowledge and human language. Rather than being stopped where your senses stop, you can use sense knowledge to go beyond sensations. To be limited all around by what can only be gained via physical contacts in various ways is a sure sign that intelligence is either completely lacking or at least dormant.

The great significance of this approach to the meaning of intelligence should be clear enough. If intelligence is taken to mean merely the ability to learn from experience, then certainly animals are intelligent as well as people, although perhaps to a lesser degree. If it is taken to mean the ability to know a means as a means, that is, a "what," the situation changes radically. No longer, then, can it be said that animals are also intelligent, but only to a lesser degree. No longer, then, can it be said that animals communicate in the same way humans do, but only to a lesser degree. It was not Aquinas who started the story about animals talking at midnight on Christmas eve.

Here we will find the basis for unifying the human species. There is no way of unifying the human race based upon the accidental developments of matter. Aquinas can do it, though, by regarding human beings as created, incarnate angels which reveal their true nature to each other by means of a distinctively human process of communication. This is not something in which animals can participate. Animals perform no operations that exceed the limits of sensation and consequently cannot be credited with subsistent souls. The obvious question, of course, is whether or not what Aquinas thought about animals so many years ago, before the advent of scientific investigation, still makes any sense today.

No one doubts that animals communicate within their species and sometimes even with creatures in other species. One type of animal will flee, for instance, when it hears a warning cry uttered by a creature in another species. Communication among animals within a species, though, is notoriously restricted. There are certain standard calls, cries, movements, gestures, and so forth which instinctively set in motion other types of action. In a way, animals have outdone humankind in this regard. The human species is still searching for a workable universal language whereas animal species already have one well established. Since animals are already engaging in communication, then, animal communication would seem to be a good base from which to begin a comparison between human and beast. Perhaps, building upon that base, an investigator could show how human language must have developed by showing how animals, when placed in the right circumstances, have begun to speak.

Winthrop N. Kellogg, for instance, summarizing attempts to get human-type language out of primates, states that the impetus behind most of the work was to give the animals tested an even break. Was it that the average chimpanzee could not speak because it lacked some necessary prerequisite power or simply because it never had the same opportunities as a normal human baby? One way to find out was to raise the chimpanzee in a regular home setting as if it were a human child. Kellogg reports on six such studies aimed at determining in a comprehensive way just how far the instincts of anthropoid apes could be modified in the direction of human culture.[44]

The interesting thing about the experiments is that they consistently failed on both counts. The apes tested never got to the point where they could speak as well as many other creatures do without any in-house training. They also never achieved any kind of communication with humans involving an interchange of ideas through the means of language.

It was found that the subjects tested were able to adapt quickly to the human household setting. In swinging from the chandeliers and matters of physical strength the young chimpanzees far outdid their human companions of the same age. The best that could be accomplished in the way of speech, however, was that a certain chimpanzee named Viki, which had been raised for many years by the Hayeses, was thought by the investigators to be mouthing, in unvoiced and hoarse whispers, the words "mama," "papa," "cup," and "up" on certain occasions. Even these, however, came about only after many months of actual physical manipulation of the animal's lips. Otherwise, any communication from any of the apes to humans was in the form of gestures which they had to be trained to perform in a regular way.

Communication from the trainers to the ape could be carried on in the form of gestures or sounds, but again only after a training period in which a one-to-one correspondence between stimulus and response had been established. Kellogg concluded that a standardized system of gestures rather than articulated speech would seem to hold the most promise for a two-way communication system between people and a home-raised ape. At the time he wrote, however, no such system had been worked out or implemented. Later the Gardners, and others such as Francine Patterson, published some inconclusive results along the suggested experimental lines; inconclusive, that is, once human intelligence is fairly defined in cognitive science.

In recent years a modification of such an enterprise has been carried out. David Premack, a follower of B. F. Skinner, tells of his experiments with a primate named Sarah. His study asked the question: Can apes be taught language? His answer is that apes are an unclear middle case. They are the linguistic connecting link between animals and people. He bases this answer upon a series of experiments in which the subject was required to perform certain intermediary tasks in order to acquire something she wanted. Premack believes that if the ape can be made to work with words, sentences, questions, the use of language itself, class concepts (color, size, shape), copulas, quantifiers, and logical connectives, then it can be said that it has been taught language.[45]

The experimental procedure basically consisted in substituting in a regular way certain colored pieces of plastic for certain objects or sequences of events and then requiring the ape to use those pieces of plastic in order to signal that she wanted or did not want that which they represented. These signals were made by placing the pieces of plastic, which had metal backs, on a magnetic board. If more than one symbol was needed Sarah was required to place them in a vertical line, one under the other.

Based upon his tests Premack concluded that Sarah really talked insofar as she was able to transfer the properties of an apple, for instance, to a little blue piece of plastic which then came to symbolize the thing itself. This symbolization, he stated, is an integral property of perhaps all learning and is what makes language possible. Once symbolization and transfer procedures are established, the subject can be said to be working with language and therefore capable of talking. Such speech is something more than mere imitation or unaltered brute signals such as crow calls or the imitations of parrots and myna birds.

Premack thinks that when studying language, one should begin with animals. He seems to think that by studying how apes can be taught to converse with humans, one can get some insight into what language is all about. He notes that we tend to assign a definitional weight to every aspect of human language. But, he asks, are not certain features more critical than others? His intention, we are informed, is to distinguish language as a general system from its particular form in you and me. This can be done, he implies, in agreement with other experimenters, by working from ape to humans rather than vice versa. In other words, in order to learn about human thinking, you study animals rather than yourself.

More recently Premack, in conjunction with Guy Woodruff, has reported upon some experiments with the same female chimpanzee, Sarah, used in the earlier tests. In the new experiments she was required to view on videotape a series of acted-out problem situations and then select a still photograph depicting the solution to the problem situation. In each case she had to choose one of two photographs indicating that she "understood" the correct solution. Altogether there were eight different problems. After a series of several daily trials, with four attempts at the solution of each of the problem situations, it was found that Sarah was very good at picking out the correct solution picture. In one case, for instance, she was shown a man trying to exit from a locked room and successfully picked out a picture of a key as the correct solution.

As indicated by the title of the report, "Chimpanzee Problem-Solving: A Test for Comprehension" (*Science*, 3 November 1978), what the authors were after was some sign of "comprehension" ability in apes. They considered their work to be a continuation of Koehler's "insight" experiments carried out many years before. However, as the authors themselves state, Sarah was no stranger to the elements involved in the tests, having practically lived with humans for thirteen years. What was special about the tests was the particular arrangement of the problematic elements and their solutions. To what extent her familiarity with the stage props determined her "comprehension" of the plays the experimenters cannot say. But, given the circumstances they described, can we be sure that Sarah's actions exceeded the limits of an ape's well-developed sense powers? This same question can be asked of other projects carried out by other members of the same team, as well as of the many similar projects undertaken by others.

Of course, animals learn. Various apes, the numerous circus acts we are all familiar with, your own pets, police dogs, seeing eye dogs, and many other instances all attest to this fact. But what does one mean by learning? Many thinkers today shy away from talking about learning in terms of immaterial concepts, that is, an apprehension of the "what" or essence of a thing or of a series of events. Many prefer a vague picture or image. But no picture or image can ever be vague or general enough to stand for a common characteristic. Nevertheless, learning is often spoken about in such terms. To many, to learn means to form certain kinds and sequences of sense images which were not present before the learning took place. Under these circumstances animals can be said to learn as well as, and in some cases better than, humans. If learning is to be defined in terms of operations which can be observed and measured, then it is quite possible and proper to speak about animal learning.

In many quarters this sort of thing is considered to be all there is to learning. Something is said to have learned when, based upon what can be outwardly observed, it in fact carries out certain activities which it did not carry out previous to the learning process. If this is assumed to be the basic definition of learning, then certainly animals can be said to learn. To go a step more, though, and say that therefore animals that learn and humans that learn are separated only by a matter of degree would not be warranted. The reason is that, although humans can learn in the same ways that animals learn (by mimicry, trial and error, "insight" into physical combinations, training), there is something in human learning which animals are not capable of possessing even to a slight degree. This something is the ability to form concepts, which are not anything like vague or fuzzy images or perceptions.

From a series of causes, such as familiarity between some people and some animals and the modern development of animal cartoons which show animals acting like humans, it is often difficult for humans to realize that animals do not exist as people do. A cow licking her calf is thought to be showing the beginnings of human affection. Birds, and in fact all animal creatures that care for their young, are regarded as doing the same. Animals have all sorts of mating, military, territorial, and play rituals. Is the jealous guarding of a certain piece of real estate by some animal species the beginning of human nationalism and private property law? Are ant societies the foundation of human tribalism and "in-group" altruism? Under the influence of writers and artists such as Walt Disney it is easier than ever to answer yes.

However, for those who are a little more careful in their observations the situation is not that way at all. One can, for instance, train a dog to associate the sound "stick" with several images of the actual item. The same could be done with "newspaper" or "shoe." The animal could then be trained to retrieve the items on cue or upon certain other memorized commands. However, can a dog ever know what a tree is, a news medium is, or a piece of wearing apparel is? It is easy enough to find out. Disconnect the memorized physical sound from the memorized physical image and see what happens. Nothing. A dog can be trained to respond to a particular clock on yonder wall, but ask it to go to "that which translates duration into space and then divides it into equal segments" and even the wisest old Rex will get nowhere. As *you* know, clocks don't measure time. They measure distance. Chronometers come in many kinds, and no one example exhausts all the possibilities. Your pet dog would never think of constructing any type of clock at all. And a request to get a copy of *The Daily Record,* when made at an unusual time and place, will elicit no response.

Parallel examples can be found in all segments of the animal world. Birds, for instance, so often praised for their counting ability, can supply some cases. The grey-breasted martin, for instance, after its nest has been moved a short distance from its original location, will return to the original position and completely fail to notice the slightly removed nest. After a while it will begin building a new nest on the original site.

The case of the cuckoo bird is also a good indication of a complete lack of human-type intelligence. The cuckoo places its eggs in the nests of other species of bird. When the young cuckoo hatches, it ejects the other little birds from the nest. What does the mother of these other youngsters do? She feeds the cuckoo and ignores her own offspring squeaking a short distance away.

There also does not appear to be anything like human affection in the animal world despite what might be read into superficially parallel cases of child care. Blackheaded gulls and penguins, for instance, after the original eggs in their nests have been replaced with other items, will just as willingly try to hatch stones, tin cans, or golf balls as their own eggs.

Furthermore, even the brooding of real eggs is, when otherwise undisturbed, no indication of parental love. During the brooding season birds develop uncomfortably warm brood spots on their breast area.

By sitting on the cool egg, and turning the egg as one side warms up, the birds relieve the uncomfortable warmth they feel. By cooling off the brood spots with cold water or some other cool thing the experimenter can cause a bird to forget completely about its eggs.

Woodpeckers, squirrels, and other animals that store food for the winter in hollow trees can also easily have the whole process short-circuited. Imagine continuing a hole started by a woodpecker all the way through and out the other side of a tree. Does the bird realize that its placing nuts in the hole is a necessary means to the end of having a winter supply of food? Apparently not. The bird will continue to ''fill'' the hole even though its food supply is obviously disappearing out the other side.

Rats, to take some final examples, show the same unintelligence. If the nerves in a rat's leg are cut, it will proceed to eat its own foot even though it needs the foot to move around. A rat will, over and over again, carry its own tail to a nest it is building even though it just as frequently carries it away again. Also, a mother rat will carry back to the nest any little rat that happens to stray away. What would happen if fifty little rats were placed near the nest? The mother will quickly seize them one at a time and attempt to stuff them all into the nest.

In conclusion, when viewed in terms of their own world, animals are wonderfully adapted to survive. They can construct with precision, communicate by body chemistry, and forecast the weather accurately. But when judged by human standards, we discover not a difference of degree but a radical difference in kind. Although people can be trained to perform many tasks efficiently in a fashion similar to the way animals can be trained, it must not be supposed that animals can be trained to do all that humans can do, even in a very rudimentary way.

As long as attempts to train animals, especially apes, to speak have been restricted to one-to-one, sense-level correspondences, they have been able to show some success. In a consideration of human beings, however, the situation changes radically. No longer are we tied to merely simple or complex perceptions. Although we certainly have sense powers, we also possess other abilities as shown by the activities of which we are capable, even though we may not be continually exercising these powers. One of these powers is the ability to know in a special way. In order to fully appreciate it, however, psychologists must first overcome the Walt Disney syndrome.

But what does this collection of information tell us about the unity of the human species? First of all, being a *homo sapiens* is not enough to make you equal to other people. Intelligence, along with all the other specifically human powers, is only a sign of something more profound. Intelligence is a power of the soul. In relation to the soul it is something secondary. If it were primary, then people would cease being people before the age of reason or when unconscious. The vast majority of thinkers on the subject of human nature have recognized the fact that mind must cover more than intellect or even consciousness. If there is to be continuity in the human person, subjectivity cannot be coextensive with consciousness. This can be explained by seeing the soul as an act with intelligence as one of its activities. The soul is an act; the primary actuality of its body. All the functions of the soul, though, are potencies to do things which are not always being done. The two—act and potency—cannot be identified.

But where, it may be asked, does the soul come from? It comes from God, created to be a *res per se subsistens*. The same cannot be said of animals and their life principles. As the material side of the human person develops more and more, the soul can more and more exercise its inherent powers through the body. All along, though, the developing creature is still a human being because of its soul.

As Aquinas was fond of saying, therefore, the human species is a separate entity in the universe just as much as one type of number is separate from another. Taking his cue from Aristotle, he points out that the difference between two and three is not a matter of degree. No number can be more or less two, three, and so on. Therefore, the soul cannot be the result of a purely natural generation process. At the end of his *Summa Theologiae* he points out that there is no way the soul can come from the semen. He presently adds,

> Similarly, the intellectual soul, since it can operate without the body, is subsistent, as was established above. And so it is proper for it to exist and to be made. And since it is an immaterial substance it cannot be caused through generation, but only by the creation of God.[46]

The alternative to natural generation, as he says, is special creation. But what if someone should claim that the intellectual soul comes about within matter by a sort of quantitative-qualitative transformation as the soul gradually goes from a vegetative to an intellectual status within the womb? This also must be rejected, thinks Aquinas:

> First, because no substantial form [of any kind] can be more or less. Rather, the addition to it of a greater perfection produces a different species, just as the addition of a unit produces another species of number. It is not possible for one and the same form to belong to different species.[47]

The overall conclusion, therefore, is that regardless of external appearances or cultural customs, there is something common to all human beings. This is the subsistent soul. Discovering its existence in any particular body, though, is another matter. The best means for doing so would seem to be to test the being for its ability to form universal ideas. The next best means would be to note whether or not the being is the offspring of creatures which are human. If so it should be presumed that the offspring has a subsistent soul as well, even though the soul may not be manifesting itself fully due to some lack of bodily development. In the end, then, if all humans are equal it must be because they are *created* equal.

Evolution and Pollution

If, as Skinner says, there is no real freedom in nature, then there really is no need to cultivate self-discipline and will power in order to avoid sin and the occasions of sin. There can be no moral pollution without a moral order to pollute. But, if there is true freedom of choice, then it becomes important to develop individual will power. The problem is, how can anyone be sure that his or her decisions will really have any practical effects on the world in the long run? Certainly, in the short run, we can all observe the effects of personal decisions. However, what, if anything, do these decisions have to do with the whole course of history? To ask the same thing in a different way, just how fixed is nature over the long haul?

From the physical viewpoint the world of medieval Europe was as small and closed as was the world of the Greeks. The small heavy earth stood still in the center while the outer sphere, which was a relatively great distance from the center but really not all that far, enclosed the universe in one neat package. In terms of time, though, things were different. For Aristotle the universe was eternal, with many cultures rising and falling over and over again. The human minds of individual people had an infinite time to discover, forget, and rediscover the same truths over and over again as well. For this reason Aristotle took seriously the need to collect the opinions of past thinkers concerning the nature of things.

This was not Aquinas' situation, however. For him the universe was of a relatively short duration, having been created by God a relatively short time before the coming of Christ. This, he said, was not something open to rational demonstration but must rather be accepted on faith and faith alone. As with the divine Trinity, "that the universe did not always exist we hold on faith alone. It cannot be scientifically proven."[48] The creation of the universe was a free act of God. It cannot be regarded as something that had to happen, much less something that had to happen from all eternity.

But what about the contents of the universe? Can new species arise from the world as created by God in the beginning of time? Without any doubt Aquinas personally did not think so. As he states, "With respect to the perfection of the universe, the number of individuals can be increased every day, but not the number of species."[49] Does this mean that each and every species, including hybrids such as the mule, had to be directly created by God in the beginning exactly as they now appear on earth? Not exactly. In fact, God may very well have used subsidiary creatures, such as angels, in order to help in the process of creation. Indeed, they may still be active today in such matters. It is quite possible, thinks Aquinas, that certain creatures were directly created by God while others were only created in some sort of embryonic form to show up later in world history as fully developed creatures. This latter situation may well have been the case with plants and lower animal forms.[50]

It may also be the case with respect to the higher animal forms. Aquinas lived in an age when the spontaneous generation of living things from nonliving matter was taken for granted. Aquinas, however, attempted to reduce the spontaneity of the process by invoking both matter and the influence of the heavenly bodies as causal principles. Could the same be true of the higher animal forms? Perhaps.

He never really says whether or not higher animals were originally formed as adults of the species. He seems to want to avoid the chicken-or-egg controversy as much as possible. All he knows for sure is that in the beginning God was ultimately responsible for everything that now exists. As far as the gradual development of the preordained species is concerned, though, it is possible that ''out of the powers originally given to the elements they are able to produce animals either from elementary matter, or seeds *(virtute seminis)*, or the stars.''[51] Such an approach would be in keeping with the way nature usually operates, namely, the production of the more perfect through the less perfect.

Is this in keeping with modern evolutionary doctrine as found in reductionistic materialism or nonreductionistic materialism? Yes and no. Insofar as things are supposed to have developed gradually over a long period of time, it would be. However, insofar as the causes for such gradual development are concerned, it would not be. Thomas cannot regard the present world as the result of ''accidental'' arrangements of the minute parts of material bodies which happened to fit ''accidentally'' into the given environment of the times when they occurred. Neither can he attribute to matter itself the creative powers of God himself. His position, with respect to creatures less than human, is a compromise. The work of creation was completed during the days of creation, but many of the things created did not become visible until many years later.

> Nothing totally new was later made by God, but in a way all later things were made during the six days....New species also, if any should appear, pre-existed in certain active powers, such that new species of animals, and animals produced by putrefaction under the influence of the stars and the elements, received their existence in the beginning. And again sometimes animals of a new species arise from a mixture of individual animals of different species, as in the case of the mule coming from an ass and a mare. Yet even here it pre-existed in its causes in the works of the six days.[52]

With respect to human nature, however, there can be no doubt, given the special status of the human soul as a subsistent principle of life, that it requires a special creation in every instance. This is shown very clearly in the way Scripture describes the creation of man as something very special in the world economy. This applies to the whole of human nature, that is, the body and the soul together. Consequently, saying that the specifically human body was formed first in time ahead of the infusion of the soul must be wrong because such a notion goes against the perfection of the first arrangement of things. God would not have created the body without the soul or vice versa, "since each is a part of human nature. And this would be especially unbecoming for the body, which depends upon the soul, and not the other way round."[53] In other words, if anything were to be created first, it would have to be the soul.[54] It is the soul which makes "this" body an individualized person.

Once the question of the origin of species has been resolved, it is possible to go on to deduce what one's position should be on pollution problems. As we have already observed, it makes little sense to affirm first the haphazard, promiscuous, and "accidental" nature of change and then to express fears over pollution. Such an attitude implies that the first step is not really taken seriously. To worry about pollution bringing about the demise of the human race is to show very little faith in the inner dynamic progression of divine matter.

However, according to psychosomaticism, with or without immortality, it does make sense to worry about pollution. When Aquinas lived, people simply did not have the industry and technology to make pollution a problem. Today, though, we can see how in any system which regards nature as a creation constructed according to relatively fixed patterns, pollution caused by humankind is something to be concerned about. Just as sin is a kind of moral pollution of the spirit, so uncontrolled abuse of the environment is a physical pollution of the body. Since human nature is both body and soul, both of which are destined for eternal survival, Thomists should be in the vanguard of those concerned with pollution. This is not something one would expect from consistent materialists. We saw that Aquinas was willing to admit that species were created in potency in the beginning and later came to actuality. This was important to him, since it would allow for both the ultimate dependence of everything upon God and the appearance of new species after the time of creation. To put the matter otherwise, even potencies, potentialities, inner tendencies, and natural affinities require God's creative power.

In contrast, such a thing cannot be taken seriously by anyone in the materialistic camps. Dobzhansky himself illustrates this point very well.

> The statement that life must have had from the very beginning the potentialities for all the evolutionary developments which did in fact occur is obviously true but just as obviously trivial. If it were otherwise evolution could not have done what it did. What is more important is that life had also innumerable other potentialities which remained unrealized.[55]

The emphasis here is obviously upon the future. There is nothing preordained about evolutionary development. There is no telling what will happen in the future or what has happened elsewhere in the universe. The ways of matter are not our ways, and the knowledge of the future is not ours to possess. How organic forms have adapted from one environment to another, whether on earth or on some distant planet, can only be known by actually observing them. And how they will adapt in the future can only be known by waiting until the future becomes the present. Certainly the inherent potentialities are there, but that is the whole point: They are just there, uncreated and eternal.

By the same token, the disappearance of species from the face of the earth might trouble a Thomist but should not really bother anyone in either of the materialistic camps. This is not always the case, however. What arguments can be put forward to justify using extraordinary means to prevent the disappearance of endangered species? Consider the following:

> There are compelling justifications for preventing needless extirpation of species. We have a common evolutionary heritage with other organisms, and find inspiration and beauty in many of them; thus, in some sense we are impoverished by the elimination of other species. More pragmatically, species are genetic and chemical resources that are useful in plant breeding, pest control, and biomedical research. Clearly, loss of species reduces this resource base.[56]

Are these arguments really "compelling" according to a materialistic view of the human person? The first argument is purely aesthetic. It could be used by either the theistic or the atheistic evolutionist. The overall beauty of nature is reduced when some of its parts disappear. But how does this *compel* us to stop their disappearance? It would seem that the theist would be in a much better position to justify such a claim than the atheist. He could argue that since God owns nature and humans are only the caretakers, they have a responsibility not to lose anything. Atheists, of course, can make no such statement.

The second argument is based upon the need to have specimens to experiment upon in order to help future generations in various ways. But again it can be asked: Why not let the future take care of itself? Nature will breed, control, and "research" until whatever happens in fact happens. For contemporary people to go out of their way to preserve a certain very small percentage of the millions and millions of different organic species in the world, when there are so many others which can be experimented upon, hardly seems compelling.

My conclusion, then, is that those who attempt to be good environmentalists and good materialists simultaneously, although undoubtedly sincere and well-meaning, are nevertheless acting very inconsistently. Put in other terms, can anyone who denies that there are fixed natures, fixed purposes, and a well-balanced harmony among things in the world really be concerned with the upsetting of such nonexistent natures, purposes, and harmonies? I think not.

This does not mean that Aquinas and his modern followers are necessarily always consistent in everything either. How, for example, can the very fact of the disappearance of seemingly well-established species be accounted for as an aspect of a well-ordered universe? Ultimately it must be attributed to some part of a divine plan for the development of the universe. This plan must involve something more than just punishment for sin, since today we can hardly claim that all such disappearances resulted from the Flood, or even from original sin. When all is said and done, the best a modern Thomist can do is to leave the question open.[57]

The issue of exactly at what time in the life history of the developing human being the infusion of the soul takes place also poses a serious problem for the Thomist. Clearly Saint Thomas taught that there is a progression of souls in the developing fetus; that is, the growth is not human from the moment of conception, but instead goes through a series of forms each of which is corrupted upon the arrival of a later one. "We conclude therefore," Saint Thomas states, "that the intellectual soul is created by God at the end of human generation, and this soul is at the same time sensitive and nutritive, for the pre-existing forms have been corrupted."[58] Consequently, some would reason, claiming Aquinas as their authority, there is nothing wrong with directly willing as the primary end the death of a fetus during its early prehuman stages.

But what exactly is the status of a developing fetus? It is certainly not a mere possible. It is a really existing and developing biological organism. After the infusion of its human soul it is a real and actual human being. But what is it before that moment? In other words, if you kill it, *what* is it that you are killing?

To begin with, in the *Summa Theologiae* II-II, 64, article 1, the progression-of-souls thesis is repeated within the context of a discussion on whether it is lawful for higher beings to kill inferior ones: "Hence it is that just as in the generation of a man there is first a living thing, then an animal, and finally a man, so also things which merely have life, like the plants, are to serve animals, and all animals are to serve man." Can beings which are actually men, then, kill beings which are not yet actually men, but only on their way to becoming such?

Later in the same question (article 6) he argues that there is no way to justify the direct and willful killing of a righteous, innocent, or guiltless human being when that act is willed as an end in itself. When speaking about self-defense in article 7, Aquinas, utilizing the principle of double effect, states that to kill in self-defense is permissible to the private individual (along with other conditions) provided he does not intend killing the aggressor as the primary end. In article 8, when discussing whether one should be considered a murderer because by chance he caused the death of someone, Saint Thomas states that he would be guilty only if he were engaged in something unlawful at the time, or, if lawful, were not taking reasonable care. In reply to the second objection, he writes: "He that strikes a woman with child does something unlawful: Wherefore if there results the death either of the woman or of the animated fetus, he will be guilty of homicide, especially if that death follows naturally from that type of blow." Although it is not clear, this passage could be interpreted as implying that if the woman died before the fetus was animated, that is, achieved its human soul, the man would be guilty of murdering only the mother, and not the child. But if the fetus was animated, he would be guilty of a double homicide.

One is bound to ask at this point how Aquinas could talk about a progression of souls in a person (or in anything else) while also maintaining that species constitute an either-or qualitative difference. How can something be a semihuman? Also, how is it possible for something to exist outside the mind as a nascent genus or species? If the fetus is not at all times a definite human being, it must be a definite something else. If it is plant, what species of plant is it? If it is an animal, what kind of animal is it? Genera and species *qua* genera and species are abstractions. They can exist only in the mind. They are one of the logical ways the mind handles external things. Externally, though, there exist only concrete individuals of some definite nature. There seems to be no reason, except for the general notion that it is often suitable for the imperfect to precede the perfect and hence that it takes time to develop a properly disposed body, for Aquinas to think in any other terms when deciding the status of the fetus. Yet he seems to do so.

Behavior Modification

Page and monarch forth they went,
Forth they went together.

What kind of social life should human beings be expected to lead, given the psychosomaticism-with-immortality view of human nature? The answer is a highly integrated social life under the leadership of a saintly monarch. In contrast with both the pagan Aristotle and the great Christian saint and thinker Augustine, Aquinas attempted to place humans in a social context that was neither overly worldly nor overly other-worldly.

Aristotle regarded women as misformed males and thought of slavery as natural as the rains in spring.[59] Augustine, for his part, tended to regard worldly political associations as necessary evils brought about by original sin and the resulting depravity of existential human nature. Man, born between urine and feces, was off to a bad start which was continued in his need for the material sanctions and satisfactions of the earthly state. Even slavery can be defended as justified in the secular state as an extension of the disordering of people and nature caused by original sin.[60]

Aquinas, however, by emphasizing both the incarnate part and the angel part of human nature cannot allow for the inferiority of women, for slavery, or for the unnaturalness of material associations. Obviously, thinks Aquinas, there are inequalities among people. This would have been the case even in the Garden of Eden. Because of differences in age and bodily disposition some people there could have done things which others could not have done. There is also free choice to contend with. People can either increase or deduct from their abilities by what they choose to do and not do. Thus inequalities can develop as a sort of second nature in people.

At no point, though, can one person say to another that the other person is his or her property. The fact that people serve different functions in society based upon their different talents in no way detracts from the fact that at base everyone has been created equal before the throne of God. What we need, then, is some system of things which will allow for the fact that each human being possesses a supernatural destiny and that each human being must work his or her way towards salvation by material means on earth.

Now, since being material means that there will certainly be differences in talents and abilities, everyone cannot be equally qualified to lead and direct others in the attainment of the common good. That is to say, it can be expected that human inequalities will show up in administrative powers as well as in the areas of relative strength, beauty, speed, and so on. Mastership, therefore, in the sense of leadership, is natural to human society.[61]

There remains now a practical question to be answered, namely, exactly how should the leader use the position and power of leadership? If we look to the historical Aquinas for a complete and detailed answer to this question, we will not find it. The only treatise on politics he wrote was the very brief and unfinished *On Kingship, to the King of Cyprus* (Hugh II of Lusignan who died in 1267 at age fourteen), begun about 1265. Recall that this was the time of the Crusades, and having an ideal Christian kingdom in the Middle East would have been appealing.

Explicitly stated in the work is the need for a monarchy controlled in large part by the educated Christian people of the realm. So long as the king acts as a good administrator, whose primary interest is in the salvation of his subjects, he is to be obeyed and respected. If he should deviate from this course a little, he should be encouraged by moral, economic, and physical pressure to return to the right path. If he should deviate a great deal from his proper course, he should be removed from office and replaced by a better person. As Ignatius T. Eschmann describes the work, the fragment *De Regno* really had only two main points to make. One was that civil society is a good and natural thing; the other was that it must have as its goal "the ultimate end of man, the eternal salvation of his immortal soul."[62]

However, there is more contained in Aquinas' thought which can be drawn out and stated. In the first place, Thomas would say, there is no way in which human populations can do away with hierarchies in society. The Marxist dream of a classless society in the utopian future is completely unfounded given the nature of the human person. Instead of no hierarchy at all being the ideal, the ideal situation would be to preserve the true hierarchy of nature. This is the hierarchy of God, angels, humans, animal, plant, and mineral. In social and political terms this means paying attention to what rules of behavior are indicated by such a hierarchy. The general rule is that the inferior should serve the superior.

But again the question arises of exactly what rules are to be followed in organizing social and individual behavior. To answer this question we must know what the superior power wants of us. Here the Thomist sees various layers of laws. At the top there is the eternal law of God's own nature, which cannot be directly known by humans. However, some of it may be known via Revelation. This Revelation takes two forms, one direct and one indirect. The direct form is Scripture. The indirect form is created human nature endowed with reason. This is what Aquinas means by the "natural law." It is the discovery of what God wants us to do by investigating our spiritual and material constitution.

Are divine (Scripture) law and natural law at variance? By no means. After all, what is the combination of Revelation and reason? Is it not theology? For Aquinas, therefore, legal problems boil down to the question: How can the conclusions of theology concerning human nature be translated into positive or man-made laws which are conducive to the fulfillment of human nature and destiny?

As it turns out, there is no one and only best means to such an end. The king must use prudence and great circumspection in working out what particular laws are best for each particular set of circumstances. What works at one time and place will not do at another time and place. In modern terms this means that what works in Canada may not work in Singapore. What is good for Central Africa may not be good in the United States. Also, what works at one time, such as capitalism when individual initiative is needed, may not work at another time in history. He must also be careful, at all times, to take into consideration the material conditions of the state and its population.

In this sense, then, Aquinas was a relativist when it came to particular human laws. With this in mind it is not surprising that he should have avoided saying anything too specific about what laws should or should not be passed. Rather than being too specific, it is better to state clearly the end to be obtained, namely, individual salvation via the body, and leave the particular laws needed to achieve the end open to variation from culture to culture.

In his own culture, dominated by massive ignorance, "democracy" could not be allowed. Democracy under such circumstances would be the same as what we today would call "mob rule." A one-man-one-vote rule would have meant chaos. By the same token, since people by and large were not able to protect themselves in commercial and economic matters, it was necessary for the monarch to make sure that rigid rules concerning profits, wages, interest charges, weights and measures, coinage, and so forth were passed and enforced. The ignorant poor must be protected against themselves and those who might abuse them. As one political scientist has pointed out, "Aquinas is perhaps the first advocate of social legislation as a main function of the state."[63]

In general it is the monarch's function to take care of the material needs of his people. Like a good father he must see to it that food, clothing, and shelter are fairly and adequately distributed to his children. This can best be accomplished by a sharing of authority. Decentralization is the best way to keep everyone happy. What Aquinas wants, therefore, is a balance of power. Force is needed to keep the irrational elements of society in line. But to the extent that reason is shared and developed by the population they should be allowed to rule.

Consequently, the best form of government is a mixture of monarchy, in which one person rules, and aristocracy, in which a number of people lead according to their virtue, and democracy, that is popular rule, insofar as the leaders can be elected by the populace and the populace is capable of electing its leaders. And this system was instituted according to divine law.[64]

What would happen, though, if everyone were fairly well educated—farm workers as well as land owners, factory workers as well as capitalists, women as well as men? The answer can be inferred from the principles of the Thomistic view of humans. Original sin did not cause any radical change in basic human nature. It is possible to have a society in which practically everyone is well developed enough intellectually to make rational decisions. In fact this is *not* likely to happen, but it is possible. Assuming such a situation, force is not the way to move people to action or keep them in line. Where rational persuasion is possible, it should be used.

In a police state the system is preserved by the suppression of individual creativity. If certain citizens are allowed to do something creative, it must always be under the strict control of the rulers. In a Thomistic society, on the other hand, the system is preserved by fostering creativity. This does not mean going to the extreme of complete license in everything. Absolute freedom is impossible in any kind of society. The most one can hope to do is to maximize freedom of action. However, whereas a Thomistic society will aim at maximization (which will vary under different circumstances), the police state will aim at a minimization of freedom of action.

But what is it about people which allows them to be creative and which is forever the thorn in the side of the would-be complete dictator? Creativity presupposes a higher than animal destiny for man. Precisely because people have an immaterial aspect in addition to their material bodies can they be creative in a material world. Creativity in human beings, though, does not always mean the creation of what is good. Abilities can be used for evil as well as good. To say this is not to say that people are evil at the core.

People are certainly capable of doing evil. But to say that every exercise of will power or natural aggressiveness must necessarily spring from evil motives, and only accidentally produces some good, is unfounded. However, even to create evil situations requires an immaterial power. The general problem in human relations is to get people to create what is good. How is this to be accomplished among politically free people freely pursuing a spiritual destiny?

We are already aware of the answer in principle. In his analysis of humans Aquinas could agree with Aristotle about the elements of a distinctively human type of freedom. Such freedom depends upon the fact that we are not irresistibly drawn towards any one finite object or situation judged as good. To move into action at all, though, in a distinctively human way, requires that we be in a position to judge. That is to say, we cannot get away from the role of knowledge in freedom. In fact, since freedom of choice depends upon having knowledge of several alternatives and also being able to evaluate each in terms of its relationship to our happiness the more knowledgeable someone is the more free that person is. It is the truth that makes people free.

The proper way to motivate someone, not already so perverse as to be incapable of willing to listen, is by supplying accurate information. A person will desire what he or she judges to be good. If we want our fellow human beings to follow certain behavior patterns, we can get them to do so by showing them that our program is the best one to follow when compared with other approaches.

It is not hard to see that a pluralistic society is the kind of political system most in keeping with human dignity. In a police state using propaganda methods, access to accurate information about all aspects of the society in comparison with other societies would be impossible to obtain openly. Depending upon the degree of isolation (the Russian biologist Ivan Pavlov found that complete isolation gave the best results) and the intensity of the propaganda, police states can be more or less successful in shaping the intellects, and consequently the wills, of the population. This could not happen in a pluralistic system.

A pluralistic system is not one in which every part is homogeneous with every other part. It is rather a mosaic in which each part agrees not to destroy any other part by physical violence. If a part does weaken or fade out of existence, it must be the result of its own shortcomings or external persuasions. Only under such circumstances can a real multi-logue take place among the advocates of different points of view. As soon as people see for themselves that a pluralistic society provides them with the greatest opportunities for personal fulfillment and happiness, they will desire to live in such a society. And if it can be shown in addition that in order to preserve such a system, certain means and conditions are necessary, these will also be desired.

Consequently, given the nature of human beings, the whip is not the only means to assure law and order. Regardless of whether the whip is in the form of direct beatings or appears as operant conditioning, it can be rejected in favor of a better and more natural way of reaching the good society.

In connection with this point, what would happen if we were dealing with a well-educated society, but one in which the Church was not the moral guardian of the secular rulers? This was certainly the case in most parts of the world other than Europe even during Aquinas' own lifetime. Needless to say, it is more the case today than it was then. According to the psychosomaticism-with-immortality position it is neither possible nor proper to force belief on someone. Even if it could be done, it would not be meritorious and conducive to the individual's salvation.

The only alternative, then, is not to even try to do it. As Thomas I. Cook pointed out in the 1930s and as Vatican II confirmed in the 1960s, the state cannot be regarded as the proper *moral* guardian of the people. The proper realms of religious and secular powers can never be identified. For the pope to become the monarch of a religious state would mean the destruction of the Catholic church, for it would necessarily then be no longer universal. The proper role of the pope is to be forever outside the political power of any particular state in order to criticize or praise its actions better.

The other side of the coin is this: Where the Church cannot offer direct moral guidance, it is not proper for secular rulers to come in to fill the vacuum. The secular state cannot take over functions which properly belong only to religion. The only alternative left is for the state to allow complete freedom of conscience and religion within the bounds of the material necessities of human nature. It would be proper, for instance, for the state legally to outlaw a religious group which advocated murdering any and all political leaders. Except for such extreme cases, though, freedom should be maximized. Clearly then, thinks Cook, "from Aquinas's teaching can be inferred the whole theory of freedom of conscience."[65]

The basis for this view is the fact that Thomists must take the body seriously. Furthermore, they must take collections of human bodies seriously. Such collections are never purely random. They are always organized into hierarchical levels going from the family up to the kingdom. At the same time, though, the soul must be taken seriously. The soul gives to human beings their rights relative to one another. Bodily might does not make right, but only God's will as revealed in Scripture and human nature. Ultimately this scheme of things rests on faith. Those who have it are blessed. Those who do not can never hope to acquire it by reason alone. Consequently they can never hope to appreciate a good King Wenceslas who together with his loyal subjects and his God form the ideal Christian community. Faith is the beginning and the end of a happy human life, even on earth.

> There are three stages in God's schooling; the first is the enlightening of the intellect by faith, and this is the most excellent lesson. It is a greater thing that a man have a modicum of faith than that he should know everything that all the philosophers have discovered about the universe. *For this is your understanding and wisdom in the sight of the nations* [Deut. 4:6], and *Blessed are they that have not seen and have believed* [John 20:29].[66]

Three months before he died of an unknown illness, Aquinas is reported to have ceased all writing, even though he had not yet completed his major work, the *Summa Theologiae*. His trustworthy friends reported that his whole life had been altered by what Aquinas considered to be authentic visions of, and conversations with, saints and scholars long dead. Echoing the epistle of Saint Paul to the Philippians, in which Paul says (3:8-9) that everything else is like dung when compared to the knowledge of Christ, Saint Thomas is reported to have said that in comparison with the direct visions and conversations he had had, everything he had written was like waste to him. He could not bring himself to write another word, and so he did not.[67]

CHAPTER 6

Vitalism

THE POSITION

Plato the Bad

At this point in the development of the six possible positions on the relative status of human beings in the universal scheme of things it would seem that we should now be ready for a nonpsychosomaticism without immortality position. In other words, it might seem that it is possible to entertain the notion of the soul as being radically separate from the body during its stay on earth, but then ceasing to exist when the body breaks down. Aristotle could not imagine each individual human form or soul continuing to exist when the body which it actualized ceased to exist as a unified whole. But why, it may be asked, could not the body and soul exist together for a time in some parallel fashion and then simultaneously go out of existence at that moment which is called "death"? The question may be put in another way, namely, is there anything in the nature of a soul—a soul which can exist separately and independently with respect to its body—that would forbid its destruction at some time after coming into existence?

We have previously seen that Aquinas could not imagine such a thing in nature. As a simple subsistent substance without parts there is no way (except through a direct and willful annihilation by God) that the human soul could possibly go out of existence once created. This was regarded as a nonserious option. In order to exist as an intellectual substance, the soul demands certain characteristics which necessarily rule out the possibility of a nonpsychosomaticism without immortality view of human nature.

However, what is not ruled out by the inherent characteristics of the soul is the possibility that it is not created in such a way as to depend upon a body for its operations in a material world. This possibility, of course, was not accepted by Aquinas. In fact, though, it has been accepted by many others. For Aquinas a human being is born into the world with nothing but his or her nude body and can look forward to taking nothing else out of the world except the body when he or she goes. Hence the importance of showing due respect for the corpse of the deceased. Others, however, although they would agree that we come into the world with nothing but our naked bodies, would say that when we go out, we will not be able to take even that with us. That is because the true "us" does not include the body. This is the position which for twenty-three hundred years in the West has been most closely associated with the name of Aristotle's teacher, Plato.

In our present age Plato must rank as one of the most maligned people to have ever lived. He has been denounced as the enemy of just about everything that is highly valued in the modern world—science, evolution, democracy, the graphic arts, emotional literature, and so forth. In a nutshell, Plato was an otherworldly thinker whose doctrine set the stage for two thousand years of contempt for everything fleshy and material. By putting the emphasis upon the world of the intelligible, the world of the senses necessarily fell into disuse and disrepute. The result of this emphasis was a long period in western history during which the development of the material side of human life was sorely neglected. Consequently, Plato was responsible for the lack of "progress" in the world until very recent times.

True, there was another side to Plato. In addition to the Plato of the *Republic,* who insisted upon the need for an absolutely transcendent "Good" beyond all being, there is the Plato of the *Timaeus,* who was very much interested in giving some account of, and some importance to, the world of sense experience. In a way, the Plato of the *Timaeus* was perhaps more important than the other one if the historian can judge by the number of translations of it, commentaries upon it, and the way it shows up in Plato's hand in Raphael's famous 1510 painting "The School of Athens."

Nevertheless, when all is said and done, if the real Plato were to stand up, it would be the Plato of the *Republic* rather than the other one. There are two reasons why. For one thing, did not Parmenides also write about the way things *seem* to be in the world of sense experience even though we know that he really did not believe that such things could be logically true? In reality the world is one unchanging mass. If Parmenides did stoop to consider the appearances of things, he did so only to placate the ignorant masses.[1]

For another thing, the two world views presented by Plato in his two works are inherently incompatible. The intelligent thinker must choose between the two. It might appear that you can have it both ways at once by invoking the doctrine of "emanationism," that is, claiming that the First Cause *necessarily* "overflows" into the making of the material world because of its intrinsic goodness and lack of any sort of jealousy or envy. However, as Lovejoy claims, such a device cannot overcome the inherent contradiction of the two ideas. It might *seem* to do so because of the "gratuitous" assumption that the inferior must come from the higher, but such an approach is totally unsound.[2] In other words, the Band-Aid won't stick. There is in fact no reason why a superior being should ever find it necessary to multiply the number of things in the universe. One thing, namely itself, should be enough—and more than enough. Anything else that might come forth from it in any way whatsoever would mean a degradation of the average value of the universe. Lovejoy emphasizes that the fullness of good is supposed to be complete in God, so that, even without creatures, "the universe would be none the worse."[3]

Later, when discussing Friedrich W. J. von Schelling's debate with Friedrich H. Jacobi in the early nineteenth century over whether or not it is reasonable to say that the more perfect can arise out of the less perfect, Lovejoy sides with Schelling. If Jacobi were right in his view that God must precede the world, reasoned Schelling, there would never have been a world. Since God is already supposed to be perfect and complete, there would be no sufficient reason for the existence of anything else. "Here," states Lovejoy, "the central contradiction inherent in the logic of emanationism—but for so many centuries persistently disregarded—was pointed out with the utmost sharpness."[4] Hence the necessity of pantheism as the only rational theology.

Look at it this way. We know that there is a changing world of sense experience. Consequently, since we cannot have both the old-fashioned God of Plato, of the Middle Ages, and early modern philosophy, and simultaneously the modern "God" of worldly matter, the only reasonable thing to do is to reject the former in favor of the latter. What Lovejoy is saying, in effect, is that to be modern, you must get rid of Plato. To the extent that Plato stood for other-worldly stability and fixity, he ran directly counter to the modern need for nonreductionistic materialism, the view which Lovejoy himself favors.

It goes without saying, of course, that any view of human nature which teaches that human beings are essentially eternal souls independent of all matter must be dismissed as well. Such notions are simply too antiscientific to be given any serious consideration. True to his nonreductionistic materialism, Lovejoy would regard anyone to the right of the second position as ascribing an unwarranted independence to the mental side of human nature. Even if there is a hierarchy of beings in the universe, composed of an innumerable series of creatures of unequal value, and of which immaterial creatures are only a part rather than the whole, the fact remains that there is still a gap somewhere between the material and the immaterial. "Thus the pressure of the principle of continuity," states Lovejoy, "tended, even in the Middle Ages, to soften, though it did not overcome, the traditional sharp dualism of body and spirit."[5] Any such dualism must be eliminated.

Plato the Good

At the other end of the spectrum of opinions about the place of Plato in the history of science and philosophy stands the monument to Plato erected by those who deem him to be the only true philosopher in world history. Some, such as Huntington Cairns, appear to be over-powered and carried away by the grandeur of Plato's thoughts. "He was poet, thinker, scientist all in one and there has been no such combination of powers displayed by anyone before or since. To understand Plato is to be educated; it is to see the nature of the world in which we live."[6]

Alfred North Whitehead, a man of mathematics and science before turning his attention to philosophy, shared some of this admiration for the ancient Greek. Whitehead regarded his own doctrine of actual entities as existing in an ever-fluent world as little more than an expansion of one sentence in Plato's *Timaeus,* in which Plato says that whatever is known via the senses never really is. He even goes so far as to say (erroneously, as we should now realize) that the whole European philosophical tradition may be regarded as hardly more than a series of footnotes to Plato. In fact, Whitehead's philosophy of Organism, according to Whitehead's own perspective, may be viewed as Platonism modified by two thousand years of human experience in the sciences, arts, and religion.[7] Although Whitehead felt he had to reject Plato's dualism of mind and body, his attempt to do so was itself carried out within the framework of Plato's own categories of Eternal Ideas and earthly participations in the Ideas.

Mortimer Jerome Adler also has praised Plato's abilities to the detriment of all other thinkers. According to Adler, Plato was a pure philosopher and scientist, in the theoretical sense, who never did allow himself to reach any final or ultimate conclusions. His whole life was devoted to the development of technique, the technique of intellectual investigation in which problems are carefully set up and their possible answers and consequences deduced by a strictly rational process. This was Plato's "dialectical" approach. In him the dialectician and the philosopher were identified. "In this sense," thought Adler, "Plato is the first and, unfortunately, the last philosopher perfectly to understand the nature of his proper task and the traits of his technique."[8]

Plato has also had his advocates in the physical sciences, although in mathematics and physics rather than chemistry and biology. In his *Timaeus* Plato goes into one of his "myths" or imaginative stories designed to maintain reader interest while getting across one or two essential philosophical and scientific points. Science for Plato meant universal and certain knowledge. Such knowledge cannot be had by the senses. Only the mind can appreciate the fixity of nature as seen in ideas. True knowledge requires absolute stability and fixity. When the mind is fixed upon the Eternal Ideas which never change, we have absolute science. But when the mind is turned towards the world of changing nature, the best we can do is mathematics. Through mathematics alone can the human mind acquire any knowledge worthy of the name about the world of sense experience. This is one of the main points Plato wanted to make in his semicreation myth.

The *Timaeus* traces back the origin of the present universe to the work of the Demiurge, or the greatest of the souls (gods) which exist below the realm of the Eternal Ideas. This "Worker for the People" brought order out of chaos. He took the chaotic jumble of disorderly sequences of whatever it was that existed then and brought into it symmetry, beauty, and uniform measures of motion, or what we call time. Using the Eternal Ideas as the models for his work, he changed the amorphous mass of disorder into the intelligible world we now know.

What was the universe like before the Demiurge set to work? It is impossible to know, since it was unintelligible. When he did set to work, though, it was *as if* the universe were simply pure extension, an empty receptacle or place (space), without any definite determinations. In order to produce orderliness, everything was gradually built up by combining together certain simple triangles. The whole material, observable universe, therefore, is at base geometrical in character.

Therefore, not much imagination is needed to realize that if the scientist is to understand the sensible world, the only way to do so is to reverse the process of creation. The orderliness of the universe can only be understood through mathematics. If the book of the world is written in the language of mathematics, especially geometry, no scientist who regards mathematics as a foreign language will get anywhere. And who understood this better than the founders of modern mathematical physics: Galileo, Descartes, and Newton.

Here we have the foundation for calling Plato the true father of modern science. This is precisely the point the famous historian of early modern science Alexandre Koyré wished to make when he pointed out that only geometrical bodies can be "placed" in a geometrical space.[9] But before you can have geometrical space, you must first have a Platonic universe. In such a world there is the unsensed real world of Eternal Ideas, the sensed world of changing images which reflect the Ideas as a mirror reflects the real person, and the surface upon which the reflection occurs. This surface is the receptacle, or canvas upon which the Demiurge paints. Such a universe is not the commonsense world of experience. To find it takes a great deal of searching and storytelling. And it was Plato who first told the story in such a way as to gain a large audience. Koyre states,

> Once more, we are so accustomed to mathematical science, to mathematical physics, that we no longer feel the strangeness of a mathematical approach to Being, the paradoxical daring of Galileo's utterance that the book of Nature is written in geometrical characters. For us it is a foregone conclusion. But not for the contemporaries of Galileo.[10]

So it would seem, therefore, that it is the otherworldly Plato who is the true father of modern science rather than the atomists or some other materialistic school.

But what of other areas of human interest, such as religion and theology? Even here we find that over the centuries Plato has been praised for his insights into some of the most profound mysteries of religious beliefs, especially within the realm of Christian influence, both early and late in the West. When speaking of Marsilio Ficino, for instance, one of the outstanding Renaissance translators of Plato's dialogues, Gilson remarks that Ficino certainly *wanted* to be a Platonist. But this was not at all unusual. Making Plato into a Christian was quite common in the Middle Ages.[11]

This does not mean that Christianity is somehow simply a variation of the philosophy of Plato. Later Christians could no more be out-and-out Platonists than the earlier ones could be. Salvation for Plato was a purely natural process in which a few exceptionally intelligent human minds found mental happiness for a while by being good scientists. This was hardly suitable to the supernatural faith demanded by the Good News.

Nevertheless, when Christian thinkers speculated upon the words of the Gospel, as they did from the very beginning, they did in fact find themselves feeling a closer affinity with Plato than with any of the many other Greek thinkers known at the time. Plato had, for example, some notion of a created universe, a strong inclination for the importance of discipline with respect to the body, the idea of the individual immortality of each soul, and some awareness of the need for reward and punishment after death if justice is to be had in the universe. Even more important than specific points which could be remade to fit in with the Gospel, however, was the overall spirit of Plato's outlook on the meaning of life. His whole doctrine, observes Gilson, was so animated with a love of truth and of divine realities that you can hardly imagine a philosophy that comes nearer to being a religion without actually being one.[12]

What was Plato, then, a great benefactor or public enemy number one with respect to humankind? The answer to this question would seem to depend by and large upon whether or not he was right when he thought that he had hit upon some very fundamental and durable truths about human nature and its place in the universe. Is it really necessary to sweat and slave in one's thinking to maintain the unity of body and soul? As we have seen, everyone up to the position of vitalism has thought it absolutely essential that we do so. But why? Perhaps we should forget about trying to maintain personal unity and simply be content with a body-soul dualism in the sense of two really separate entities.

Such an approach, of course, would require some arguments in its defense. Do such arguments exist? If so, why have they been so widely overlooked in modern times? Is it really only unfamiliarity with the facts of science, as Dewey said, that keeps large groups of people in the world from accepting his (Dewey's) position? Are there no essential human traits, as Skinner said, which are not open to scientific (in the sense of laboratory, test-tube-type science) investigation? Is the trans-migration of souls such an impossibility? Is it not possible to have out-of-body experiences in such a way that the soul, even when separated from the body, can have sensations? That is, how can we be sure that the body is really necessary in order for us to have knowledge of the world ordinarily said to depend upon the five external senses of touch, taste, smell, sound, and sight? To answer these questions, we must look more closely at what the vitalistic position means to say about the human person, and also at the evidence, as well as the methodological status of the evidence, which can be brought forward to establish such a position.

The Person Is the Soul

If one were allowed to make reference to *Alcibiades I*, it would be especially easy to show that for Plato the person is to be equated with the soul. The purpose of the dialogue is to try to convince a young Athenian that he should give up his pleasure-seeking in a bodily way and turn all his efforts to perfecting his intellectual talents. In the course of doing so Socrates must first convince him that his true self is not his body but his soul alone.

A comparison is developed between a workman and his tools, and the soul and the body. Basing his argument upon the way we use ordinary language, that is, the way we naturally speak in terms of "My hand," "My foot," "My body," and so on, Socrates argues that the true "me," "I," "myself," and so forth cannot refer to the body but only to that which directs and uses the body. Consequently, the workman is to his tools as the true self, or soul, is to its body.

Clearly, then, they must be separate and independent of each other. And of the two only the soul can claim to be the real person. One consequence is that it is improper to think of love as including the other's body. To love a person is to love only the person's soul, not the body. We would thus also have a good foundation for speaking about "Platonic love" as a bodiless sort of affair.

However, unfortunately for the sake of neatness, a reference to the *Alcibiades I* cannot be made without being challenged by an expert such as Alfred Edward Taylor who has spent his whole life studying Plato. According to Taylor, this particular dialogue reads like a manual in ethics. But writing textbooks was something Plato never did and never wanted to do. As a result, the work is either a very early, immature dialogue and so should not be taken seriously, or it is the work of one of Plato's immediate disciples and so not actually written by Plato himself. Taylor himself thinks the latter is the case. "I agree, then," he concludes, "with those who hold that *Alcibiades I* is a careful exposition of ethics by an early Academic, written well before 300 B.C., and possibly, though perhaps not very probably, even before the death of Plato."[13]

It must be observed, though, that Taylor's rejection of this dialogue is not as well founded as he thought. Indeed, one would think that he surely would have realized this in view of what he himself had to say about another dubious work, the "thirteenth book of the *Laws*," or the *Epinomis*. Taylor wants to accept the *Epinomis* as authentic and does so with the explanation that the dialogue, although apparently indicating a falling into atheism by Plato in his old age, has generally been "admitted to have been at any rate composed immediately after

Plato's death by a disciple for circulation along with the *Laws,* and is therefore, in any case, likely to be faithful to the master's teaching."[14] Why cannot the same be said of the *Alcibiades I?*

The situation is even more unusual in light of two other considerations. One is that there is evidence in at least one of Plato's undisputed dialogues that the first *Alcibiades* may indeed be a very early work in which Plato rather bluntly states his position without the sophistication he later developed. The situation might remind one of Aquinas' *On Being and Essence,* the basic notions of which he so greatly elaborated upon later in life. In the *Phaedo,* which may fairly be regarded as Plato's "Bible" or work on how to achieve personal salvation, Socrates states:

> Did we not say some time ago that when the soul uses the instrumentality of the body for any inquiry, whether by means of sight, hearing, or any of the senses (because using the body means using the senses), it is drawn away by the body into the realm of the variable....But when it investigates by itself, it passes into the realm of the pure, everlasting, immortal, and changeless.... (*Phaedo,* 79cd)

When was this "some time ago," and where was it that he said that the body is the tool of the soul?

A second point concerns the fact that even if the blunt statement of the first *Alcibiades* is ruled out because it is unauthentic, there remains in several other places sufficient evidence to show that such a doctrine is truly Platonic. Examples of passages in Plato which either state or imply that the true personal self is the soul and nothing but the soul would be the following:

> Socrates: I will explain. Every seeker after wisdom knows that up to the time when philosophy takes over his soul is a helpless prisoner, chained hand and foot inside the body, forced to view reality not directly but only through the prison bars, and wallowing in utter ignorance. (*Phaedo,* 82e)

Cebes [while describing Socrates' view before raising an objection to it]: The tailor makes and wears out any number of coats, but although he outlives all the rest, suppose he perishes before the last one wears out. This does not mean that a man is inferior to his coat, or has a weaker hold upon life. I believe that this analogy might apply to the body-soul relationship, and I think that it would be reasonable to claim in the same way that while the soul is long-lived the body is relatively weak and short-lived. (*Phaedo*, 87d)

Socrates: That will help Crito to bear it [trying to decide what to do with my body] more easily, and keep him from being distressed for my sake when he sees my body being burned or buried, as if something terrible were happening to me. It will also prevent him from saying at the funeral that it is Socrates whom he is laying out or carrying to the grave or burying. (*Phaedo*, 115de; Cf. *Laws*, 959c)

Socrates: But the truth of the matter was, as it seems, that justice is indeed something...which is within...and having linked and bound all three [appetite, emotions, reason] together and made of himself a unit, one man instead of many, self-controlled and in unison, he should then and only then turn to...taking care of the body.... (*Republic*, 443de)

Socrates: Tell me, are all these instruments by which you perceive what is warm, hard, light, or sweet parts of the body and of nothing else? Theaetetus: Yes. (*Theaetetus*, 184e)

In all these cases the notion of a body-mind dualism is strongly stated or hinted at. The imagery of a prison complete with bars and chains certainly indicates this dualism. Not by accident does Plato open the *Phaedo* with a picture of the prison wardens removing Socrates' chains. Soon his real chains, his material parts, will be removed when he commits suicide by voluntarily drinking the poison. In the same way, the imagery of a man in his clothes, the fire in which the fake Socrates (the corpse) is being burned, the soul as a bundle of functions, and again the body as a tool, all point to the same conclusion.

Taylor himself indirectly admits this when discussing what Plato considered to be the most "original and important" part of his

Timaeus. As we are told in the *Phaedo* (78c), the soul is not a composite, even though it may have several functions. It is divine, while the body is composed of many parts and is subject to dissolution (80b). But what exactly is the nature of the composite body? Ultimately it must be open to geometrical analysis just like every other material thing in the world. What Plato envisioned was the reduction of all worldly phenomena, including the material parts of living things, to geometry. As far as the body of a living thing is concerned, Plato was a mechanist. "The human organism," reports Taylor, "as he conceives it, is a machine directed and controlled by mind or intelligence, but the machine itself is made of the same ultimate constituents as other machines and the workings of it follow the same laws as those of the rest."[15] By recognizing this aspect of Plato's doctrine for what it is, namely, a summary of vitalism, Taylor rather clearly confirms the traditional view that the soul is a ghost in a machine, or like a person in his or her clothes, a pilot in a ship, and so on.

Where Plato does seem to talk in terms of the body and soul as a unit rather than as two separate parts accidently fallen together, he always does so within the context of his doctrine of recollection as the only way to explain the human person's rational knowledge. In the *Meno* (86a) and the *Phaedo* (76c, 79b), for instance, Plato is obviously concerned with the current practical state of affairs. The fact is that while on earth humans are stuck with a body whether they like it or not. Through the very possibility of intellectual knowledge, however, which cannot come from the senses, we can understand that the soul must have existed as a self-sufficient substance before falling into the prison of the body. Consequently, to the extent that the words and deeds of others are capable of arousing in us recollections of the Eternal Ideas which we (our souls) were allowed to see directly after we (our souls) were created by the Demiurge, our bodies can be regarded as a real part of our person. As a practical necessity, although not as an absolute necessity, we are required to use the instrumentality of our bodies for the purposes of stimulating our mental powers. However, once the innate knowledge of the Ideas is possessed by the soul, it can easily dispense with the body without any loss of content.

Indeed, if one is to take seriously the story of the soldier named Er, who dies and who then returns to life, as related at the end of the *Republic,* the soul is capable of all the sense powers of the body even without its body. Er was capable of seeing and hearing everything that went on around him even though separated from his body. Such powers may even be retained, says Socrates in another place, by those sad individuals who in life were so heavily weighed down by their bodies that they could not completely escape even after death. They can sometimes be seen hanging around tombs and graveyards. Such ghosts are doomed to wander the earth until at last they are once again imprisoned in a body and continue their evil ways.[16]

The Nature of the Soul

"As far as the body-soul relationship is concerned," concludes T. M. Robinson in his study of the soul in Plato, "the *Charmides, Alcibiades* I, and *Protagoras* are united in asserting that self and soul are one and the same, but differ in their accounts of its relationship to the body."[17] Robinson considers these three dialogues to be early works. Even at the end of his life, though, Plato maintained the same view. Although there are various changes in emphasis, the *Epinomis* says nothing basically new about the soul. "In particular, the dichotomy of soul and body is trenchantly reaffirmed (980 D 6 ff.), and we are treated to a number of familiar epithets."[18] Between the early and the late periods in his life Plato, it cannot be denied, modified his positions on the different gods or souls which made up the third most important aspect of the universe (below the Ideas and the One Beyond Being) in several different ways, sometimes becoming involved in some minor inconsistencies. Throughout his life, however, at least one thing appears to have remained constant, his conviction that the true person is the soul and nothing else.

To define the soul, consequently, is to define the true person—the true you. And as the principle of life, there is no doubt that the soul must have life as the basic element in its definition. But what is life? Is it not to be capable of self-motion? A living thing is that which can move itself from within. But, if a thing can move itself from within by its own power, how could it ever lose such power? It doesn't seem possible that it could. In Plato's summary:

And now that we have seen that whatever is moved by itself is immortal we will feel no problem in affirming that self-motion is precisely the essence and definition of soul. Body that has an external source of motion is soulless, but a body moved from within is alive or besouled, which implies that the nature of soul is what we have said. If this is true, namely, that whatever moves itself is exactly equivalent to soul, it must follow that soul is not born and does not die. (*Phaedrus,* 245e-246a)

The same point is made in the *Laws* (896a). "Clinias: You mean that the selfsame reality which we call soul has self-movement as its definition? Athenian: I do."

The soul, the true person, the source of life in the human body, and the power of self-motion are therefore all the same thing. From this it can be easily seen that death can be nothing other than the separation of the soul from the body. There can be no doubt about the fact of death. This is a fact of experience familiar to anyone of experience in the world. Yet the vast majority of people, in fact "everyone except the philosopher" (*Phaedo,* 68d), regard death as an evil to be avoided for as long as possible. The philosopher, though, while admitting the fact of death, has no reason to fear it. The body and soul may be separated, but since the soul continues to live there is no *real* dying. This is true for all human beings. Certainly there is nothing to be feared by the real philosopher who has fully developed his powers of speculative reason. For him death is simply the release of the soul from the body so that it may pursue its proper function of contemplating the Eternal Ideas which exist outside the "back of the world" and "beyond the heavens" (*Phaedrus,* 247c).

What can be noticed here is that for Plato the definition of the soul as a self-moving, immaterial substance is not really his main point. In the *Phaedrus,* after defining the soul, he goes on to say that he has spent enough time on the immortality of the soul and must now say something about its nature. On this topic the main point is the affinity between the soul and the Eternal Ideas. What Plato wants to tell us, and what he does tell us over and over again, is that the soul is a god in its own right. It is divine. By this he does not mean only that it is immortal and everlasting but, more importantly, that its proper place is in the presence of the Really Real, the realm of the Eternal Ideas. We come to know the nature of the soul by knowing what it resembles. And what it resembles is the realm of the Eternal Ideas, the proper object of all its attentions.

After creation by the Demiurge, the soul is allowed to stand on the outer sphere of the universe and view the Eternal Ideas. What it observes is forever deeply imprinted upon the soul. Forevermore, after observing the Eternal Ideas, the only way the soul can ever achieve true contentment and happiness is by returning to its source of knowledge. This can only be found beyond the heavens.

> It is there that true Being dwells, without color or shape, that cannot be touched. Reason alone, the soul's pilot, can behold it. And all true knowledge is knowledge of it. Now even as the mind of a god is nourished by reason and knowledge, so also with every soul that wishes its proper food. Therefore when the soul has beheld Being it is well contented, and is nourished and prospers while contemplating truth, until the revolution of the heavens brings it back full circle. (*Phaedrus,* 247d)

An obvious question then as now, and one to which Plato never did find a satisfactory answer, is how a soul whose gaze was fixed upon the World of Truth would ever find its way into a material body. In the *Phaedrus* (248ce) the reason for this strange reversal of fortunes is said, although in a myth, to be the result of some weakness within the soul itself. As long as the soul can maintain its steady gaze upon the World of Real Being, it is fine. But should it relax its concentration, it is doomed to lose its "wings" and "fall to earth."

Now, since no soul which has beheld the Eternal Ideas for even a short time is fit to inhabit the body of an animal, it must "fall" into the body of some human-type thing. The exact sort of body and material condition into which it falls will depend upon the amount of knowledge absorbed while viewing the Ideas. From highest to lowest, Plato lists the following as possibilities: Philosopher, law-abiding king, businessman, athlete, priest, artist, farmer, Sophist, tyrannical ruler. Finding itself in a body, the soul has no choice but gradually to work its way out by studying mathematics and the Eternal Ideas.

In the *Timaeus* (42a) it is said simply that souls were implanted in bodies in the first place by "necessity." The use of the term "necessity" by Plato means that the whole affair is really unintelligible to him. By "necessity" he is referring to the fact that there are several irrational aspects to the universe and that this is one of them. The soul has no business being mixed up with the senses and the flesh. Yet it is. Other examples of irrationality in the world which the Demiurge could never adequately overcome would be the way in which the hypotenuse of a unit right triangle can never be made commensurate with its sides, as well as the irregular and retrograde motions of the planets which exist in the supposedly perfect heavens. Such elements of chaos can be explained only as being carry-overs from that period in the universe before the Demiurge brought order and measure into things. Why they *must* be there Plato never did come to understand.

Souls, Matter, and Evil

Are those traces of chaos which are still preserved in the world the only source of trouble for human nature? Apparently not. There would seem to be at least two other sources of difficulty: The knowledge *not* possessed by individual souls and the material aspect of the world. It would also seem, though, that only the soul can count as a source of true evil. For something to be evil it must violate a divine rule. Now, as it happens, the only eternal standards are to be found in the realm of the Eternal Ideas. Even the Demiurge, the greatest of the gods, is subject to these patterns of perfection. Goodness or virtue, therefore, means acting in accordance with them, while evil or sin means to act out of step with them.[19]

All this is very intellectual; the only mortal sin is ignorance. To act well means knowing what is right and wrong, which in turn means concentrating upon the Ideal Type for each of the actions to be performed. Once the knowledge of the proper Idea, say of justice or courage, is known, human nature (the soul) can be counted upon to act accordingly. No one voluntarily does evil. It is impossible, thinks Plato, for someone who clearly sees what is good to choose the opposite deliberately. "To prefer evil to good is not in human nature," says Plato. (*Protagoras,* 358c)

What role, then, is left to the will? It would seem to be only a preliminary one. The soul can either choose to concentrate on the Ideal Types or not.[20] This first step requires the real effort. However, with repeated efforts, the task becomes progressively easier. After a while, the human being becomes so much at home in the realm of the universal and abstract that any attempt on the part of others to pull him or her back into the realm of ever-fleeting sensations is regarded with the greatest disgust.

If death is merely the separation of the body and soul, then it can truly be said that the philosopher or speculative scientist is practicing dying even while still in his body. For the vitalist, to the extent that he has managed to pull away from his body in thought, he is already dead. This is not a bad or evil thing. On the contrary, it is the best thing that could possibly happen to the human person. Once true scientific knowledge is achieved, which can only occur after death, the soul or person has risen to the height of his potentialities as a human being.

Some later followers of Plato, such as Plotinus in the third century A.D., allowed for the possibility that such bliss might occur for short periods of time even while still alive. However, short of death, such states of ecstasy cannot be permanently maintained. Plato himself, however, in the *Phaedrus* myth, makes things even more difficult. To obtain a final and everlasting release from the body, a soul must choose the speculative life at least three times in a row for periods of a thousand years each. This allows for a very interesting possibility, of which Plato himself must have been aware. Could future great minds in science, mathematics, or philosophy be Plato himself reincarnated? And was Plato perhaps the reincarnation of Pythagoras or Parmenides?

Evil doing, therefore, is the result of ignorance which in turn is self-induced by the person's own will. Aside from some inherent fault in the soul as created by the Demiurge and the residue of anarchy left over from the prechronological universe, the only other extenuating circumstance which might help explain the existence of nonscientists in the world is the very existence of matter itself. Later followers of Plato came to speak about matter itself as somehow basically evil.[21] To Plato's own way of thinking, though, this was not part and parcel of the overall scheme of things. If anything, the evil of the material world is due to some evil soul, greater than human souls, which perhaps deliberately created the conditions which produce evil actions and results. Since soul is superior and prior to all the material manifestations of the universe, it must be responsible for all happenings in the world. Plato writes:

> Athenian [talking with Megillus and Clinias]: Hence are we not driven to conclude that soul is the cause of good and evil, of the fair and the foul, of right and wrong, and in fact of all contraries if we mean it to be a universal cause?
>
> Clinias: Certainly.
>
> Athenian: So then, if indwelling soul is thus in universal control of all things that move anywhere are we not forced to say that it controls heaven itself?
>
> Clinias: Of course.
>
> Athenian: Is this done by only one soul, or by more than one? I will answer for you both. By more than one. We must assume no less than two, one good and the other capable of the contrary effect. (*Laws*, 896de)

When Plato wrote this dialogue, he was an old man still struggling with the problem of evil in the world. Did an evil spirit somehow create the material world, thus making it evil also? Or did some evil soul somehow interfere with the work of the Demiurge so as to introduce some evil arrangements of things into the world so that the world of matter is constantly at war with the human person or soul?

Although it is true that Plato does not directly call matter evil, he certainly seems to hint at the idea often enough, even in his younger days. In his *Phaedo* (66, 67, 94), for instance, he claims that the body "contaminates" the soul, that the soul is "infected" by the body, that it is "shackled" to the body. In every way the soul, which is the source of goodness, is opposed to the body.

Between the *Phaedo* and the *Laws* came the *Statesman* (or *Politicus*). In this work he seems to want to combine "necessity" with the inherent evilness of matter. What could cause the clamors and confusions which we observe in the world? How can a world fashioned after the Eternal Ideas show signs of irrationality and warfare among its elements and parts? How can there be any degree of failure in the universe? The vitalist reasons,

The bodily element in its constitution is responsible for its failure. This bodily element belonged to it in its most primeval state, for before it came into its present state as an orderly universe it was a complete chaos of disorder. From god's act of setting it in order it received all its virtues, while all its wrongs and evils arise from its primeval chaotic state. These evils in turn show up in the living things within it. (*Statesman,* 273bc)

As he goes on to say, there is no way in which this inherent tendency towards evil can be eradicated. Wherever there is matter, there will be the tendency towards disorder and irrationality. Matter then, it would appear, *can be* considered as a source of evil, at least insofar as it sets itself up as an obstacle to the soul's vision of real Being and preserves the omnipresent possibility for disorder in the world.

What makes the situation so strange, and what perhaps best explains Plato's lifelong anxiety over the topic, is that there is a very good basis for saying that the material universe does not even exist in the first place. How can something unreal be a cause? In his late dialogue *Timaeus* Plato found that he had to introduce the notion of the receptacle. "This new beginning of our discussion of the universe," explains Plato, "requires a fuller division than the former. Before we recognized two classes [Being and becoming]; now a third must be revealed." (*Timaeus,* 48e) This "third nature" is pure geometrical space which is as uncreated and eternal and indestructible as the Eternal Ideas themselves. The visible, sensible (material) universe is a projection of the Ideas, in a mathematical form, upon this surface or screen.

But how real are such moving images? Not very! They are as real as someone's reflection in a mirror. This is the same as saying that the images are totally unsubstantial. Except for the light, the surface, and the human being the image would be non-existent. The material world of Plato is consequently a world of shadows. Although not *per se* evil, it is perhaps something even more worrisome—it is very close to not being there at all. Rather than being evil in themselves, the shadows we call matter, or the world of sense experience, are the occasions of evil. They constitute the quicksand which impedes the progress of the soul towards salvation.

A strange situation indeed. It is hard to condemn something as evil when it is hardly there at all. Plato might have thought to declare the whole substantial material world of the senses an illusion, as did Berkeley, if he had had any idea of a true Creator-God. However, such an idea never crossed his mind. He could never get rid of the material world completely because, as far as he knew, it was always there. The best he could do was to force and press it into geometrical patterns and molds. In so doing he managed to reduce its significance to mere insubstantial shadows. A reinterpretation of matter was the outer limit to which his natural abilities could carry him. Like that of his pupil Aristotle, Plato's world was composed of several parts which ran along parallel tracks. The One Above Being, the Ideas or Being, the Demiurge, the Shadows, and the Receptacle—all equally eternal.

Sandwiched in between the Demiurge and space, and all mixed up with the shadows, we find human souls: queer things, out of joint with everything else. Why such things should exist at all, and why they should exist in such a disagreeable situation as found in the world of shadows, nobody really knows. All we know for sure is that there must be a radical difference between the sphere of influence of the body and that of the intellect. For everything else the best we can do is to dream up likely stories. It is no historical accident that not many years after the death of its master the Academy fell into several hundred years of skepticism.[22]

Of the Necessary and the Universal

When speaking of Plato's True Being or Ideas George Sarton notes, "The terms used by Plato are *hē idea* (idea) and *to eidos* (form, shape). The second term is semantically curious, for its original meaning is 'that which is seen' and the Idea cannot be seen. All our abstract terms have necessarily concrete origins."[23] If, by his last line, Sarton meant to say that Plato had built up his universal notions from sense perceptions, he was certainly mistaken. Sarton may have wanted to say something like this; note the way he bestows praise on "nominalism" two pages later. Nominalism, he says, is scientific while Plato's Ideas are not. Sarton, like some others interested in the philosophy of science, thinks so because of the way in which nominalism emphasizes the existence of, and hence the study of, unique particular individual entities. We will see a little later whether or not Sarton may have lacked some philosophical sophistication here.

However, regardless of the verdict on that point, there is another way of looking at what Plato was trying to do and where he started the process of doing it. Plato was simultaneously aware of two things concerning knowledge. One is that he did in fact know things in a universal and necessary way. Some knowledge is absolutely true. Secondly, he could not possibly have gotten such knowledge from or through or by his senses. While the mind unites through ideas, the senses constantly divide through ever fleeting perceptions. How could two such radically different operations belong to *one* person? And furthermore, if one is to dominate and rule, should it not be what is of the universal and necessary rather than the other? Of course. Aristotle was aware of this when he pointed out that the main function of the Eternal Ideas separate from matter was supposed to be to *explain* the world of sense experience.[24] To Plato and his followers the Forms were not expedient and poetical devices for avoiding science, as Sarton implies. Quite the contrary, without the Ideas there could be no science at all.

This point is important to understanding the force of vitalism as a standard view of the human person, and the reasons why it keeps coming up over and over again despite the charges against Plato for having defended such an old-fashioned position. Like Socrates, at the end of the *Phaedo,* vitalism as a doctrine keeps slipping through the fingers of those who would crush it out once and for all.[25]

According to Plato the need for the Divine Ideas is demanded by experience. They are the way ''experience presents the matter'' and are the result of ''looking the facts of experience in the face.''[26] To appreciate vitalism we must therefore try to put Plato's insights into as good a light as possible. To do so requires making a serious attempt to see the connection between the world of sense experience and the world of intellectual experience.

Science

In one way or another a great many animal species surpass people in sense abilities. If the mere size of the nervous system, especially the brain, is to be assigned a predominant role in forming sensual complexes, porpoises and dolphins, with brain sizes comparable to that of humans in terms of the ratio of brain size to body size, should have the same level of sense awareness as human beings. Furthermore, if any one sense power is singled out as a basis for comparison, the human species usually ends up behind in one way or another. Birds can see much better than people. Some fish can hear better. Fish are also thought to be better at tasting. Dogs, deer, mice, and bears have a keener sense of smell. Some species have special powers, such as their own "radar," which allows them to travel where humans fear to tread.

Others have the ability to combine all their sense powers so that they never get lost. Foxes and horses, for instance, have much better place memories than people. If science were nothing more than sense knowledge, there is no reason to suppose that certain species of animals would not also surpass people in certain sciences. But in fact none do. This is not to be interpreted to mean that the senses are unimportant to the human scientist, even the mathematician. What it means is that sense knowledge is only part of the process.

The human power to know intellectually as well as sensually is a prime datum in understanding the difference between you and your pet dog. By the use of their intellect people arrive at a thing's meaning. They can know a thing's nature, *what* it is, as well as sense it. Rather than being stopped at the level of sequences of sensations, which merely show activities rather than a knowledge of essences as the causes of those activities, the typical member of the human species can understand the meaning of the events. We can understand the relationships among the parts. We can work with meanings and use symbolic language as a way of expressing knowledge to other creatures with powers the same as our own. To work with meanings and to work with language are quite different undertakings. Animals might be trained to do the latter without in the least being able to do the former.

But what is this thing called "science" that we hear so much about? Is science really a thing? Is science more like light or more like a lead weight? Is someone who asks whether or not science can save us speaking about a person? In what neighborhood does this person live? Has anybody ever seen science? Is it ever possible to study science as science?

As soon as such questions are put, of course, it becomes obvious that science is not some sort of tangible thing. Students of physics do not study physics. What they study are various kinds of motions, forces, and changes in connection with material bodies. Physics as a science is the result of such study. A physics text contains a summary of what was discovered plus whatever postulates and principles are necessary in order to weld the discovered laws into a coherent system. A mere systematizing or classification of diverse information, such as a telephone book, is not enough. Neither is merely being experimental enough. One can perform as many specific experiments as many times as one likes, but no science will ever result as long as the specific inquiries are not directed towards some central theme or hypothesis.

Likewise, no mere collection of data, however carefully carried out, will ever produce by itself even one scientific proposition. "Showing it as it is" has a place, but it is not the scientific place. Observing that columns of mercury here and there stand at about thirty inches is a good start. One does not get scientific about it, though, until one begins to talk about the weight of the air. In time, the cause or causes may even become visible, for instance by the freezing of the gases that compose the air. Actual sensing, however, is not a necessary condition. Similarly, *observing* that certain ways of behaving are common to all people or that people go through certain stages of development as individuals, constitutes a good beginning, but science does not enter the picture until some reason why this is so is advanced. The first step in appreciating the great value and glory of science is to eliminate the illusion that "empirical" science itself is in any way empirical.

Science in and of itself, regardless of how much it may be immersed in specimens, microscopes, accelerators, litmus paper, and the rest is first and foremost a mental activity. It is a human being using the mind that is engaging in scientific activity. In order to arrive at scientific results, the scientist may require varying amounts of material aids, but when scientific propositions are finally enunciated, they are never material things. And if the scientist should publish his or her results in one form or another, it is always to be understood that the material record of this work is an expression of the person's thinking and that it (the record) does not constitute the primary content of science.

But what kind of activity is science? Is it simply any kind of knowledge? Again, even as the questions are asked it becomes clear that "knowledge" is a broader term than "scientific knowledge." All consciousness involves some sort of knowledge. Merely knowing about something, though, is not sufficient to have scientific knowledge. Both Plato and Aristotle could agree that both a man and his pet dog can look up at the night sky and see that stars twinkle. Both would then know something in this very low-level way. This can be extended to a host of other examples. In many cases both men and animals can know the same thing. In many other cases two or more men can know the same thing. But does this sort of notebook level of knowledge justify calling a creature a scientist? Of course not. Something more is required. What is it?

Assume you were asked to treat scientifically the fact that chlorine gas is green. Would it do to repeat that "chlorine gas is green, is green, is green" or "chlorine gas is green because it is green because it is green," etc.? To do so would be to simply repeat the data. No one would mistake such repetition for science.

By the same token, no one would take a repetition of the data on a different level for science. To say, for instance, that chlorine gas is green because it is made up of little parts, each of which is colored green, will not do at all. We see here the bind in which all would-be scientists are caught. You can either simply *repeat* the data, and end up being trivial, or you can offer to *explain* the data, and thereby be on your way to being scientific. To complete the task the explanation must be:

1. well supported by evidence, and
2. in terms different from the data to be explained.

What has been said should not lead you to suppose that there is only one way to explain, or only one level of explanation. Those who have engaged in philosophizing will realize that there can be different levels of explanation. It is a characteristic of the philosophical approach that it is radical, that is, it goes to the root, to the most fundamental level possible for human reason. A scientist might explain rust, for example, in terms of oxidation and red in terms of different wave lengths and be satisfied, but a philosopher keeps asking about what does it mean to be, to change, and to die. This is perhaps the most obvious feature of Plato's overall approach to the world.

To explain, then, requires going to a different level for your explanation. This is scientific. But this is not to say that there are only two or three different levels. There may be many. In biology, for instance, we deal with molecules, cells, organs, systems, and wholes. But is this all we have when it comes to saying something about humans as a species? Perhaps we need levels which are not part of the biological sciences, or, for that matter, not part of any physical science. But again one must be careful. Does this mean that the levels can continue to multiply forever and ever? Not necessarily. Sooner or later, if one is really broad and searching in one's curiosity, one will terminate in the realm of something immaterial, a place which the materialists would find very uncomfortable.

It might be objected that one has a right to feel uncomfortable since, if we continue our line of reasoning, this realm would also require a scientific explanation. This may be the case, but if it is, it is something to be argued in philosophy and not in the physical or social sciences. In any event, the objection is irrelevant. Such a problem would be concerned with *that* level of data seeking an explanation and not with some previous level demanding an explanation. To say "it's just there" for some previous level requiring an explanation would still remain a nonexplanation.

Scientific knowledge, therefore, is something relatively fixed or "tethered" as Plato says in the *Meno* (97e-98a). It must give an account or reason for the ever-shifting sands of sense experience. This can only be done on the intellectual or intelligible level. The scientific thinker, that is, one who possesses true and certain knowledge of a given state of observed occurrences, must proceed from the observed data to an explanation of the data stated in terms different from the given data. As Whitehead has stated in our own day, such an approach is simply the "ordinary scientific method."[27]

But why is it necessary to move from the material to the immaterial? Why cannot the scientist, regardless of how profound the levels of explanation become, forever remain in the material world? Plato, the supreme epistemologist, would answer that such a situation would not correspond to the factual evidence. Through a careful and complete reflection upon our own mental and physical modes of knowing the world, we come to realize that it is strictly impossible to explain the mind in terms of the body. Being radically different in characteristics and modes of operation, the mind and the body must be radically different in existence. It is the only hypothesis which agrees with the facts of experience and with the proper methodology of rational science.

Universal Ideas

When it comes to thinking, no one begins from scratch. We all begin with knowledge of some kind or another. An Eskimo might not know about bats but he or she knows seals. An Australian aborigine may not know seals but he or she knows bats. This is true of all of us. What we know will vary, but we all *know*. We have all "taken in" a tree, a car, a desk, or whatever, which can act as the basis for a self-experience about our own knowledge.

With this in mind, perhaps the most obvious thing we notice about our ideas is that they can be widely used. That is, we do not need a new idea for each and every particular thing we run across. We can refer to this property of our ideas as their universality. Universality is not something we create or invent. We discover it just as a chemist finds that iron rusts or an astronomer finds that stars twinkle. What we find is that concepts or ideas can be predicated of many individual things, but that no individual thing can be said of another individual thing. We say quite naturally that "John is a man" and that "Sam is a man," but we cannot make sense of "John is Sam." No one particular thing can be predicated of another precisely because the universality of our concepts expresses what is common, not what is particular.[28]

This is not to say that you think without any individual, particular images whatsoever. What it does tell us is that no image or picture, no matter how fuzzy, can be a concept or idea. A universal image is a contradiction in terms. Every graphic, auditory, or other sign is always something physical and material which can exist at only one place at a time. Every year at Christmastime some brighter children wonder how it is possible for Santa Claus, who is supposed to be one individual, to show up simultaneously in every department store and on every other street corner. Short of some kind of miracle, bilocation is not possible to exactly one and the same material thing.

The fact of universality can be witnessed in both the mathematical and physical sciences. Consider *a* triangle as opposed to simply triangle or triangleness. Every individual triangle has a definite size, shape, and color. If one wanted to, I suppose, one could even scrape off the material used to draw the triangle and taste it. The concept of a triangle, however, as expressed in its definition, has *none* of these traits. It has no size, no shape, no color, and so on. Although everything about the picture and word "triangle" is material, there are no material characteristics attached to what the picture and word stands for, namely, triangle.

Consider next some physical object such as an apple. Again we find that every individual case of an apple has a whole series of definite physical characteristics. Our idea of an apple, which applies to all apples, on the other hand, has *no* physical traits whatsoever. Again, although everything about the material thing and symbol "apple" possesses physical traits, the meaning of apple has none.

We note this same state of affairs in every one of our concepts. The number five in a child's picture book is big and red, but what color is five? The clothes you are wearing have definite colors to them but what color is color? The table or chair you are using has some definite size to it, but what size is your idea of size? How much shorter than your concept of a mile is your concept of an inch? How heavy is your idea of iron? What is the second derivation of calculus? How much DNA does biology have? If physics is the science of measure, how long is physics?

When tied down to images there is no way in which a creature can break away from particular things or states of affairs. It makes no sense to talk to animals about mathematics because mathematics depends upon having something more than sense images, regardless of how many blackboard drawings are needed as material aids. It makes no sense to talk to a horse about raising apples, even though the horse may have eaten a thousand apples. Observing one apple at a time or seeing a whole bushel of apples in its stall will never make a horse into an apple scientist because there is a world of difference between sensing apples and being able to universalize about all apples, that is, appleness.

Take the case of a brick. We sense a heavy, solid, reddish, 3 x 4 x 10 inch, rough block and say it is "a brick." We, the brick, and our words are all open to various kinds of physically measurable and recordable investigations. However, the meaning of the word is not necessarily connected to our English "brick" or to some particular speaker; hence the possibility of foreign languages and conversation. If there is one thing the meaning of "brick" is not, it is the voice or handwriting of the speaker. We understand meanings; we do not physically hear, or see, or touch, or smell, or taste them. It makes no sense to talk about breaking off part of the meaning of a word, for you cannot break up something immaterial.

Our experiences tell us that we do generalize, that a material general thing is impossible, and so our knowledge cannot be material. To the extent, therefore, that general intellectual knowledge is a mental fact, it must be an immaterial mental operation. And to the extent, therefore, that scientific understanding is a mental operation, it cannot be material. Insofar as a science is intramental, a scientist never studies the knowledge of science. To study knowledge requires a subjective or introspective approach eliminated beforehand by those who wish to work with only material things. Regardless of how pure a sample of copper is, it will never be a mineralogist. Regardless of how complex a structure all the natural elements come together to make, it will never be a mineralogist either. As simply matter, there is no way it could universalize.

For the same reason animals cannot be held responsible as moral agents or looked to for inspiration in the sense of showing us how one can transcend a particular physical place and time. Since they are not quantitative to begin with, moral traits such as prejudice and justice cannot be handled by creatures restricted to sense knowledge. To have knowledge of such occurrences one must universalize.

The same holds for the realm of time. To escape time one must be able to move on a level different from the material. Although we cannot do this physically speaking, we can intellectually. What it means to be a triangle or apple is not restricted to one space-time coordinate but can exist in one space at many times or at one time in many spaces. By being radically different from the material images of sense knowledge, concepts allow those creatures which have them to become eternal to a certain extent. No animal has ever been observed to act in such a fashion. Consequently, it is safe to conclude that they lack the power to do so.

But how in the world is it possible for one and the same term to apply *equally* to many different particular things? Or again, how is it possible to classify or categorize? Once the fact of universality is fully appreciated, one can attempt an answer. No one has ever denied that people do in fact use universal language. It is an obvious datum of experience to anyone who looks. In logic, mathematics, all the natural sciences, in ordinary day-to-day discourse, and so on, people do it without giving it a second thought. John is a student, Sam is a student, Mary is a student. Water has been found on Venus; Water has been found on Mars; Water may be found on the moon. How is it possible for John, Sam, and Mary to all be *equally* students? How is it possible for the *same thing* to exist on the moon, Venus, and Mars?

The answer to this problem is that the items classified must be *identical* with respect to the characteristic used as the basis for the classification. This, of course, helps show the immateriality of ideas and the minds that form concepts. No material thing can be identical with another material thing. They could be similar, but similarity means both identity *and* diversity. In classification, it is the identity aspect that is emphasized. To claim that the items classified are merely similar does not do justice to the data of experience. Each of the students in the class is not *like* a student; each *is* a student. If everyone were only *like* a student, then there would be no students at all! Is this apple edible? No, it is like what is edible. Is this hamburger edible? No, but it is like something edible. Imaging doing this for every edible thing that passes your way. In a month or so all arguments over universals would become moot, since you would have starved to death.

When communicating with one another, it is very important that human beings make every effort to make sure that they are talking about the same thing. If all sameness of meaning, as well as that part of analogous usage which is the same, were merely based upon similarities, such efforts would be impossible of fulfillment. How then could two zoologists ever talk about the same seal or bat, or two dietitians ever discuss the same menu? If one's stock is placed in the virtue of likeness or similarity or family resemblance, then communication, science, induction and deduction and classification become impossible. As a matter of fact, though, these activities are extensively carried on. The major precondition for such activities is that universal predication expresses identity and not merely likeness.

There is no imaginable way matter can give rise to thought. There is a radical difference in kind between the one and the other. This difference is not one of different material characteristics as you would find, for instance, between chlorine existing as a gas and as it exists in table salt. The difference is much more radical than even that. Both in and out of salt chlorine, whether actual or potential, is still localized in one place at one time. This is not the case with the difference between your sense images and your ideas.

Faced with this situation you can do one of two things. You can insist that thought is really material after all. That is, you can deny the data. Or you can admit, based upon your own personal experience, that there is an immaterial side to human nature. This alternative gives rise to problems of its own, such as how to preserve the unity of each human being as *one* thing. However, they represent separate issues and should not be used to deny the evident data.

For those picking the first alternative there is a traditional and standard way of attempting to rematerialize ideas. This is the name-ism or "nominalistic" approach.

The nominalistic approach directs everything towards the *names* of the objects. The name-ism view, or some variation of it, is necessary for those who take a materialistic view of people. Nominalists cannot deny that people use universal language. Yet, since universals, or concepts as opposed to complicated sensual pictures, imply immateriality, those holding a materialistic view of people must somehow deny the existence of universal ideas. This feat is accomplished by reducing generality to mere names. The meanings of universals, they claim, are nothing but physical vibrations or graphic marks. These names are attached to *similar* things to suit the needs of the speaker. The terms student, seal, menu, edible, and so on, consequently, represent nothing more than the similarities among individual specimens. All specimens of anything in the world really have nothing exactly the same in common except either the label or some group of characteristics arbitrarily decided upon and lumped together under one term.

If nominalism were taken seriously, which generally speaking it is not, the results would be far-reaching and devastating. It would mean that all communication, whether in the same language or via translations, would be impossible. Inductions which aim at generality and deductions which begin with universals would be impossible. Logic, mathematics, and every science which depends upon univocal usage would be impossible. Every law defending social and political justice would have to be thrown out, since such laws apply to classes of cases and, especially, to all members of the human sort or type of creature. According to nominalism, all classification, in any strict sense, including placing all humans in one human species, would be reduced to meaninglessness. Economic, sexual, and political exploitation would then not only be widely practiced but would be philosophically justified and encoded into the law as the norm.

Needless to say, we are fortunate that nominalists do not practice what they preach. We are also fortunate, thinks Plato, that we have the reflective power to be sure of the universality of our concepts. Merely looking at the meaning of similarity should make the nominalists realize that there is something radically wrong with their proposed solution. Similarity is *both* identity *and* diversity. There is no escaping the need to explain *identity* in the world outside your own mind. Appealing to similarity does not do away with the need to posit the identity factor in universal ideas.

Also, when considered with respect to itself and without reference to its consequences, the doctrine would do away with all meaning. Words would have to be signs of themselves or somehow stand directly for things without being the product of a human mind. We know that in fact we convey meaning when we communicate; that we are not talking about literally nothing. Our ideas are not merely negative. They have a positive content. Any purely negative explanation will not work. Saying, for instance, that things are alike because they are not different, or they are alike because of a common difference, leads nowhere. Consider the following parallel with mathematics:

I am not a stone	A is not equal to C.
You are not a stone	B is not equal to C.
Therefore I am you?	Therefore A is equal to B?

In all, as an alternative to the position which shows the existence of immaterial mental experiences, nominalism completely fails.[29]

Know Thyself

Plato also appealed to another power possessed by human beings in order to prove the radically different status of the knowing soul in comparison with the dumb body. In the *Republic* (509d-511e) Plato talks about the hierarchy of the sciences as corresponding to a line divided into various sections. The bottom section represents pictures of pictures (the arts), the next the visible world, the next the mathematical realm of knowledge (which matches the visible world as later justified in the *Timaeus*), and finally the realm of the Ideas which can only be reached by philosophical contemplation. It is really only the two upper divisions which stand for real science, since only in mathematics and philosophy do we find the necessary and universal. That we have such knowledge is obvious from experience, and numerous references to this fact are found over and over again in the *Theaetetus*.

But how is knowledge of the existence of the necessary and universal possible unless we know what we know? Hence the need for self-knowledge. Plato takes it as a fact of experience that we can explicitly think about our own thinking. We can form concepts of concepts. This power of self-knowledge is an amazing ability and can be used as another positive proof of the immateriality of the human intellect.

Literally, reflection means to bend back. Physicists talk about how light bends back from various surfaces according to certain laws. More solid materials can also bend to various degrees. A piece of paper can be folded back onto part of itself. Acrobats can bend their bodies in such a way as to bend one part back upon another part. Regardless of how subtle the substance, though, or how thin the paper, or how flexible the acrobat, the one act no material thing can perform is to reflect upon itself in a complete or total manner. The part of the material thing which is touching another part can never touch itself. The same terminology may be applied to actions. The ability of a thing to "touch" itself in its very activity has traditionally been called perfect reflection and no physical thing has been found to have this ability. In humans this ability is called self-consciousness, self-reflection, or self-knowledge.[30]

To see this in ourselves demands the use of the very power itself. If we did not have the power of introspection, we would not be able to so much as begin a discussion about it. However, it is not unusual for people, including professional philosophers, biologists, sociologists, and others, to miss the forest because of the trees. Since self-consciousness is so much a part of our daily lives, we often overlook its existence and its implications for our status as a species. It is just always there. We take it for granted.

What do we find when we look at the act of self-consciousness itself? Consider the following set of statements:

A. I am now reading a book.
B. Epidermidolysis bullosa dystrophica is a rare and fatal skin disease.
C. The earth and the moon were formed about the same time.

Implied in the enunciation of the first statement is that I know that I am now reading this book. In the second, that I do not know about the disease is implied. In the third, that I think or believe so is implied.

But there is more to it than this. If someone kept asking you over and over again about something you did not know about, what would be your intellectual reaction? If pushed and pressed, sooner or later the response would be something along the lines of "Leave me alone—I *know* I don't know anything about this strange disease." The same is true in the cases of the other statements. When fully and explicitly stated each statement expresses:

1. something about entities and/or states of affairs independent of our knowing power,
2. that we know, do not know, or have an opinion about them, and
3. that *we know* that we know, do not know, or have an opinion about them.

    Thus:

I know	I know	A
I know	I don't know	B
I know	I guess	C

In each case the human knower is judging his or her own acts of intellection. Not only can the intellect focus on the things about which it forms concepts (the book, the disease, the earth and moon), it can also focus *simultaneously* on the intellectual status of its own knowing. If we could not do this, we would never know the difference between knowledge and ignorance. Not only must a student know what the square root of 4 is, not know what the square root of 5 is, and think he knows what the square root of 625 is, he must also know that he knows, does not know, and only thinks it's true if he is to rest in the knowledge he already possesses and go forward to acquire the knowledge he lacks.

Hence, in order to say anything significant about human mental life or to make any advances in any field of knowledge, including psychology, introspection is imperative. As soon as this is realized, it makes a great deal of sense to decry, as did Carl Jung, those psychologies without psyches. Not only is introspection an option which may be used, it is a necessity which cannot be avoided, especially by those interested in the status of the person. Its results can be ignored, played down, and wished away, but such a denial of experience cannot be maintained for long.[31]

It is sometimes heard that introspection is to be avoided because it involves us in an infinite regress. That is, the process is said to depend upon something else, and so on, so that the series never ends. Such an argument, however, is based upon several misunderstandings. Introspection is not an explanation but a datum of experience which implies something about the nature of mind. Also, what is actual is at least possible. Since we are in fact aware of our own states of intellection, it certainly cannot be the case that introspection is impossible due to an infinite regress.

Finally, the objection rests upon a materialistic view of people which insists that all phenomena, including intellectual ones, must be regarded as ultimately deriving from a material base. Since perfect reflection is impossible for anything material, it must be impossible, period. The first part of the last sentence cannot be denied. A million relays added to a computer will not produce a self-conscious machine. A metal spring in a thermostatic feedback mechanism does not reflect upon its own expansion and contraction. Neither does the sealed glass tube have any knowledge of its tilting, nor the enclosed mercury of its own flowing. Why, though, must we begin with the assumption that a human being is a totally material thing? If the facts indicate an immaterial aspect to knowledge which cannot be reduced to a material complex, why not accept it? If you do, there is no longer any problem of an infinite regress. Knowing and self-knowing could then be possible simultaneously.

I think that we can now better understand the durable significance of vitalism. Several of the key insights into the human person, first brought into prominence by Plato, have remained with us ever since. Plato knew that in order to be scientific about human knowledge, he had to preserve the data of experience and attempt to explain it. Furthermore, based upon the way the human person actually operates in the knowing process, he realized that the explanation, which must be different from the data to be explained, must move into the realm of the immaterial. Exactly how all the parts and aspects of the universe fitted together he did not know. With respect to details he gave us myths and dreams. With respect to the sense-intellect relationship, though, he gave us hard evidence. If he were alive today (in one way or another), he could do no better than to do what he did thousands of years ago, to wit, encourage us to see it for ourselves by doing some really serious thinking about ourselves.

Some Variations

There is no reason to doubt that René Descartes was always a loyal son of the Catholic church. After achieving fame throughout Europe at a relatively young age, he had ample opportunity to repudiate any such connection with a minimum loss of either fame or fortune. Numerous Protestant princes would have more than welcomed him in if he had so desired. However, he remained true to his religious tradition, even in spite of provocation to do otherwise. As with Galileo, his attitude towards the small-minded conservativism of many church leaders was one of paternalistic sympathy and resignation rather than condemnation. It would seem that his desire was more to reform gently rather than destroy outright the traditional structure. In a way he would be a one-man church council doing what the many bishops could not do.[32]

In 325 the Council at Nicaea condemned as heretical any attempt to identify Christianity and Platonism. It was the first time that the whole structure of the Church was mobilized against a particular philosophical doctrine. But it was not the last. Over and over again in later centuries the meaning of Christianity had to be defined and redefined relative to some philosophical doctrine. The same sort of thing occurred during the fifth Lateran Council of 1514-1517, a weak attempt to introduce some much-needed reforms into church prac-tices. At this council the bishops condemned the proposition that the immortality of the soul was beyond the competence of reason to es-tablish. In the dedication of his *Meditations* to the Faculty of Theology in the University of Paris Descartes explicitly referred to the council and its invitation to Christian thinkers to work on the problem of immortality to the best of their abilities. Descartes saw himself as fulfilling this highly important task.

As a Christian who accepts on faith the infallible truth of divine revelation, as he says in his preface to the *Principles of Philosophy,* it follows that he must believe in the essential goodness of the material world. It was created by God, and recreated, so to speak, by the second person of the Trinity in the Incarnation. Consequently, the fact that the soul can be shown to be a separate and independent thinking thing with respect to the body in no way prejudices the status of the body. The material world will preserve its intrinsic value regardless of the body's relationship to the soul.

No wonder, then, that Descartes felt uncomfortable about his position on the soul. Working on the principle that everything can be doubted except the fact that he was a thinking thing, Descartes found it easy to show that the proper definition of himself is that he is essentially a self-conscious being. In his sixth *Meditation* he summarizes the situation as follows:

> And therefore, merely by knowing with certitude that I exist, and because, in the meantime, I do not observe that anything other than my being a thinking thing necessarily belongs to my nature or essence, I rightly conclude that my essence consists only in my being a thinking thing....So likewise if the body of man be considered as a kind of machine, made up and composed of bones, nerves, muscles, veins, blood, and skin, even though there were no mind in it, it would still exhibit the same motions which it presently manifests involuntarily.

The mind is spirit; the body a machine. It would seem that the indivisible essence of the soul can in no way get together with the divisible essence of the body. Yet Descartes cannot get rid of the primitive feeling that he is one unified being. How is such a primitive feeling possible if in fact the body and soul are two separate elements? As he says in a letter (May 21, 1643) to Princess Elizabeth of Bohemia, how the body and soul can possibly constitute one being is "the question people have the most right to ask me in view of my published works."[33] Descartes has no satisfactory answer to this question. What he does is to repeat that the unity of each individual human person is an undeniable personal experience. Ultimately though he must refer to the combination of the body and soul as a mere mixture of heterogeneous things. Near the end of his Synopsis of the *Meditations* he tells his readers, "The human mind is shown to be really distinct [separate] from the body, but, nevertheless, to be so closely conjoined to it, as together they form, as it were, a unity." This "as if" approach is Descartes's final philosophical word on the subject. No other conclusion is to be expected given his initial definitions of mind and matter.

When discussing the nature of the soul, Descartes is quite satisfied to depend entirely upon his own internal self-knowledge to determine that he is essentially a thinking thing. This approach is quite different from Plato's arguments. He does, however, come much closer to Plato's approach when discussing the difference between man and beast, as he does in *Discourse* V. There he claims that there is no gradual transition from monkey to man. His reason for saying this is that he can find no trace whatsoever of human-type intellectual knowledge in animals. Invariably animals will fail when put to tests requiring the use of universal concepts. Although sometimes superior to humans in sense powers, no animal species can think in universal and necessary terms. This also explains why humans cannot hold intellectual conversations with animals. True language depends upon immaterial concepts. The fact that animals can do no better than perform sensual imitations of human speech is a good indication of their utter lack of mind power. In fact they are merely soundless machines, mere bodies without minds of any kind.

From this Descartes concludes to the special creation of each human soul. As soon as it is created as a rational soul, its essence is thought, and so it must think even in the womb. Again true to Christian Scripture, it cannot be said that the soul preexists the body as Plato said. Neither can the body be considered as a mere prison or trap for the soul. As a creation of God it must be a good and wholesome thing. In agreement with Plato, though, once created the soul is destined for immortality. By its very nature the soul is "entirely independent" of the body and thus not liable to death along with the body.

The body, on the other hand, is material and as such is pure extension. It is exactly comparable in essence to Plato's receptacle, pure geometrical space. This is the realm of physics, as opposed to metaphysics which deals with the soul and God. Our idea of matter is, in practice, hardly different from the mathematician's blackboard. Once broken up into pieces, the particles of matter possess the same mathematical qualities as the atoms of the atomists. All qualities except size, shape, and position are to be removed from matter. However, whereas for the atomists the atoms possessed an unexplained eternal motion, for Descartes God originally had to put matter in motion. Once in motion, though, there is no natural way of stopping it. What we end up with then, as we did with Plato and the atomists, is an ideal world on which the scientists can carry out their calculations. Remove, now, Descartes's souls from such a world and we find ourselves back in the universe of reductionistic materialism. In such a world there can be but one matter and one science.

This explains, perhaps, why so many modern scientists are drawn to Descartes like a moth to a flame. What alternative is there? Back to Aristotle?[34] If we do not adopt his view of the material universe what becomes of our conceptions of nature, and of the place of mathematics and mathematical physics in our studies? What will become of physics? Alas, what will become of biology? Won't any rejection of reductionism pull the rug out from underneath most of modern biology which prides itself on being mechanistic? In other words, without Descartes's arguments, how will we know for sure that the natural universe is really and truly nothing but matter in motion?

Certainly we do not literally experience such a universe. Should we call upon the "tradition" of science? But is this not a little bit too much like the superstitions of old so often condemned by science? Is it because such a view of things "works"? But maybe taking some other view of the way things really are would "work" just as well. After all, "working" is only a pragmatic term indicating that the world of experience agrees with the formulas and predictions of the scientists, not that the world must necessarily be a certain way in order to have such agreement.

Like it or not scientists seem to be stuck with the Cartesian model of matter in motion. It would be no exaggeration to say that they have a tiger by the tail. The irony is that the very doctrine regarded as so useful derives from a doctrine regarded as abhorrent by many of the same scientists, namely, vitalism. How can a self-critical and thoughtful scientist accept one without the other? Or are we to go back to the old Parmenidean doctrine, the context for the original vitalism of Plato in the first place? Perhaps this explains why those concerned with human nature forever appear to be starting over again and again.

Like Descartes, Immanuel Kant wanted to start out fresh. In 1756, after he had already written several scientific works, Kant read Hume and came to the shocking realization that Hume's skepticism concerning religious matters would apply equally well to science. But science was on the upswing. How could the conclusions of the great Newton be doubted? One might be skeptical about any number of things, but not about the truths discovered in natural philosophy.

What Kant decided to do, after thinking about it for many years, was to save science, throw out metaphysics, and protect religion by insulating it against any possible encroachment by science. Kant outlined his plan in the famous *Critique of Pure Reason,* first published in 1781. Kant never doubts that there is an extramental, three-dimensional material world out there. What it is, though, taken in itself, cannot be known. Everything we do know about it is the result of our imposing upon it our own internal intuitions and categories of organization.[35] These are first and foremost the intuitions and forms of space and time through which we perceive all sensible things. Once constituted as being in some place at some time we can and do impose judgments upon sensible things according to the categories of unity, plurality, totality, reality, negation, limitation, substance and attribute, cause and effect, reciprocal action, the possible and impossible, existence and nonexistence, and necessity and contingency.[36]

When these possible forms of thought are applied to something with a foundation in sensation, we get science. But, when applied to something without such a foundation, we get only metaphysics. Furthermore, it is exactly this latter sort of application which accounts for all the problems in the history of philosophy. According to Kant the human mind is made for physics, not metaphysics. Doing metaphysics results only in empty formulas and contradictions. This is the result of a proper evaluation of "pure reason" for Kant. Thus he explains why scientists are always agreeing with each other and philosophers are always disagreeing.

And what about theology? Well, that is not a part of science at all. Proper reasoning is restricted to the sensible. By definition, then, science cannot go beyond the sensible. We can *think* about religion, but we cannot have a *science* of it. With physics, though, that is not the case. When there is a basis in sense knowledge, there is something to be "informed" by the mental judgments and categories. And, since thought is fixed in advance by God, science will always come out the same. In religion, however, there can be no "proofs" as there are in the sciences.[37]

What, then, are we to say about the soul—its freedom, immortality, and union with God? In this regard Kant was hardly different from Descartes as far as his main conclusions are concerned. Tenaciously devoted to his mother, and raised in the strict Pietist tradition of her beliefs, Kant's whole early emotional life was directed toward the defense of religion and nondenominational Christian virtue. To do this required a soul which could exist independently of the body, which could make free choices in moral matters, and which could be united with God forever in heaven.

Obviously the human soul is of much importance to Kant, and consequently he devotes many pages to it in his works. In the *Critique of
Pure Reason* he is at pains to show that the whole point of
philosophical or rational psychology is to set limits—absolute limits—
to what we can scientifically know about our souls. The purpose of
rational psychology is to discipline us so that we will not be tempted to
go to extremes. We must stay in the happy medium between a soulless
materialism and an overly exaggerated spiritualism. In this way we will
avoid much idle speculation and time-wasting theologizing. Such is
"reason's hint" to us to steer us away from wild theories and keep us
on the narrow path leading to the fruitful and practical employments
of life. Our present life is, after all, for Christian action, not scholastic
debates.[38]

Nevertheless, we do know enough to define the person as primarily
a soul. The soul, secure against any hint of materialism due to its existence as a thinking ego,[39] is conscious of its own numerical identity
over a long period of time. Such a consciousness, by definition,
according to Kant, makes the soul a person. Being self-identical as an
immaterial substance is the very meaning of being a person.[40]

As a matter of experience, of course, the soul is also connected with
a body. We cannot escape a certain amount of materialism in our
natures, even if only in regard to the way we must have recourse to the
world of the senses in order to have a firm basis for science. Exactly
how, though, the extended three-dimensional world of matter can
have any communion with the thinking unextended world of the spirit
is another issue. It is, in fact, a problem that has no current answer and
never will have an answer in the future. There is a gap between the
senses and the mind that no speculative theory can fill. Furthermore,
how a mind could think before, or after, being in contact with a body
is also an open question. There is no way we can imagine life before
conception or life after death. Worse still (or better still from Kant's
perspective), we can't even imagine the *possibility* of obtaining
answers to these questions. Such is the state of our knowledge in this
life.[41]

For all that, though, we are not left completely helpless with respect
to our knowledge of the immortality of the soul. There is such a thing
as a "rational faith" even in this life. In his *Critique of Practical
Reason* Kant proceeds to build the only possible bridge from the
sensible world to the supersensible world, namely, one based upon the

absolute and necessary law of our will to duty. In Kant's view, pure reason alone is the only driving force the human soul needs to please God. This moral law of reason is as fundamental and binding as any physical law. Even without church buildings, clergy, sacraments, or traditional prayer the moral law remains in full force within our own reason. There can no more be a break in the moral imperative than there can be an interruption (for example, a miracle) in the physical laws of nature. Based upon this moral law, and in conjunction with the fact of human freedom and the existence of God, the immortality of the soul follows as a necessary conclusion.[42]

Kant reasons thus. The absolute end of the will is the highest good, which is its own perfection as a moral agent freely choosing good out of a sheer sense of duty. Such an agent will *never*, under any circumstances, violate the principle that he is not to do anything which could not be made into a universal law for everyone to follow. In other words, when it comes to morality you are never allowed to make an exception for yourself. Now, as it happens, it is practically impossible to achieve such perfection in this life. Hence there must be immortality in order that the soul will have an opportunity to do what it must do according to the moral imperative.[43]

The time required to do this is infinite because the only highest good is God himself. We are under an obligation to be "perfect as your heavenly Father is perfect" (Matt. 5:48). But this is impossible to achieve in any finite time. As a result we are bound to be *forever* on our way to perfection. One and the same personal rational being must endure forever. And "this is called the immortality of the soul."[44]

For Kant, then, there is no boredom in heaven. The soul, which is the true person, will strive forever to fulfill its destiny. And so we see that, although there is no scientific proof, which by definition requires a basis in sense data, there is a "dialectical" proof, that is, one within the boundaries of reason alone based upon the moral side of man. Thereby we can know to be true what no scientist can ever hope to prove by any sort of laboratory experiment. By the same token, however, neither can any scientist ever hope to disprove it.[45]

In the twentieth century the most interesting development of Kant's solution to the problem of relating human knowledge to the world, and thereby simultaneously making a great contribution to the body-mind problem, has been the Transcendental Phenomenology of Edmund Husserl. Transcendental Phenomenology is both a philosophy and a philosophy of methodology. During his own lifetime Husserl's primary concern was to elaborate a *program* or guide for philosophizing. Whether or not he actually produced a definitive body of knowledge, in the sense of some all-comprehensive philosophical system of things, was of secondary concern to him. His intention in this program was to give new life to what was in fact a very old undertaking but which, in his opinion, had never succeeded in the past.

The objective to be conquered was to fulfill the old dream of finding an absolutely dependable methodology for achieving true and certain knowledge within the bounds of our earthly existence. Transcendental Phenomenology was to be the means by which this goal could, and would, be reached. Beginning with Plato, who was the first to appreciate fully the importance of *Geist* in the effort to achieve absolutely certain knowledge, human intellectual history has moved through the Cartesian period, with its emphasis upon the subjective *starting point,* and the Kantian phase, with its emphasis upon the mind as the ultimate *source* of scientific, that is, true and certain, knowledge. All that remains now is for the human race to realize finally that only if it goes beyond or transcends Kant, by completely and unreservedly plunging into a hitherto untried radical subjectivism, can human beings finally reach the much desired destination of an absolutely perfect scientific knowledge of man in the world.[46]

Getting such a program across is no easy task. Obstacles abound. As it turns out, the main obstacles to be overcome are precisely the same ones faced by Plato so many years ago. Everywhere one turns one meets relativists, pragmatists, naive naturalists, and empirically oriented psychologists who flatly refuse to allow for the scientific value of introspection. Everywhere in modern times science is perverted and forced into materialistic modes of thinking which, in the end, actually render science impossible. All over the world there are the so-called learned academics who refuse to admit that it's even possible for the human mind to know essences or to know what a thing really is in itself. It seemed to Husserl in his day, just as it did to Plato in his, that the errors of empiricism and nominalism reigned supreme throughout the whole academic world.[47]

And yet it is all so foolish. If, instead of having a situation in which "The philosophers meet but, unfortunately, not the philosophies,"[48] people got together and really talked *and listened* to each other, things would be very different indeed. In that event everyone would realize that it is strictly impossible to have science without essences, that empirical psychology without introspection is not even good empirical psychology, and that nobody could ever be a nominalist in practice. Husserl is utterly amazed at the way modern philosophers and psychologists are constantly pouring out so much energy—and words—debating the obvious. Of course people have minds. Of course the same idea can be expressed in different words. And of course we must know that we know in order to carry on any kind of research whatsoever. The absurdity of the situation is such that the very aspects of the world which these modern Sophists seek to deny are the very same aspects which they must employ in their vain attempts to make their case.[49]

But even when the obstacles are finally overcome, it may be asked, what are we left with? What exactly is the criterion of truthfulness and validity which we are to follow in our continuation of the Copernican Revolution in philosophy and science? In rejecting Sophism in all its forms, we may well learn what is wrong, but how shall we then learn what is right? Like Descartes, Husserl must find an incontrovertible jumping-off place, something which even the most radical skepticism cannot destroy.

According to Husserl there is one and only one correct method for fully realizing the goal of absolute certitude, namely, to go back into yourself, into your own consciousness, in order to really "know thyself," and thereby to rediscover ("reconstitute") the whole world anew. This must be done in a radical way. It is not sufficient simply to pay attention to appearances *qua* appearances. Such an approach would be a terribly superficial phenomenology, the kind of thing one would expect from an unphilosophical empiricist but not from a true seeker after truth. No, the attention paid to one's own consciousness must include *all* that is implied in the acts of consciousness as well. Mere descriptions of the "I see red here and now" type must be transcended. A Transcendental analysis of phenomena cannot be a simple-minded phenomenalism.

Taking his lead from Franz Brentano, his "gifted" teacher, who had an insight into the significance of Intentionality "apart from which phenomenology could not have come into being at all," Husserl finds in the clear and certain fact of Intentionality the key to this more profound form of phenomenology.[50] By Intentionality

Husserl means the way in which all our conscious acts always "intend" or refer to something beyond themselves. Even when thinking about our own thoughts the content or matter of the self-reflective act of consciousness is never identical with the act by which the content is cognized.

To Husserl this dual aspect of human thought was both reassuring and frightening. It was reassuring because it allows us to be certain that every thought will always be about something; but frightening because it leaves him open to the charge that our thoughts are so self-contained that there may in reality be nothing beyond them. Like the teacher who asks students on a test to state their own views on a question, and then belatedly realizes that unless it can be proved that the students are lying, they must all be given the top grade, the self-contained thought, bearing *within* itself its own reference, in no way proves beyond a shadow of a doubt that the "intention" or content of the conscious act really exists independently of the thought itself.

Nevertheless, it is this dual aspect of our ideas which most impressed Husserl. As he finally came to conclude, *regardless* of whether or not the contents of our ideas actually subsist on their own, we can be absolutely certain both that we are having such thoughts and that we can know the essences of their contents. So let us restrain ourselves with respect to asserting whether or not anything exists other than our own thoughts. Such a "bracketing" of existence will in no way prevent us from being scientific, that is, from having a knowledge of essences, from possessing "eidetic" (certain and universal) knowledge.[51]

At this point a new revelation, most pertinent to the nature of the human person, shows itself. Husserl is now in a position to make a contribution to the body-mind problem. How can dualism in nature be overcome? Can the human mind be seen as a part of nature? How can there be any intercourse between mind and body? How can Kant's out-there, the thing-in-itself, be brought into the subjective mind? Where is the bridge between the objective and the subjective? Immensely difficult issues to be sure, and with no hope of clarification without the techniques of Transcendental Phenomenology.[52]

Based upon Intentionality, however, something of importance can be said on the subject. Is there really any such thing, asks Husserl, as given in absolute un-theory-laden consciousness, as a parallel between reason "in here" and a "reality out there"? Do we really need Kant's noumena——phenomena distinction to save us from a Berkeley-type Idealism? Isn't absolute being or reality identical with appearing reality or being? Are there really any such things as "things in themselves" or "I know not whats" in the whole universe?[53]

What Husserl proposes doing in effect is reinterpreting the meaning of "object" or "thing." The universe is not composed of things and minds—at least not the universe of the pure ego concentrating all its energies upon *bewusst-sein* ("being in consciousness"). As "constituted" or discovered in absolute consciousness the thing out there and the conscious act in here are united in one and the same psychic act. The essential nature of the thing appearing in consciousness cannot be anything other than what in fact it appears to be. As far as the conscious person is concerned, reality is what is conceived by the mind.

Nonetheless, Husserl does not deny the existence of unperceived things. What he denies is their importance in our understanding of the human person. The existence of rocks, trees, and dogs cannot condition the knowing mind precisely because it is a fact of consciousness that the situation is just the other way around. It is *they* that are the correlates of consciousness and not vice versa.[54] In itself consciousness is a self-contained system of being which cannot be penetrated by foreign elements deriving from psycho-physical connections.[55] Yet, at the same time, no object or thing is ever out of relation to an active consciousness.[56] Furthermore, is it not the case that we must think that something now under the gaze of the mind's eye already existed before that gaze was turned upon it, and that it will continue to exist later? Is it not a fact that an analysis of Intentionality shows that it is part of the intrinsic nature of things as given to us in consciousness to be perceivable, that is, capable of being perceived but not always actually being perceived? And thus are not *all* things essentially oriented towards the conscious ego?[57] Husserl of course says yes, and on that basis can, for all practical purposes, forget about whether or not there is a three-dimensional extramental world existing independently of mind.

The value of Husserl's analysis, though, cannot be forgotten. Where is the connection between mind and body? It is in the idea. *In* the idea the twain shall meet. The act of "intending" by which the complete human person cognizes *is* an idea, a psychic event, a pure act of Geist. Yet *in* that very act there is contained a reference to an objective world which is not a product of the mind's own creation. Thus there is no hint of a metaphysical Idealism à la Berkeley. There is, though, much more than a hint that we are now experiencing the fusing of body and mind such that the "life of the soul is made intelligible in its most intimate and originally intuitional essence."[58] Such a life is forever changing and yet essentially stable. Every moment is fresh and newly organized, and yet in the center of all rests the self-conscious ego supreme in its scientific certitude. In the idea there is no possible distinction between reality and illusion, being and appearance, out there and in here. In the idea the mind and body, though remaining distinct, fuse together in the unquenchable flame of Intentionality.

Now, after this has been said, what can Husserl tell us about immortality? At the beginning of his *Cartesian Meditations* Husserl says that his whole program is a sort of neo-Cartesianism insofar as it aims to build upon a radically subjective foundation.[59] At the same time, though, he finds that he must reject nearly all of the well-known Cartesian doctrines. Was the existence of a separate and immortal soul one of these rejected doctrines?

When all is said and done, and despite Husserl's constant emphasis upon the importance of spirit and mind, it would seem so. Reminiscent of Pietro Pomponazzi (1462-1525), Husserl's emphasis upon the essential relatedness of knowledge to material content of some kind or another would seem to forever tie the soul to the body for its existence. It was Pomponazzi's position that there is no foolproof purely rational way to prove the immortality of the soul. One of his main arguments against a separately existing soul is the fact that all knowledge employs phantasms. But the soul, in order to have an operative imagination, requires a body. So, with respect to the soul, "in all its knowing it needs imagination. But, if this is so, it is material. Hence the intellective soul is material."[60] Consequently, thought Pomponazzi, one should give up on the philosophers and turn instead to Scripture. There you will find all the "proof" of immortality anyone will ever require.

It seems likely that Husserl, if he ever did believe in immortality, would have had to take the same approach. We know that near the end of his life, while under house arrest by the Nazis, he sent his family to a Benedictine monastery for safekeeping. Yet, as far as anyone has been able to determine, his final thoughts on the soul still remain unknown to us today. As far as his stated philosophy is concerned, in the search for an absolutely dependable foundation for truth he found himself so intimately connecting the knower and the known that the human person was as absolutely unified as a geometrical figure and its properties.

We cannot even appeal to his "school" for an answer. With followers as different as Max Scheler (an on-again, off-again Catholic), Edith Stein (a martyred Carmelite nun), and Maurice Merleau-Ponty and Martin Heidegger (both non-Christians), our task would only be *more* difficult. All in all, then, I would have to agree with Dorion Cairns that according to Husserl "every mind is necessarily connected with a body and could not exist apart from one."[61] Beyond this point, to press Husserl for an answer to the question would really be unfair.

BACKGROUND

The Undeniable Data

When discussing the question of whether or not the soul is corporeal, Aquinas in his main work has recourse to only one proof. The old philosophers *(antiqui Philosophi)*, by which he means the Greeks, in many cases could not rise above their imaginations. As a result they taught that for something to be real, it must be a body. Such a universal judgment, of course, must apply to the soul as well. But, he goes on to say, "This opinion can be proven false in many ways. However, I will use only one which is both universal and obviously convincing in showing that the soul is not a body." The core of this one proof is that if it were possible for a body *qua* body to be alive, *all* bodies would be alive. "Obviously, to have a life-principle, or to be a living thing, cannot be due to a body as body. Otherwise all bodies would be alive or possess life-principles."[62]

Earlier, when discussing the nature of God, Aquinas argues that God is not material. One way of proving this is to note that God is supremely alive. "But," observes Aquinas, "a living body is not alive insofar as it is a body, otherwise all bodies would be alive."[63] Consequently, it must be the case that God is at least as immaterial as any soul.

The second article of Question 75 in the *Summa Theologiae* goes on to show that the human soul must be subsistent as well as just immaterial, as we have already seen. Since things cannot be differentiated by what they have in common, the soul cannot be corporeal. In addition, though, since the human soul can perform intellectual acts in which the body does not (and cannot) share, the soul must be capable of existing in its own right. It is here that we find the strongest common element among Plato, Aristotle, and Aquinas. The human mind does in fact possess universal and necessary (that is, scientific) knowledge. Even one of the greatest critics of human knowledge, Immanuel Kant, took this fact for granted based upon the way scientists actually operate.

Nevertheless, how this fact is to be explained in terms of the relationship of body and soul is another question. Plato argued for their complete separation, Aristotle for their unification without immortality, and Aquinas for their unification with immortality. According to Aquinas, the reason Plato could so argue was that he thought the soul capable of sensing on its own without a body. However, since God created both the body and the soul together, Aquinas could not imagine of what use the body would be if what Plato thought were true.[64]

Today, in light of the nonreductionistic materialism position, we know that Aquinas' one proof is no longer very strong. True enough, it is obvious that things cannot differ by what is common to them. This is a perfectly sound logical principle. To gainsay it would introduce a contradiction into the proposition. Someone such as Hegel, though, would not be bothered by such a situation. You cannot accuse Hegel of unconsciously committing a violation of the principle of noncontradiction when the whole point of his answer to Parmenides is to begin by doing precisely that.

In addition, in the case of someone such as Dewey, it can no longer be said that *all* materialists want bodies *qua* bodies to be alive. We must rather say today that it is the case that some bodies *qua* organized a certain way are alive. Consequently, even though the logical principle can still be maintained, Aquinas' approach is no longer good for factual reasons. The microcosmic world which we today take for granted was unknown to Aquinas. It was also unknown to Plato and Aristotle.

For this reason most of the arguments employed by Plato to convince his listeners of the soul's subsistence, and so of its immortality, are largely unconvincing today. To talk about the way in which everything runs in cycles, and so the way in which death and life must alternately replace each other, can just as well be explained by nonreductionistic materialism as by any other view (*Phaedo*, 70); likewise for the argument that the soul must participate in the Form of Life in order to be alive (*Phaedo*, 103; *Republic*, 608). Such talk today can be regarded as being either a mere tautology or as simply a shorthand and trivial way of summarizing the wealth of biological data on the differences between living and nonliving things.

In terms of contemporary knowledge the one argument which has not become threadbare is the one in which Plato argues that the mind is akin to the Eternal Ideas and so must somehow share in their incorporeal nature (*Phaedo*, 79). This approach, which is in fact the central argument running through many of the dialogues, is still the foundation for Plato's claim to philosophical fame. His firm grasp upon the radical difference between sense knowledge and intellectual knowledge has never suffered any substantial weakening from the time of the ancient atomists to the contemporary "family resemblance" of Ludwig Wittgenstein. Despite all attacks and criticisms there has always remained that certain residue of data which any viable theory of the human person must somehow take into account.

Father Parmenides

But this is all hindsight. Plato himself did not appear to be especially concerned about concentrating all his efforts on just one approach that would outlive all the critics. To see the actual historical genesis of the vitalistic view as expressed by Plato, we must look into his relationship with the same historical figure who produced as his offspring Lucretius, Hegel, and Aristotle.

Parmenides, says Plato, is the one thinker he respected above all the others that civilization could boast of (*Theaetetus*, 183e). Practically everyone else, including all the great poets of the Greeks, were little better than Sophists who failed to see the limitations of sense knowledge. It is with great regret that Plato comes to part company with Parmenides. Yet he feels he must do so in order to allow for the reality of change in the world. The information from the senses cannot be denied. Notwithstanding, it is still like killing his own father (*Sophist,* 241d).

Plato began where Parmenides left off. For Parmenides the world was one unchanging, spherical mass. The immutable is the really real. Plato continues this approach. He must, however, agonize over the way in which the reasoning of the true scientist, who is forever looking for the permanent, eternal, and fixed, can be reconciled with the existential fact of change as given in sense experience. To be a true "being" must mean that the thing (the really real, the beingly being, the thingingly thing) is forever fixed and unchanging. If the object of knowledge were not eternally stable, the knower could not even begin to grasp it. It would not even be an "it" to be grasped. That which is constantly changing, as revealed through the senses, is no fit object for science at all.

Furthermore, if what Parmenides said about the true nature of reality *(ousia)* were the full and complete statement of the matter, how could anyone ever make a false statement about anything? To make a false remark means saying what is not the case. But did not Parmenides show quite well by reason alone that it is impossible either to think about or to express yourself about nothingness or "what is not"? If to say something wrong means invoking the unthinkable and inexpressible "nothing" or nonbeing, nobody can ever make a wrong statement. But surely this is opposed both to all common sense and to all the certitudes of reasoning itself. To say "two plus two is five" is universally recognized as wrong. And to say that it is wrong is true.

In his dialogue *The Sophist* Plato brings up the basic question about the meaning of "to be" or being *(ousia).* Could not the Sophists, who were leading Athens astray with their moral relativism, use Parmenides to prove their case? Plato says no. Why? Because Parmenides was wrong in certain ways. In the first place, Parmenides could not have been right when he said that everything was *one* and unchanging. Is not language itself dual? Does not every proposition contain a subject and a predicate? In addition, how can the mass of the world really be one? Does it not have a whole series of differentiated parts from the center to the circumference? *(Sophist,* 244-245) Indeed so.

Consequently, Parmenides must be modified. To hear Plato talk, one almost feels he was wishing that his "father" were still alive (unless Plato himself is the "corrected" reincarnation of Parmenides) so that he could explain to him why he had to leave home. Sense experience cannot be denied. It can, though, be reduced to as low a level as possible. The really real things are the Eternal Ideas, multiple yet corresponding to Parmenides' Being insofar as they are non-sensual, fixed, and eternal. Immutable self-identity is the prime trait of true being. At the same time, however, sensible and changeable phenomena also exist in a certain way, as reflections in a mirror might exist. What we regard as material things, then, may be regarded as fleeting and passing "participations" of something (Plato does not really know what this something is) in the Ideas.[65]

But wait. How do you account for both the internal self-sufficiency of each Idea and simultaneously for their many mutual internal relationships with one another? Do not all Ideas share in Reality, in being real? Do not they all share in Otherness, in being different from each other? Does not Equality share in the Odd and the Even, and so on and so forth through a countless number of cases?

To explain this dual character of things which are supposed to be absolutely simple Plato is forced into postulating the One Above Being. This is the Source from which the Ideas (Being) somehow derive. To call it mysterious would be an understatement. If the Ideas are Being, what could the One or Good possibly be if not nonbeing? No wonder the scientist must remain hushed and quiet at the edge of the Good. It is as if Plato had come to the edge of the earth and, while gazing out and down at the great abyss, drew back in a combination of horror and stunned amazement at what he had come upon. Beyond the intelligible lies the infinitely unintelligible, the ultimate irrationality upon which hangs all that is rational. Everything that *is* depends upon what *is not!* Indeed hyperbole can go no further (*Republic*, 509).

Poor Plato! If the greatest Good is the greatest because it gives rise to what we *know* to be good (the Ideas), what can it be if not the very thing father Parmenides said was impossible? If the Ideas which dwell beyond the heavens are true being, and what explains them cannot be of the same nature, their Source must be the very "nothing" rejected by Parmenides. It seems that Plato has betrayed his father on two fronts. On the one side he allows in change, while on the other side he is forced by reason itself to allow in nonbeing.

Even as he talks of the Good as Being, he knows that it cannot be Being. Just as the sun is the cause of generation on earth but is not itself generation, so the Good which is the source of knowledge and truth (the Ideas) cannot itself be an Idea. Yet in the very process of speaking about such a thing (that is, a no-thing) Plato must clothe it with the very attributes which he must, in order to be scientific, deny to it. It would be better perhaps not to speak of the situation at all. "And Glaucon said with a laugh, heaven save us, hyperbole can go no further. The fault is yours, Socrates answered, for forcing me to say anything about it at all." *(Republic,* 509c)

The Happy Medium

Plato felt that if he were to say (as did Parmenides, Lucretius, Aristotle, Aquinas, and Hamlet) "to be *or* not to be" he would be playing right into the hands of the Sophists. Hence he worked out a scheme of things whereby he could say "to be *and* not to be." This was accomplished by making Otherness or Difference one of the Ideas. In this way everything which differs from anything else must share in the Idea of Otherness. So, whereas the perfectly negative or nothingness *(me on, kenon)* is unthinkable, the notion of Difference *(heteron)* is thinkable and therefore capable of occupying a place in the realm of the Eternal Ideas.

We see, consequently, that it is possible to make a false statement. To do so we must use a term which is other than what it should be. In other words, what appears to be perfectly negative is really something positive in that it shares in the positive Idea of Otherness. This was the best Plato could do *(Sophist,* 258b).

From Plato's own point of view, though, it wasn't really all that bad. Given the scientific atmosphere in which he found himself at the time he could honestly view himself as striving for some sort of compromise position which would preserve both the senses and the intellect. This was in fact how he looked upon himself. On the one hand he had to contend with those such as Parmenides and some Pythagoreans who wanted to deny any change whatsoever. On the other hand were those such as Heraclitus who wanted to deny all stability and eternal immutability. Both sides must be partly right and partly wrong, thought Plato. How could it be otherwise if we are to accept the evidence presented by both the mind and the body? As Plato puts it, using the Stranger as his spokesperson:

> For these reasons it therefore seems to me that there is only one
> course open to the philosopher who values knowledge and the
> rest above all things. He must refuse to believe those who cham-
> pion one or several forms teaching that all reality is changeless.
> He must also refuse to listen to the others who teach that all real-
> ity is always changing. Instead, like a child begging for both he
> must say that reality, or the sum of all things, consists of *both*
> the changeable *and* the unchangeable. (*Sophist*, 249cd)

What could be more natural, therefore, than to regard the soul as
akin to the unchangeable and the body as akin to the changeable? To
put them together, in the sense of regarding them as being one thing,
appeared to be neither necessary nor convenient to Plato's way of
thinking. But don't they *appear* to be one thing in terms of actual human experience? Yes, but only to the extent that we are paying attention to the material world of shifting sensations. Under such circumstances the mind is not acting according to its godlike nature but degrading itself by allowing itself to be absorbed in the sensual. This is
not the right way for human beings to act.

When acting rightly the situation is quite different. By concentrating upon the Eternal Ideas, the mind discovers its true nature and will,
if it perseveres, finally achieve a complete and final separation from
the body forever. How can such a thing be achieved if the body is an
essential part of the human person? What role and place could there
possibly be for a material thing in the world of the purely intelligible?
None at all is the only answer which makes any sense to Plato. Only
that which is akin to the intelligible can have any intercourse with it.
And this can only be the soul, the true human person, the god
imprisoned in flesh.

SOME CONSEQUENCES

Reincarnation

One of the most obvious features of vitalism as a view of what it
means to be a human person is that the soul or true person must exist
before it comes into the prison of the body. This aspect of vitalism was
something which Plato never ceased advertising. References to the way

the soul moves from one body to another can be found throughout many of his dialogues, both early and late.[66] Plato regarded such trans-migrations as unavoidable. Except in those few cases in which the soul devoted its whole adult life on earth to nothing but the study of the Eternal Ideas, the ordinary human soul must accept the fate of being doomed to continue the process of returning to some body or other over and over again.

This is obviously a form of immortality. It can be found strongly stated in Hinduism, Buddhism, and Pythagoreanism, as well as in Platonism. As we have seen, the one great problem in life for Plato is the fact that we are stuck with a body. If only the mind or soul could be free of the body, how wonderful life would be. It could then enjoy eternal bliss without any kind of material interference.

This was Plato's doctrine of salvation, the religion of the few. For the many Plato thought in terms of setting up some kind of worship of the sun and stars. The intellectually weak need images and pictures that they can sense. The true philosopher, though, does not require such things. And for those few who did succeed often enough in be-coming true abstract thinkers the reward at death would be to pass beyond the stars to the realm of the pure Ideas and dwell there forever.

However, for those who failed to find salvation, and in practice this was everyone, the situation would be quite different. They would have to return to the material world in one form or another. If you are a male and do not lead the proper sort of scientific life, you may return as a woman. If given to violence, returning as a wolf might be your fate. If you are a nonintellectual, yet hardworking and fair in your relationships with others, you might return as a bee or an ant in the next life. For Plato anything other than being a true abstract scientist was a crime. And his aim was to have the punishment fit the crime.

These notions were not invented by Plato. As with Plato, for the Hindu reincarnation is a form of punishment. It is the failure on the part of a human being to realize that he is an illusion in the all-encom-passing Brahma. But there is an escape. Each person must live out his or her role in society to perfection. This allows their vital energies to return in the form of someone in a higher caste. Finally, if those in the highest social status do as they should they are finally completely reunited with Brahma thereby returning their vital energies to the great common pool of universal energy rather than having it concen-

trated in some one creature in another life. The evil of material existence is finally overcome. Once the self-delusion of personal individu-
ality is gone, so is the pain and suffering of human lfe.

Buddhism preserves these essential elements of Hinduism. Buddhism has been called the Protestantism of Hinduism. The first "intellectually enlightened one," which is what "Buddha" means,
wanted to do away with all the mythical gods, rituals, and social-polit-
ical intrigues which were saturating Hinduism. Plato and Buddha
both had at least this in common, namely, they wanted each suffering
human person to pull himself up by his own boot straps. In this sense
they were both very intellectual or rational plans for human salvation.
Ignore the evil material world, do not attempt to either improve or
destroy it, was their advice.

For Buddhism the main cause of human ills is that we want and desire things. Do away with desires and you do away with disappointments and suffering. By sheer personal will power reduce your expectations to zero and so reduce your disappointments to nothing. As
long as we desire things the flame of life and passion is fed. We will
then continue to return our vital energies to the universe in new re-
births. Each last thought before death conditions the next new form of
vitality in the world. But once eliminate desiring, and the life which
causes us so much pain will go out like a candle flame. This is Nirvana,
the return to Brahma from which there is no return. The personal conquest of human misery is the true and final realization of our own personal nothingness.

In contrast to vitalism there is no separation of body and soul, and
so there is no death because you were never really alive as a separate individual person in the first place. Once the will is killed through contemplation, you return to what you really are all along before you
started opposing yourself to Brahma through your will. The apparent
opposition and conflict is overcome and you sink back into the all-con-
suming sea of Brahma. Through meditation you may transcend the
variety of sensible things and move back to the One of Brahma.[67]

It may sound strange to Westerners to hear of such an identification
between people and nature. This is because we derive our scientific
orientation from the Greeks who by and large never identified their
religious gods with their explanations of the material universe. The
gods may have been "big men" but they were always immortal per-
sonalities clearly separated from impersonal physical nature. Plato's

abstract world of eternal, unchanging Ideas was divine in the sense of immortal, but he never thought of calling abstract formulas gods. Gods were like people. Each had its own separate enduring personality. Each god had to be a somebody as well as a something. The result of this in the West was that the stage was set for the attitude that mind could *control* nature (science and technology), something not endemic to the East. When combined with the biblical command of Genesis to go out and subdue the world, the "man of science" became a real practical possibility.

No Evolution

Plato's explanation of how universal and necessary scientific knowledge is possible and the atheistic versions of evolution are incompatible. A completely materialistic version of evolution, whether of the reductionistic or nonreductionistic type, demands the doctrine of nominalism as its philosophical foundation. This is just another way of saying that the biologist must first deny that there are such things as species in any Platonic sense of the term before he can speak about the alteration and changing of "species" by some process of common descent. This fact has been clearly recognized by modern evolutionists. Ernst Mayr, for instance, has stated that Darwinian-type evolutionary doctrines could not become widely accepted as long as scientists continued to engage in "typological" thinking. However, with the decline of this type of thinking and the rise of flux or process philosophy (that is, the very type of thing which Plato spent his whole life opposing), modern evolutionary doctrines could become the orthodox and standard scientific theory on the origin of living species.[68]

As a matter of history this is certainly true. Even at the very hour in which Darwin was publishing his *Origin of Species* some of those knowledgeable in science were rejecting the premises needed to support Darwin's hypothesis. Such a person was William Whewell (1794-1866), the master of Trinity College in the University of Cambridge from 1841 until his death. Whewell was the world's first important historian of science. The third edition of his *History of the Inductive Sciences* was published in three volumes in 1857 and reissued in two volumes in 1859.

As an historian of science he was well aware of the significance of induction, but with a difference. Pure Baconian induction was not productive of scientific progress. Merely accumulating heaps of data would lead nowhere. To be scientific the data must be unified, and to do that sort of thing requires the active use of the scientist's mind. There must be some unifying concept or theory which will allow all the facts to fall into place. All the facts in the world will not produce science, but the right idea, regardless of how it is discovered, will lead on to innumerable factual discoveries and applications.[69] This in fact is what explains why the Greeks, despite their avid interest in the observation of the world around them, produced no great scientific theories comparable to Newton's. "The defect was, that though they had in their possession Facts and Ideas, *the Ideas were not distinct and appropriate to the Facts.*"[70]

When speaking of Plato, Whewell is careful to note how Plato's Ideas served a very useful scientific purpose. They were the basis for unifying the many facts of observation. There is no way this can be done via the senses alone. Although this theme is developed in much greater detail in his lesser known work *The Philosophy of the Inductive Sciences* (1840), the *History* is clear enough on the point. If Plato's approach was unproductive, it was not due to the wrongness of searching out the unifying Idea. It was due instead to the lack of application of the right Ideas to the right observations. Although he encouraged the study of mathematics, he was not an experimenter. However, once let the experimenter and the man of Ideas come together and good science is inevitable. In the end, and overall, it is the Idea which is preeminent. If only Aristotle the observer and Plato the Idea-man could have gotten together, Whewell seems to have been saying, how different the history of science might have been.[71]

When applied to organic evolution by common descent, it is clear to Whewell that the role of Ideas in physical nature rules out any kind of Darwinian doctrine. Can species be transmuted into one another? Yes, but only if there are no true species in the first place. Based upon what we today would call the ecology of nature, Whewell sees the scientist as caught up in a dilemma. Either he can admit that nature is balanced and unified according to certain relatively fixed types or he can claim, against all evidence, that nature is all promiscuous and amorphous. If the former, evolution is impossible because the Ideas which determine species are fixed. If the latter, you can call yourself an evolutionist, but only at the price of throwing aside any real care for the facts. As Whewell states,

> And the dilemma in which we are placed is this;—that if species are not thus interchangeable, we must suppose the fluctuations of which each species is capable, and which are apparently indefinite, to be bounded by rigorous limits; whereas, if we allow such a *transmutation of species,* we abandon that belief in the adaptation of the structure of every creature to its destined mode of being, which not only most persons would give up with repugnance, but which, as we have seen, has constantly and irresistibly impressed itself on the minds of the best naturalists, as the true view of the order of the world.[72]

Whewell was not alone in his position. On the very eve of Darwin's coming fame he was calling upon the great scientists of the time to support Plato against Heraclitus. He wrote,

> I refer to Mr. Lyell, Dr. Prichard, Mr. Lawrence, and others for the history of the discussion, and for the grounds of the decision; and I shall quote very briefly the main points and conclusions to which the inquiry has led.
>
> It may be considered, then, as determined by the over-balance of physiological authority, that there is a capacity in all species to accommodate themselves, to a certain extent, to a change of external circumstances; this extent varying greatly according to the species. There may thus arise changes of appearance or structure, and some of these changes are transmissible to the offspring: but the mutations thus superinduced are governed by constant laws, and confined within certain limits. Indefinite divergence from the original type is not possible; and the extreme limit of possible variation may usually be reached in a brief period of time: in short, *species have a real existence in nature,* and a transmutation from one to another does not exist.
>
> Thus, for example, Cuvier remarks, that notwithstanding all the differences of size, appearance, and habits, which we find in the dogs of various races and countries, and though we have (in

the Egyptian mummies) skeletons of this animal as it existed three thousand years ago, the relation of the bones to each other remains essentially the same; and, with all the varieties of their shape and size, there are characters which resist all the influences both of external nature, of human intercourse, and of time.[73]

These statements represent his main theoretical objection to evolution. In addition, though, he detected other problems with it. For example, there must somehow be the unaccounted-for production of the very beginnings of the things which were supposed to evolve by common descent into what we have today. What started the process? In other words, Whewell asks, what accounts for the production of the first creatures in each species? When he lived, no evolutionary theory could supply an adequate explanation for the generation of the first rudimentary plants and animals. We must also assume a necessary *progressive* development in nature. Moreover, we must assume that changes brought about by external circumstances can be carried on into future generations. In other words, heredity, which is essentially a conservative force, must be used to explain innovation as well. And finally, we must assume that in every period of world history nature is constantly producing those elementary forms out of which all higher types supposedly develop. So where are they? Such assumptions, ends Whewell the Platonist, are "altogether gratuitous and fantastical."[74]

Behavior Modification

Whereas Descartes stayed away from ethics and politics, Plato appears to have seen the vitalistic doctrine as being of great practical significance in these areas. In his *Theaetetus* (172-179), for example, Plato hints that the whole purpose of his discussion about the nature of knowledge, and the nature of the human mind that is capable of possessing knowledge, is social. How can a state aim for what is good if it does not know what is good? Can it really be said that something is good for the state simply because it has somehow become a law? Is there not a parallel between a good doctor and a quack on the one hand, and a wise lawgiver and a sophist on the other hand? And how can someone be a wise lawmaker unless one first of all knows what is good? And so we come to the importance of fixing our attention upon the Ideas and those who study the Ideas.

This all seems simple and straightforward enough. However, as with all theoretical schemes the practical problem is precisely the problem of practice. How do you put into social and political practice the vitalistic view of the human person? First of all you need a true philosopher, that is, someone who knows clearly and distinctly all the Ideas pertinent to civil government. This knowledge must be possessed while the mind is still alive on earth. Secondly, you must provide such a mind with absolute power over the affairs of the state and its people. As Plato was well aware, such a combination would be extremely hard to produce. If it were to come about at all, it would be only after an extremely long, hard process of training and education. Not only must such a ruler be trained, but so must the people he was to rule. No one who studies Plato today is surprised to learn that what he wanted never did come to pass. A long time ago, though, Plato was not willing to give up easily. As he has Socrates say to Theaetetus: Nothing ventured, nothing gained (*Theaetetus,* 187c).

The political consequences of vitalism are discussed at length by Plato in three of his dialogues: *Republic, Politicus* (or *Statesman*), *Laws.* In the first, Plato describes the relationship between the individual and the state. The various "parts" of the individual (mind, emotions, bodily appetites) are reflected in the various parts of the state. There are the philosophers who rule with wisdom, the soldiers who fight with courage, and the many different sorts of workers who work with devotion and diligence.

How are the rulers obtained? By a long weeding-out process involving many years of carefully supervised, compulsory education. Music, physical training, and mathematics are especially important. Those who survive the training would then be allowed to study the Ideas or dialectic. After many more years of this those who again pass the test would be allowed to become rulers. Because of his doctrine concerning the true nature of the human person Plato could feel secure in his belief that education, the "e-duction" or "leading-out" of the innate Ideas, would indeed sooner or later produce the philosopher-king.

In the *Politicus* Plato comes to emphasize more the personal nature of leadership. The state must be a unified society of common ideals.

This can only be achieved through the agency of one perfectly knowledgeable mind. A nation of laws will not do. Laws are too remote and inflexible to be of much practical value. Injustice is bound to spring up everywhere due to the different interpretations and applications of the codified laws. Hence the need for one living mind in contact with the Ideas of Justice and Equality. Such a mind may be hard to find, says the Stranger to the young Socrates, but once let him appear and he will immediately be acclaimed king *(Politicus,* 301d).

But he did not appear. And so Plato decided to do the next best thing. He would imagine himself as the God-sent ruler and attempt to codify what he would say to the people of the state. Plato does not unsay in his *Laws* what he had said in his previous two dialogues. It must rather be imagined that he was making a last attempt before dying at describing the perfect state in terms of the laws that he himself would enact if he were the actual ruler with absolute power.

Many commentators have not looked with favor upon the results. He has been called a "fanatic" who wanted a "crazy commonwealth" in which the state was supreme. In Plato's utopia individual persons were to be only imperfect copies of the eternal state. Such an attitude is "good communist and totalitarian doctrine."[75]

If Plato's ideal republic, and Marxism in practice, do come out as look-alikes, it is not because one of the two is really in the other's paradigm but because they both possess a near-fanatical desire for *neatness,* one which is willing to destroy all individual creativity and initiative in the name of law and order. There is nothing inherent in Plato's "spiritualism" to restrain such a desire. Free choice *per se* for Plato (as for Skinner, Marx, and Aristotle) is not of great value. Results are what count, not love and will.

Those who criticize Plato along these lines are largely correct. He did in fact propose a kind of *Animal Farm-1984-Rollerball* society long before anyone ever heard of Karl Marx. He was especially aware of the importance of mind control through the popular media. The use of forced education, slaves to help the economy, lies to the public on the part of the rulers, "iron curtain" techniques of isolation that would have made Pavlov proud, and the heavy, complete censorship of literature were all recommended by Plato as suitable tools for the rulers to employ. In addition, a state religion was to be strictly enforced, and genetic manipulation was to be used as much as possible in order to assure the generation of the best bodies. Moreover, the size of the population was to be carefully controlled, and no "capitalistic" money enterprises were to be allowed.[76]

How can such views be consistent with Plato's so otherworldly, "spiritualistic," position on the human person? Does not the independence of the soul insure the maximum of freedom and creativity for the person? Apparently not. Why not? For one thing most people are not aware of their true personhood. They are so immersed in matter that they have thoughts for nothing but food and sex. Can such people be allowed to share in the rule of a great and prosperous nation? Of course not.

Secondly, in any doctrine propounding reincarnation the death of the nation's citizens is not really of any great lasting importance. Sooner or later they will all be back. Consequently, if the state deprives someone of life for crimes against the state, it is only removing that person temporarily. Hopefully, after some time, that person will return as a much more loyal and scientific citizen. In vitalism, as in all the other positions studied so far except position number four, the individual human person really counts for very little. It is the species in the long run that counts (if anything at all is to count), not the temporary individual. This is not what some thinkers may *want* to be the case but what the various theories necessarily entail.

In the third place, but most important, is the very nature of Platonic salvation. Only the best and truest scientific minds can escape the eternal return by concentrating upon the unchanging Eternal Ideas. In such a view of human nature, inevitably great weight will be placed upon the need of the state to imitate the stability of the realm of true being. And this is exactly what Plato does.

There are two means for achieving such stability. Either have a master-ruler obeyed by everyone in unison, or have a rigid set of laws obeyed by everyone together. In either case central planning is imperative. In his *Republic* and *Politicus* Plato speaks of the former. In his *Laws* he pushes the latter. In order to imitate the perfect stability of the Eternal Ideas, the state must also be as unchanging as possible within its material conditions. If all possessions, if all women and children, if all personal talents and abilities, if all individual senses and emotions that acted and reacted, if all judgments about right and wrong, and if all sources of pleasure and pain were held in common, we would come as close to political perfection as possible. Where there is unity in the institutions of society, there is joy and happiness. Where there is one body, there is *social* immortality.

How then do you perpetuate the good life in the good society? You have the good society imitate the good life by first getting it to conform to the Ideas, and then getting it as free from change as possible. This can be done by having a nation of laws which apply to everyone without exception. This is the "nearest to immortality" that Athens can expect to come on earth *(Laws,* 739).

If what Plato had to say sounds strikingly similar to what Skinner had to say, it is because they are very much alike. Both approaches envision a state run by experts. The scientific expert is king. Plato cannot see turning the control of the state over to the ignorant masses any more than he can see turning a fine race horse over to just anybody to be trained. He would no more go to an ordinary citizen for advice on how to run the government of the state than he would go to a quack doctor for advice about how to care for his body.

If the ruler has to use devious means in order to assure law and order, even if he must deny the populace knowledge, then so be it. This is simply how experts operate. The end is what counts, not the means for achieving the end. For those who do not see this, for those who think that freedom and salvation mean variability rather than stability, Plato has no sympathy. They must be suppressed so that the experts can do their job without interference.

We see, therefore, that the vitalistic position on human nature in and of itself is no guarantee of a democratic society. At the same time, though, we cannot fail to realize that when it comes to an analysis of the human person, vitalism has in fact pointed out certain important aspects of human nature, especially with respect to knowledge, which no complete theory of the human person can afford to overlook if it would be truly scientific.

CHAPTER 7

Reductionistic Immaterialism

THE POSITION

The Law and Morals

It is sometimes said that Marxism practices what Christianity preaches concerning the sharing of material wealth. It is also heard now and then that Plato's rejection of the flesh was the precursor of Christian moral principles concerning the body. The two statements are connected, and Aquinas would strongly disagree with both of them. Morality at sword point (or gun point) is no morality at all. And a scientific salvation for the few would not be in keeping with the Christian message to the many. Both nonreductionistic materialism and Platonic vitalism agree on the need to use police-state tactics in order to insure that the material wealth, as well as the educational institutions, of a country are distributed according to the plan of the leaders. Aquinas, however, while admitting the importance of the body, would not use psychosomaticism with immortality to justify the use of force in order to have people fulfill their spiritual destinies. To the extent that you are forced to be moral by the pressures of external police power, the virtuous acts you may do are not really virtuous.

We can see this in our own society as well as in the communistic states. Much of our tax money goes towards the support of the needy—the unemployed, widows, orphans, and so forth. Some of it goes to give everyone the benefits of education and medical care. This is a variation on the tithing system, as it used to be called in religious circles, and is not a matter of choice on our part. It is something forced upon us. We are taught by the example of government practices that to hold back money from the tax collector is the most deadly of sins. Sometimes it appears to be the *only* sin recognized by the modern state.

Consequently, can we say that such "donations" are really meritorious and virtuous in a religious sense? It would seem not. You mean not even a little? Indeed, if we are to listen to the parable of the Pharisee and the Publican as recorded in Luke (18:9-14), even some of those who give voluntarily cannot be considered as pleasing in the sight of God. As a result, even though it may be wise to force people to do what they should do anyway as good Christians, Aquinas would say that such legislation can in no way be regarded as a substitute for a truly spiritual motivation.

This is the true meaning of the saying that governments cannot legislate morality. It means that laws alone will not change the hearts and minds of people. This is quite different from saying that the laws themselves are nonmoral or do not presuppose some definite ethical foundation. Every major piece of legislation, anywhere in the world, is in fact founded upon some set of philosophical or religious moral principles. In this sense every law necessarily legislates morality. In the sense of inner motivation, however, laws neither can nor should make people moral.

All this does not mean that a thinker should stop trying to motivate people to be moral through either faith or reason or both. As we have seen so far, everyone discussed has assigned an important place to behavior modification in his system of thought, being careful of course to adjust the recommended methods to his view of the true nature of the human person. Our survey of the possible positions, however, is not yet complete. There is one more possible paradigm on the human person that must be given serious attention, especially in view of the reductionistic theory, the view of the good and well-meaning George Berkeley, an Anglican bishop who died in 1753.

Matter

What is matter? That which has weight and occupies space? This definition of matter comes to us from the ancient atomists and is still to be found in many modern science textbooks in use around the world.[1] The original Greek atomists thought of the atoms as constantly falling through space. When an atom occupied a certain place, there was "being" in that place, but where there was no atom, there was the void or empty space. Exactly what the atoms were in themselves these thinkers could not say; at least it could not be determined by the use of the senses. The nature of the atoms could only be determined by reasoning. Today, even with electronic microscopes, we are no better off. The best the modern physicist can do in terms of direct observation is to see bright reflections of something or other. It also seems that regardless of how great the magnification, there is always something more to be observed and some background to that which is observed. This is the case on the concrete level of seeing.

Even on the theoretical level, though, there is deep trouble with the traditional view of matter. Cannot geometrical figures, which in the fashion of Descartes can be regarded as pure extension, occupy space? Descartes identified matter, extension, and space. What are geometrical figures if not mere two-dimensional extensions? Therefore, do not geometrical figures occupy space? And yet they have no matter, no body, and no weight. There is really nothing "solid" about such things, not even in solid geometry.

In a similar way it may be asked whether or not having weight is really a "solid" property of bodies. In modern times is not the experience of weight explained in terms of geometry? What we call weight is the result of the pull of gravity. But what is gravity? In the modern view of Albert Einstein the existence of gravity is due simply to acceleration. All bodies in the universe are in constant motion along curved paths of one size or another. Whenever a body moves in such a fashion, it accelerates. In one type of acceleration bodies are constantly "falling" to a center point. This "falling" is what we call gravity. Furthermore, it can be represented geometrically rather than in terms of unseen forces. Consequently, even weight does not express anything "solid" about a body.[2]

What is it then that we are talking about when we speak of matter? For the atomists it is unperceived and unchanging Being, for Plato it is the mysterious receptacle, for Aristotle and Aquinas it is the no less mysterious potency, for Dewey it is ambiguous and complex "Nature"—and for Berkeley it simply isn't! If no one knows what matter is anyway, including the modern scientist who is supposed to know these things, why do we bother with the notion at all? Perhaps we can eliminate it entirely and be none the worse off for having done so? And this is exactly what the good bishop did.

The Principles of Human Knowledge

What do we know, and how do we know it? These are the key questions Berkeley raised and answered in his main work *A Treatise Concerning the Principles of Human Knowledge*. It was first published in 1710 and saw a second edition in 1734. The work is divided into two parts: An Introduction and a Part I. There was supposed to have been a Part II, but Berkeley states in a November 25, 1729, letter to Samuel Johnson (the first president of Columbia University in New York City) that he had lost the partially completed draft of the second part in 1715 while traveling in Italy.

The same ideas contained in the 1710 *Principles* were somewhat later (1713) cast anew in a playlike form called *Three Dialogues Between Hylas and Philonous, In Opposition to Sceptics and Atheists*. Hylas comes from a Greek word meaning "matter," while the other name means love. This process of first writing a more scholarly work and later writing a more popular version was carried out later by Hume and Kant also.[3]

Part I is composed of 156 short sections, and indeed the whole thing is not very long. In the same letter to Johnson mentioned above the bishop also states that he had no desire to burden the world with large volumes of words for readers to wade through. Instead, he wanted to give the really intelligent people of the world some hints as to what the true state of affairs concerning matter really is so that they might go ahead and think things out for themselves—refreshing thoughts in any age.

The various sections break down into some main subdivisions. Sections 1 to 7 give the key argument and conclusion. Sections 8 to 15 raise and answer the main scientific objection of the time. Some secondary objections are brought up and answered in sections 16 to 21. Sections 22 to 24 give a recapitulation. God is discussed in sections 25 to 33. Some other philosophical and scientific objections are handled in sections 34 to 81. Sections 82 to 84 deal with certain religious objections, mainly that the Bible supposedly teaches that God created a material world. Some consequences of his position are discussed in sections 85 to 132, and the knowledge of spiritual entities is taken care of in sections 133 to 156.[4]

Abstract Ideas

Berkeley sets the stage for his position in the Introduction to his *Principles*. The whole of the Introduction is concerned with "abstract ideas." The entire contents of the mind, says Berkeley in section 1 of Part I, is exhausted by three types of ideas: Sensations, passions (love, hate, joy, grief, and so on), memories and imaginings. Where in this collection is there any room for abstract general ideas supposedly represented by general words and terms? Thanks to the analysis done in the Introduction, he can proceed with his reasoning process as if there were none. The whole point of the Introduction is to show that there are no such things as abstract general ideas. As strange as it may sound, in order to destroy matter, Berkeley must first destroy abstractions. Nevertheless, this is exactly how he attacks the problem of whether or not matter is an unnecessary hypothesis in the explanation of the universe.

What is an abstraction? It is one quality of a body considered as separate from all its other qualities. Such abstractions are carried out exclusively by the mind. It is the mind which takes apart a given combination of qualities and considers one to the exclusion of the others. Building upon this process of separation and segregation the mind can then look for what is common to all of the separated qualities (such as extension, color, and motion) and thereby frame abstract notions of each one.

The same can be done for more complicated things, such as a man or a dog. For such things the mind keeps leaving aside all of the noncommon qualities which are encountered in different examples and specimens until it arrives at the abstract idea of a man or some animal.

Berkeley is careful to speak about what the mind *can* do, not what it *must* do. He does this so that he can identify himself with the ordinary person in contrast with the overeducated know-it-all. Who deals in abstract ideas? The learned and pompous in education. Who takes things just as they are without becoming all entangled in metaphysics and logic? The ordinary person, the simple and illiterate man in the street. Such people may have general ideas insofar as they recognize one thing as the same type of thing as another thing, but they do not fool around with *abstract* general ideas. That is to say, they do not pretend to be able to take things apart and consider one part as existing separately without all of the other parts. Berkeley is proud to count himself among those who cannot do such things.

Let the so-called learned scholars busy themselves with such nonsense, but he will have nothing to do with it. When he possesses the idea of "man," claims Berkeley, it is always of some particular man. Each such "idea" will have very definite qualities with respect to color, shape, size, and so on. Likewise for a body in motion. Berkeley cannot get an idea of motion without there being some particular body in motion pictured before his mind's eye. Surely he can imagine apart things which can exist apart, such as a rider and his horse. But he can in no way *picture* apart things which cannot exist apart, such as the nature of a human being and some particular case of a human being.

The same would be true for the relationship between, say, a triangle and the nature of a triangle or triangleness. How in the world can we hold in our minds an "idea" of a triangle matching each and every particular triangle? As Berkeley goes on to point out, the ordinary person can get along quite well without such contrivances. Let the learned toy with their abstractions if they want to, but such toys, says Berkeley, are in no way necessary for either communication or science.

If at times abstractions do seem necessary for communication or the enlargement of knowledge, it is only because we are fooled by the way we use language. We think that words must stand for abstractions so that both words and abstractions must exist in order for people to talk to each other. Not so, declares the bishop. Every word, if properly analyzed, will be found to be the expression of some determinate and precise picture. Words do not represent abstractions but only concrete situations to be brought to the attention of the listener.

The great deception worked upon the ignorant by words is that the unlearned think they are missing something when they do not immediately apprehend the meaning of some fancy phrase used by a scholar. In fact, though, it is the other way around. The learned are the losers. They talk in abstractions and forget the concrete source from which all abstractions come and to which they must all return in order to make sense. What do we mean by a man? We mean John or Peter. What do we mean by motion? We mean the moving body. The attempted separation of human nature from John, or of motion from this moving body here and now, is the great False Principle which must be destroyed before the great True Principle can be appreciated.

To Exist Is to Be, or to Be Capable of Being, Perceived

With respect to human knowledge, what is the greatest example of the False Principle at work? It is the attempt to separate the existence of a material world from the mental perceptions by which it is present to us. Do mountains and rivers and houses really exist independently of our knowing minds? To say so would be an outright contradiction, thinks Berkeley. He states:

> For what are the forementioned objects but the things we perceive by sense. And what do we perceive besides our own ideas or sensations. And is it not plainly repugnant that any one of these, or any combination of them, should exist unperceived. (I, 4)

Therefore, the existence of anything is only in the mind. If a thing is unperceived by either a created spirit or by God, then it simply does not exist at all. And existence is to be precisely identified with such perception. Consequently nothing in the world exists except individual minds or spirits. All reality is in individual perceptions and all perceptions are in individual minds, either created or divine. "From what has been said it is evident there is not any other substance than spirit, or that which perceives." (I, 7)

It does no good to throw against Berkeley the criticism, as was done in the form of a humorous limerick, that his view entails the disappearance of anything you may not be thinking of at the moment.

> There was once a young man who said, God
> Must think it exceedingly odd
> If he finds that this tree
> Continues to be
> When there's no one about in the Quad.

Berkeley could very well reply, as did an anonymous defender of his in the twentieth century, that things do have a continuous existence as long as they continue to be perceived by God. As long as at least God thinks of something it continues to exist. Hence the reply:

Young man your astonishment's odd.
I'm always about in the Quad.
And that's why the tree
Will continue to be
Since perceived by
          Yours faithfully,

                              God.

Matter an Unnecessary Hypothesis

After proving, based upon his psychological definition of existence, that there is no such thing as matter at all, Berkeley goes on to answer the main objection against his rather radical conclusion. We can now understand, because of what is coming in sections 8 to 15, why he devoted the first pages of his book to the destruction of abstract general ideas. The main objection runs thusly.

"To be" may mean to be perceived as far as subjective experience is concerned, but what about the objective existence of matter, either in discrete amounts as the atomists taught or as continuous quantity as Descartes taught? Bearing in mind that Descartes was known as a scientist at the time and that atomism was adopted by such great scientists as Newton, the rebuttal seemed a strong one. In effect it said that you must be wrong, my good bishop, because your contemporary scientists say so.

At this point Berkeley achieves his greatest glory. Not only don't the scientists prove him wrong, he gloats, they prove him right. In order to establish his reductionistic immaterialism, all he must do is seriously and honestly take the scientists at their word.

How do the scientists define matter? It is said to be mere extension with various shapes and sizes. In themselves the pieces of matter are inert, senseless, and dead. By pushes and pulls they rearrange their positions relative to each other. We know about these properties through the process of abstraction. In the observed world we have a colored shape. We then proceed to separate the color from the shape and say that in the world outside of our minds bodies have various shapes just like the ones we actually observe. The same is said for extension, size, and motion. We attribute to unobserved matter characteristics like some of the things we observe around us.

But that is not all. Certain other traits of bodies, such as their color, hardness, smoothness, smell, taste, sound, and in fact anything other than the qualities supposedly really in the matter of the bodies, we attribute to the knowing subject rather than to the extramental material body. In other words, certain qualities are supposedly really *only in us* while certain other qualities are supposedly really only in matter. Our "ideas" of these latter qualities, which are said to be really only in matter, cannot be directly perceived by us but are said to be known by a sort of analogy with those qualities which are in us and so are capable of being observed by us.

Now that the scientists have so obligingly stuck out their necks for him, Berkeley finds it an easy task to chop off their heads. How are we supposed to know about these "primary" qualities, the ones which are said to really be in material bodies? Is it not via the "secondary" qualities, the ones which are said to really be in us? If so, then does this not mean that all of the so-called primary qualities are really in us as well?

If all cases of extension, figure, motion, and position are ideas, and all ideas are in the mind, how can you avoid the conclusion that all cases of extension, shape, motion, and position are also in the mind?

> But it is evident from what we have already shown that extension, figure, and motion are only ideas existing in the mind, and that an idea can be like nothing but another idea, and that consequently neither they nor their archetypes can exist in an unperceiving substance. (I, 9)

In short, what do we know first and foremost? Our own ideas of sensible qualities. And where do the scientists themselves admit them to be? Only in the perceiver. How then do we know about the primary qualities? Only through the secondary sense qualities. Where are these primary qualities then? Only in the perceiver.

To try to understand better what Berkeley is getting at, imagine that you are asked to state the type of triangle that is drawn on an unmarked blackboard. You of course say that you cannot possibly answer the question until you actually see the triangle drawn on the blackboard. However, to do so would mean coming up with some color differentiation between the blackboard and the triangle. The shape or figure of the triangle must somehow stand out against its background. Hence, the knowledge of the shape *depends* upon a knowledge of the color. But where is the color? In us. Hence, the shape is not really "out there" either but really only in us as well. This is true for all the other so-called primary qualities also. Consequently, *everything* material is really only in us. In truth there are no such things as outward material things at all. (I, 15)

The Person

Berkeley begins where Plato left off. Plato was willing to admit the existence of a material body along with the soul. Berkeley is not. For Berkeley the only reality is the soul. Everything else is *in* the soul. It is a fact that we have ideas of a sensual, passional, and imaginative nature. These ideas cannot exist alone somehow suspended from sky-hooks.[5] They must be the property of some subject. And "This perceiving, active being is what I call mind, spirit, soul, or myself." (I, 2)

It is plain to Berkeley that the human person must be identified with nothing more or less than the soul. An obvious objection to this position is that if "to be" means to be perceived, should we not have ideas of our own souls, the souls of others, and of God as well? That is to say, why is not the existence of spiritual entities obvious rather than a matter of hot dispute? Here one might suspect that Berkeley would begin to worry that there was something wrong with his identification of intellectual ideas (concepts) with imaginative pictures (Berkeley's "ideas"). It is clear from his later writings that he greatly respected Plato. Yet, he seems to have missed Plato's main point in his analysis of knowledge, namely, that there is a radical difference between an idea and a picture.

Berkeley tries to escape the difficulty by introducing a new word into his scheme of things. We may not have an idea of the soul but we can have a "notion" of it (I, 27, 142). He wants to say that the soul is a substance. This cannot be done in terms of ideas. Ideas are not substances, only passing modifications within individual minds. Consequently he must find some way of telling an idea apart from a substance.

His method for doing so is to appeal to activity. The soul is a substance because it acts. As a substance it is "that which perceives ideas, and wills, and reasons about them." (I, 139) To say "I" is the same as saying "soul" or "spiritual substance." And what am I if not a center of activity?

Ideas, on the other hand, do not act. They are simply the results of the interactions between two or more minds. This is something we know about by living within ourselves. It is something we either know about or we do not. No one else can tell us about it. If we have any doubts on the subject, we can prove it to ourselves by trying to deny our own existence. If we should try saying something like "I am not here" or "I am nothing," we would immediately see how absurd it is to try to deny that we are the center of our own activity. In contrast to ideas, then, there can be no doubt that I am a substance and that there is a vast difference between myself and my ideas. Berkeley tells us:

> All the unthinking objects of the mind agree in that they are entirely passive, and their existence consists only in being perceived; whereas a soul or spirit is an active being, whose existence consists, not in being perceived, but in perceiving ideas and thinking. (I, 139)

The main source of error in saying that there is a material world existing independently of each mind is the fact that the mind normally does not go around trying to say things like "I don't exist." Usually we take no notice of our own minds but simply pay attention to the ideas which are given to the mind. If and when we do pay attention to our own mental operations, it is very easy to see that there must be a mental substance underlying the ideas. Every mental operation must of necessity involve a mind. So, even though there is absolutely no need to invoke matter as the cause of my ideas, there is no possible way I can avoid invoking myself as the active subject of my own ideas. (I, 23, 24)

Equally important with our ability to think is our ability to will. The human person or bodiless soul, even though without matter, can still perform acts of will power. A spirit is one undivided active being. Insofar as it perceives, it is a knowing thing. And insofar as it acts on other spirits or on itself, it is a willing thing. These are the two principal powers of a person: Thought and Will. (I, 27)

It is important for Berkeley to emphasize the will. How else would we know about other minds if they were not capable of spontaneous actions? How would we be able to explain evil ideas (that is, occurrences) if they were not given to us by God to test our wills? As spiritual beings all minds possess the power to change things by their wills. This can be accomplished either internally, as when we choose to concentrate our attention upon something or when we use our powers of imagination to rearrange ideas into some new combination; or externally, as when we project ideas to other minds. Whether it is God or some created spirit which exercises his will upon us is unimportant to Berkeley. The same principle still holds. Without matter, the will becomes the element of prime importance when analyzing how it is possible to have any activity at all in the universe. (I, 145)

Everything is therefore very nicely rounded off and explained. I have ideas, they are *my* ideas, they are only in my mind, and I can act both on myself and others. As a person I am an active soul, and the whole of the material universe insofar as it is said to exist independently of any mind is both a contradiction in terms and an unnecessary supposition in the explanation of nature.

BACKGROUND

Spirit Versus Matter

Berkeley begins his argument against the independent existence of matter by giving the same list of ideas as John Locke had done before him. Ideas derive from three sources, namely, sensations, internal reflections, and a combination of the two. There are no innate ideas. We do, however, possess innate abilities, such as the power of reasoning itself, which are born within us as part of our human nature. Thus said Locke.

In addition, Locke had gone ahead and added the primary-secondary sense quality distinction to his list of things necessary in order to account for human knowledge. We have already seen from chapter 2 why this was necessary, not only for Locke but for any atomist who wanted to be consistent in his thinking. In order to avoid an infinite regress which merely repeated the data to be explained, the principles of explanation (the atoms) cannot possess the same characteristics as the things to be explained (our ideas). So it is that bodies really possess certain qualities and not others. Among these qualities for Locke were bulk, figure, number, situation, motion and rest, the power to produce sensations in sentient creatures, and the power to produce changes in other bodies.

As far as the static traits of bodies are concerned, it is easy to see, as in the case of Descartes as well, that they are precisely the traits needed to make it easy for the scientist to handle the physical world in a strictly mathematical fashion. The talk about "power," though, is something else. This was needed by Locke in order to explain how one body can affect and change another body. It's a matter of common observation which Locke could not afford to leave out.[6]

Berkeley was not about to leave out powers and causal connections either. He was, though, going to restrict them to spiritual souls. Those who think in material terms like to go around saying that fire, for instance, is the cause of pain in my hand when I touch it. Not so, claimed Berkeley. "To all which my answer is, first, that the connection of ideas does not imply a relation of cause and effect, but only a mark or sign with the thing signified." (I, 65) Having ideas, supposedly produced in us by material things, in no way proves that matter exists. What we call a cause-effect relationship in the outside world is merely a certain orderly array of ideas produced in us by God or his agents. Nonexistent matter cannot be the real cause of anything. And so-called effects are only the signs or marks by which I become aware of the presence of some active and willful spirit.

Neither was Berkeley about to allow the view that matter existed in a perfectly powerless state, that is, as a purely passive medium through which God acts upon human minds. If in fact every idea I have comes from God anyhow, as some such as Malebranche maintain, then why must there be some intervening third party between God and me? If God alone is the real cause of anything and everything that happens, why worry about a material medium at all? What purpose does it serve? Is this not to also multiply entities without need? Berkeley thought it was and called such a weak attempt to save matter an "extravagant supposition." (I, 53, 67-72)

In all, then, Berkeley took as his adversary anyone who said that matter really existed independently of any mind. In doing so he thought of himself as merely bringing to its proper logical conclusion the line of thought started by the scientists themselves. If his view appeared foolish, it was not his fault. Berkeley was simply pointing out to the reductionistic materialists that what they were really advocating was reductionistic *im*materialism. Such a conclusion was the inevitable outcome of thinking consistently on the subject. If his adversaries failed to think their position all the way through, *they* are to be held responsible for a lack of intellectual honesty, not the good bishop.

If they should ever go all the way in their reasoning, and find that they cannot stand the conclusion, let them either change their starting point or retire from the field. Berkeley, for his part, will fight on sure of victory. And why should he not be confident of winning; he is after all using the same weapons forged by the materialists. The difference is that Berkeley is using them with great skill, while they are using them clumsily. With such superior firepower he cannot lose.

SOME CONSEQUENCES

God Must Exist

Berkeley says that his whole demonstration of the nonexistence of matter can be given in "a line or two." (I, 22) By the same token the existence of God can be established quite easily. In truth, "nothing can be more evident to anyone that is capable of the least reflection than the existence of God." (I, 149) This is not to say that we *see* God. We can no more see God directly than we can see other minds. (I, 148) No, we must demonstrate the existence of God. However, the demonstration is so simple that anyone who tries can easily understand it.

We begin with the fact that matter does not exist. Also, we note that only spiritual things can be active. Moreover, we observe that we are not in complete control of the ideas we possess. There are many ideas we want to have but do not. Conversely, there are many ideas we want to get rid of but we cannot. There are also many cases in which ideas of a more or less neutral nature come to us whether or not we want them.

For instance, assuming that I have normal vision, when I open my eyes in a lighted place, I will see. Much of what I see is not dependent upon *my* will. After observing things for a while I also become aware of something else. The perceptions which impress themselves upon me are of an orderly and lawlike nature. Their very regularity is something over which I have no control. These regularities are studied in the natural sciences. Yet more, we observe that *no one* of a human or lesser nature can exercise any great control over the scientific series of events.

What are we to conclude from all of this? Since the constant and regular sequences of events in nature cannot be the work of my will, nor of any other finite creature, they must be the doing of the divine will. The creative scientist at work is the divine will or spirit. "There is therefore some other Will or Spirit that produces them." (I, 29) And this Spirit we call God. By God's will they come to be. As Berkeley likes to repeat from the *Acts of the Apostles* (17:28), it is the Supreme Active Principle, the All-Wise Spirit, the Author of Nature, "in whom we live, move, and have our being." (I, 66, 149) His argument in a nutshell is that without God we could not explain our lack of control over much of our experience. No human or angelic mind would be adequate to explain the wonders of nature.

Furthermore, as Newton showed so well, the universe is unified according to one set of all-pervasive laws. This must mean that the divine mind which continues to give us the vast array of perceptions we call the world must be one also. Monotheism is secure in Berkeley's system thanks to science. More than anything else, though, it is the intimacy with God which Berkeley likes to emphasize. The one God, each mind, and the world are all inseparable. (I, 32, 150, 155)

Consider the general intensity and vividness of our ideas of the world as compared to the general weakness of our own self-generated ideas. To Berkeley this means that God is closer to us than we are to ourselves. The mere fact that we normally pay more attention to the world than to our own internal operations should indicate to the intelligent thinker that God is always with us. This is certainly what Scripture has always told us. Yet the doctrine of Deism, which teaches that God is some kind of absentee landlord (and maybe a slumlord at that), is widespread among the learned.

There is absolutely no need for such a situation. Reductionistic immaterialism is the perfect remedy. No one can claim to do away with God for even a second. He is as close to us as our ideas of the wonderful world of color and sound. Driving home this truth about the intimacy of God and his people is Berkeley's main purpose in all of his labors. Referring to his arguments for a complete immaterialism, Berkeley says that he shall regard them as altogether useless if they should fail to inspire his readers "with a pious sense of the presence of God." (I, 156)

Immortality

"The natural immortality of the soul is a necessary consequence of the foregoing doctrine." (I, 141) As with Plato, the immortality of the human soul is a foregone conclusion once the nature of the soul is known. However, as with Descartes, Berkeley was also a Christian working with Revelation in mind. This meant that although the person (soul) could be immortal with respect to the future, he could not preexist the body. Each soul is the individual creation of God. And, even if there is no body in reality, the *idea* of the body will serve the same purpose. The impressions we have of the new soul (that is, the newborn baby) reveal to us its existence, first to the mother and then to the other spirits in the world.

The nature of each soul is to be an unextended, indivisible unity with the powers of intellect and will. Since the soul has no parts, there is nothing to come apart, and hence the soul is incorruptible. The only way it could possibly be destroyed is through a deliberate act on the part of God. But this is not about to happen given what we are told in Scripture. By the forces of nature alone, however, there is no room for any sort of dissolution. This is what Berkeley means when he says that each soul is naturally immortal.

Explaining the resurrection of the body is also rendered quite easy based upon his doctrine. The whole argument and debate over resurrection centers around whether or not we can have the *same* body after the resurrection as before. But, as anyone can plainly see, once the body is eliminated, the whole problem disappears. Berkeley, to verge on a pun, doesn't so much solve the problem as dissolve it. There can be no question about the identity of two material bodies if there are no such things in the first place. Instead of listening to endless debates among the learned, why not take "body" to mean what every plain person takes it to mean? asks Berkeley.

The learned talk about some inert extension which remains the same while undergoing all sorts of variations in position and motion.

The ordinary person, on the other hand, when he speaks about body, simply means that which is immediately seen and felt. Body to him is only a combination of many sensible qualities. Why, then, could not God see fit to reproduce these same ideas, in a glorified state, at the time of the resurrection of the body? (I, 95)

The End of Skepticism, Atheism, and Irreligion

You can't very well be a materialist if there is no matter in the first place. Or can you? The whole point of Berkeley's attack on that worst of all abstractions, matter, is to pull the rug out from underneath the enemies of religion. Do away with matter and a new wave of religious inspiration will sweep the world. He announces:

> For, as we have shown the doctrine of matter or corporeal sub-stance to have been the main pillar and support of scepticism, so likewise upon the same foundation have been raised all the impious schemes of atheism and irreligion. (I, 92)

Beginning with the materialist's own assumptions Berkeley devised a way of removing this pillar of support. Rather than an eternal, stu-pid, unthinking "I know not what" resting at the root of all reality he saw the world as composed of nothing but God, created souls, and their mutual interactions. He hoped that such a new scheme of things would prove so uncomfortable to the skeptics and atheists of his age that they would soon all perish. We must not underestimate his dislike for such people. Their views are "monstrous" and as human beings they are "wretched." (I, 92) It was his fond desire to see them utterly disgraced in the view of the public.

Berkeley looked upon himself as the champion of all religious thinkers. Indeed, it would be hard to imagine his doing more in the way of undermining the materialists. Without independently existing and unperceived matter to appeal to the Epicureans, "Hobbists and the like" will never again be able to trouble a true seeker after truth. Berkeley sincerely believed this. (I, 93)

When matter is pushed out of the universe, it drags with it a whole host of skeptical and impious doctrines. No longer will it be necesary to waste so much time disputing with the impious dregs of mankind.

In the future the time of good men and women can instead be spent upon the great and large religious enterprise of bettering the human race.

This, at least, is the dream, says Berkeley, when he sets out his demonstrations against the impious. And, he adds, even if his arguments are not fully cogent, "I am sure all friends to knowledge, peace, and reason have reason to wish they were." (I, 96)

Unfortunately for such people the bishop's arguments are not overwhelming when it comes to their practical consequences. In order for Berkeley to make his case useful for religious purposes, it is important that he clearly show the need for a cause behind the ideas or perceptions. If he harbored any self-doubts about his case, as indicated in the passage just quoted, they were most likely due to precisely this point.

It is all fine and well to do away with matter and then appeal to God in order to explain appearances, but what if someone refuses to take that all-important step from the obvious existence of his own perceptions to some cause of those perceptions? Why not simply stop with the fact of ideas and simply ignore the question of origins? This is what David Hume did. Hume even backed up his case with arguments to show that, not only are all perceptions only within the mind, but that all causal relationships are only in the mind as well.[7]

As a result mankind was plunged into a worse form of skepticism than that from which Berkeley proposed to save it. The fate of his position is therefore sealed. The human person may be only a naked soul, but it is a very lonely and isolated soul. It may not have any causal links with matter, but then it cannot have any causal links with anything else either.

Behavior Modification

The typical objection against Berkeley's position was that it denied all the ordinary human experiences of material things. Berkeley always emphatically denied this charge. He was not destroying the reality of nature. He was only doing away with the unperceived substratum of nature. He was concerned only with the *causes* of the appearances. It never entered his head to destroy the appearances themselves. Do away with appearances and they will certainly be missed. However, do away with the unobservable substratum of the appearances and it will never be missed. (I, 35)

By the same token science is saved. What does science deal with anyway? Only with the appearances of things. It deals with how they are ordered and related to each other and nothing more. The wise scientist will stay away from speculations about the hidden causes of things. He will leave that sort of question to be answered by the philosopher and theologian. The scientist's job is to observe carefully and order his observations in terms of comprehensive laws concerning the harmonious workings of nature. As long as the scientist does this and no more, he will have no quarrel with Berkeley. (I, 105)

B. F. Skinner, the reductionistic materialist, made a point of saying that even though his view of the human person was the true one, the way things *really* are, life would still go on as usual. He could see no reason for insisting that people have new and different perceptions of things. A wise move—and one taken by Berkeley as well many years before Skinner.

It was Berkeley's aim to follow Sir Francis Bacon and think with the learned but speak with the vulgar. What constitutes a learned person, of course, must be reinterpreted. The truly learned person is the one who follows Berkeley. But, the fact that he knows that there is no matter in reality is no reason to stop talking about it. Berkeley cites Copernicus as an example of someone who, although he knew that the earth goes around the sun, did not hesitate to talk about the *sun's* coming up in the morning. In a similar fashion everyone is free to go ahead and talk about matter, just so long as they know that matter means no more than what is immediately perceived by the senses. In ordinary life nothing need change (I, 51, 52).

Skinner has said basically the same thing. Surely one reductionism is as radical as the other. Yet nothing in ordinary life need change insofar as ordinary experience is concerned. We can still go ahead and talk about mind if we wish. All we must admit, says Skinner, is that such talk is unscientific; that it is not about the way things really are. What Berkeley calls reality Skinner calls superficial appearance and vice versa. Neither man, however, would deny the other the right to go on using ordinary language and having ordinary feelings about himself and the world.

Nevertheless, there is a great difference when it comes to modes of behavior and the means for changing modes of behavior. We have already seen the consequences of reductionistic materialism in this regard. We should not be surprised to learn that Berkeley's position has precisely the contrary effects. In a universe of spiritual minds with no bodies there is nothing else to appeal to except the minds and wills of these persons. The right *knowledge* of reality will provide each person with the motivation to *do* what is right, with the main standards for what is right coming from the Bible.

With continued practice and self-discipline willing what is right is bound to become easier and easier. The use of images in helping the formation of spiritual character is not forbidden, but people must always be aware of the true nature of the images. People can continue to enjoy their food, workers can continue to use their tools, and scientists can continue to carry on with their experiments. However, everyone must know that their ideas of things do not come from matter. They come from the only active principles in reality, namely, spiritual minds. Any lasting changes in the world for the good must therefore come through the spirit. All the money in the world will not produce the good life in the good society if the minds of people remain unaltered. This is something every politician should know before he sets about trying to buy his way into heaven—even if it is just a heaven on earth.

CHAPTER 8

Conclusions

ALL ROADS LEAD TO ELEA

Great minds are troubled by little things and details or at least by ordinary things. The average person does not give a moment's thought to whether or not he is dreaming when he is awake or vice versa. Neither is he ever at pains to prove the existence of the external material world. A great mind like Descartes's, though, gave a great deal of thought to such things. If a great mind like Descartes's thinks great thoughts, thoughts worthy of contemplation by other great minds, it is because they are stimulated by things the ordinary person simply takes for granted.

Another great mind of the past was Parmenides. He lived in Elea, a little town on the western coast of southern Italy. His disciples became known as the Eleatics. As we have seen over and over again, when it comes to the question of what constitutes the human person, it is the issue of the meaning of existence raised by Parmenides which dominates the various answers given.

As we have also seen, when it comes to answering the question about the status of the human person relative to other things in the universe, none of the six basic positions is haphazard or accidental. Each one represents a carefully worked out system of things with a beginning, a middle, and an end. One part flows from another part so that the whole makes up a self-contained set of principles and consequences. These premises and conclusions are not based upon mere feelings or some bad dream someone may have had the night before the theory was worked out. Rather, they are serious attempts at establishing a rational and scientific edifice capable of sustaining the weight of the experiential data. If some tuning up or readjustment is required in order to maintain the edifice in a solid and stable condition, it is never the result of a mere whim or fancy. There is a reason behind each and every readjustment deemed necessary. If it were not deemed necessary for rational and scientific reasons, it would never have been insitituted in the first place.

To say this, however, does not mean that there is nothing at all which is arbitrary in each one of the six possible theories discussed. Indeed there is something arbitrary in each case. Exactly what it is, though, is often overlooked because it occurs at the very beginning of the reasoning process. The roads leading to the various final views on the human person diverge early in the game. If you are not quick, you are likely to miss the turnoff completely. Like traveling by car through unfamiliar territory, the signs you need to give you directions are very often passed before you are even aware that you need them. If those well-meaning investigators who wander into the area of trying to decipher the human person often get hopelessly lost, this is probably the reason for it. To be a successful traveler, in one way or another, you must know the territory. This means in practice either making your own map or depending upon somebody else's map. The aim of the foregoing chapters has been to draw you a reliable map.

THE MANY FACES OF SCIENCE

As we have learned, there is no such thing as *the* scientific method. With due consideration and circumspection the vast majority of those who think about it will sooner or later realize the truth of this statement. Nevertheless, even while thinking it to be true the tendency is to back away from it and not act upon it. An example of this attitude would be that expressed by Edna Heidbreder in the "Afterthought" to her admirable work entitled *Seven Psychologies*.

Writing earlier in our century, she states that psychology as a science still has a long way to go. It has not yet made its great discovery that will put it on a par with the physical and biological sciences. Physics has its laws of motion, chemistry has its atomic theory, and biology has its evolutionary doctrine. Psychology, however, is still waiting for its

Newton, Dalton, or Darwin. "Nothing that gives it a unifying principle has yet been discovered or recognized," she says.[1] The situation
has not changed very much since these words were written in 1933,
except perhaps that scientists are now a little less sure about whether or
not the *other* sciences have really found *their* unifying principles.

Yet, the fact that psychologists fight among themselves more than
do those in the other disciplines should not, she thinks, be regarded as
being to their discredit. Zestful rivalry may be the best way to achieve
good and lasting results in the long run. Mutual intolerance may be
just what the doctor ordered when it comes to stimulating new experiments and subsequent discoveries. For what is science anyway? It is
neither the means nor the conditions of its own production. Then
what is it? The scientific end product is the only thing that counts. To
be scientific it must be impartial and impersonal. But how do we get
from pre-science to science? That is of secondary importance, claims
Heidbreder.[2]

This sounds good—but then she proceeds to retract all the good
things she has just said. What is it that all the schools regard as the
proper test of a doctrine? It is nothing other than "experimental veri-
fication." It is *only* by making actual trials of their assertions that the
various schools of psychology have come to make whatever acquisitions
they actually possess. This emphasis upon the laboratory test-tube
approach to the meaning of science—the only true science—seems to
me to contradict directly the open-mindedness hinted at in the earlier
part of her statement on the nature of science. Unfortunately there are
still many people in the world today who will claim not to understand
what I am saying. "But," someone is sure to ask, "what other
meaning can science possibly have?"

Such a question implies an adherence to the reductionistic materialism view of the human person. For people like Skinner science is
simply the method for obtaining ostensive definitions of things. It is
here that the arbitrary element comes into the system. Once it is decided that the only approach proper to science is the test-tube approach, it is quite easy to eliminate from science anything that cannot
be so measured. The methodology implicitly becomes the standard of
reality. Whatever fits the methodology is real, and whatever does not
fit cannot be taken seriously.

From this point on there is an easy and natural step from what is im-
plicit to what is explicit. The obvious question is why does the meth-

odology work? The obvious answer is that it must work because the world is amenable to exactly such an approach. But what kind of world is it? Obviously it must be one composed solely of matter in motion in which everything is on a par. Consequently, what was a methodology easily becomes an explanation of why things are the way they are. In other words, instead of reality dictating the methodology, methodology determines reality.

Nonreductionistic materialism cannot be satisfied with such an impoverishment of reality. Common sense cannot be ignored. All the important, yet nonmeasurable, aspects of life must also be allowed to find a place in one's scientific explanation of the human person. This necessarily involves a reinterpretation of science. No longer can the "scientific" be identified with the measurable. There must instead be a movement in our thinking in the direction of the underlying causes of the things experienced. Science is broader than material laboratory methods. This must be our attitude at the beginning of our inquiry rather than something we get around to later on.

Yet how can the investigator accept feelings, mind, freedom, and so on as being on a par with matter in terms of their reality without becoming involved with the spiritual or at least with the immaterial? Solving this problem means putting a heavy emphasis upon evolutionary doctrine. Some mechanism must be found whereby we can account for the true novelty of things in the world without giving up our materialism.

Thanks to Hegel such a mechanism was discovered. The leap from quantity to quality allowed for both continuity and discontinuity in nature. There could be radical differences and material continuity at the same time in the same universe. Now the nonreductionistic materialists could both have their cake and eat it too. They could share with their reductionistic brothers the desire to discover "missing links," some human traits (such as social behavior and language) in the primates, and in general to find shades of gray up and down the whole scale of living things. Since there must be a material buildup before the qualitative leap occurs, it appeared to those in position two that they could have the best of both worlds: The continuity of human features in lower species *and* a unique status for the human person as a higher species.

The psychosomaticism without immortality position, however, has no predisposition to remain materialistic in any strict way. According to this third theory science is a certain type of knowledge. How it is acquired is of secondary importance. No one single methodology is dictated. The aim of science is to find the causes behind occurrences. How this is to be done is another question altogether. It could be by pure reasoning alone. Or it could be by some combination of reasoning, ordinary experience, and deliberately contrived experimental work. In any event, it is the end product that counts. And, if it should turn out that part of one's discovery about himself or herself includes the immaterial as well as the material, then so be it. Let the chips fall where they may.

The remaining three positions continue this attitude. In psychosomaticism with immortality we find the added feature of Revelation. Theology is now also regarded as a science. Its subject matter is different; yet its aim is still to discover why things are the way they are. This much at least remains the same. In this fourth view we found that we must take existence itself seriously if we are to discuss the possibility of rationally proving the immortality of the human soul. Starting with God's revelation of himself as pure existence, everything else follows. All creatures must be ratios of essence and existence. By conceiving of the soul (a notion introduced in the previous theory) as a substance of essence and existence the investigator can rationally discuss its continuity after death as well as its reunion with its body at some time in the future.

Obviously this is a paradigm in which it is impossible for someone to be a follower of the living God of Abraham, Isaac, and Jacob and then go on reasoning as if Scripture did not exist. For Aquinas Scripture, which is the source of the problem on how to reconcile religion and science, is also the source of the answer. If it were not for Scripture, we would never know about the free creation of a good material world. But then neither would we have the problems of trying to explain how a necessarily good material world can contain so much evil, or how there can be so much routine stability all around us.

Just here, though, Scripture comes to the rescue, for if it were not for Scripture, we would never have learned God's *nomen proprium*: He Who Is. But now we do know it, and it no longer makes any sense to pretend that we do not. "Existentialism" cannot be avoided by any Judeo-Christian thinker. It is the intelligibility of existence *(esse)* and its superiority over essence (the "what") that simultaneously account for *both* the possibility of a created universe inhabited by human beings living with the burden of free choice and original sin *and*, because of the existence of essences, for the possibility of scientific knowledge in the human person. Truly then, for psychosomaticism with immortality, Scripture is the solution.

As we saw, in contrast to psychosomaticism without immortality, the fourth position was able to set apart human souls from all others in the material world. Aristotle saw no need to do so. In his eternal world with its eternal species the existence of human persons was as much to be taken for granted as the rest of the universe. Human beings were regarded as coming about via a process of natural generation from previously existing specimens just as everything else in the higher biosphere. To talk of the need for the special creation of each human soul would have seemed ridiculous to the Greek. Likewise for human culture. Everything went in eternal cycles, including learning. How many "Aristotles" have existed before me? Aristotle must have often wondered to himself.

Not so for Aquinas. For him not one thing was to be taken for granted. For him the universe has a beginning; it was created. Now, regardless of the actual age of the universe (and even one a trillion years old would still be as nothing when compared to eternity), this one fact alone was enough to sever completely any really fundamental doctrinal affinity Aquinas might have had with the Greeks. And once one special creation is admitted, why not others when the evidence seems to call for them? This was the situation as Saint Thomas saw it with respect to the human person. He had to leave Aristotle if he was to agree with Saint Paul in his letter to the Colossians that no longer was there any difference between Jew and gentile, master and slave. People could only be equal by being created, and being recreated through Christ, equal.

Vitalism, the fifth theory, also prides itself on the way in which it is committed to science, or necessary and universal knowledge. It is not, however, very much interested in preserving the unity of each individual human person. For Aristotle and Aquinas the soul is necessarily related to a body. In fact, if it were not, it would be improper even to call it a soul. For this reason, if one were to be strictly technical, it would not be proper to call Plato's "soul" or mind-substance a soul.

However, be that as it may, science in this view is a purely intellectual and rational enterprise. It has nothing whatsoever to do with the senses. There is a radical break between the intellect or mind on the one side and the body with its material senses on the other side. To know something scientifically means to grasp its causes in terms of its corresponding Eternal Idea in the realm of unchanging Being. The senses cannot contribute to such an enterprise in any way. In fact, if anything, they actually cut down the chances of success. They are nothing more than distractions leading the knower away from his innate knowledge of the Ideas.

No wonder the only science Plato showed much interest in was mathematics. But even this was only propaedeutic to his real interest in a higher wisdom. This higher wisdom, or philosophy, was the only true science for a vitalist such as Plato. The reason is that only in the Ideas can the investigator be sure to find necessary and universal knowledge. Since it is only the mind which can achieve any contact with this realm of Ideas for even short segments of time, it is only the mind which has any right to be called a person. In its own way, therefore, vitalism is as scientific as any other position on the human person. It would be a gross error, consequently, to make Plato, the great fact-respecting student of human knowledge, into a purveyor of some strange oriental mysticism.

After all, the vitalist might ask, if you are going after intelligible causes, why not go all the way to the top? After all, does not each of the other positions aim at exactly the same thing? They all want an ultimate explanation in terms of ultimate causes. To achieve this end requires a knowledge of reality. Regardless of how the really real is viewed, therefore, whether materialistically or not, we must not overlook this basic point of methodological agreement among the various theories.

Finally, reductionistic immaterialism is no exception to this pattern of events. Berkeley lived at the junction of two streams of events in England. One stream was the widespread acceptance of atomism by the learned and scientific segment of society. The other was the spread of atheism. There was a need to reestablish the values of the Judeo-Christian tradition. By 1700 Europe had seen the optimism and hope which so dominated the thirteenth century being washed away. Whereas Aquinas was representative of the combination of faith *and* reason, Berkeley could see that his own times were becoming more and more dominated by skepticism and atheism.

What to do? He reacted against this trend by sharply criticizing the skeptics, atheists, and all other "freethinkers" both on a personal basis and on a scientific basis. As Plato before him, he saw the need for a moral reformation in the materialists before they were even open-minded enough to discuss religious matters rationally. He had no patience with those who only took and never gave. He was intolerant of those who freely used the interest from a capital investment but who denied the very existence of the capital funds themselves.

If someone were to injure an atheist, he would be the first one to cry "foul." The materialist is the sort of person who expects others to treat him according to Judeo-Christian values but who does not expect the same of himself toward others, claiming that such standards are too high, too scientifically unproven, or otherwise too uncertain for him to act upon. Would that all such wretched hypocrites could be removed from society altogether! Thus thought Berkeley.

Also with respect to the atheistic claim that the standards of the Bible are too high for ordinary people, Berkeley agrees with someone such as Aquinas that such a claim cannot be taken seriously for at least two other reasons. In the first place, if the speaker were ever to realize fully the debt he owes to the Bible, he would also have to realize the uncompromising nature of Scripture. Jesus pronounced several "hard sayings" concerning moral behavior. Should these be taken seriously at face value? Of course, thinks the bishop, and no amount of juggling with the texts by half-baked theologians can eliminate them.

Secondly, such an attitude is highly impractical. To those who would go around saying that it is better to "aim low but be sure of hitting your mark," Berkeley would respond that "if you would hit a low mark, you had better aim high." The overwhelming evidence from human experience is that the vast majority of people are lucky to achieve even 50 percent of their goal. If the goal itself were to be lowered to only 50 percent, on average and over the long haul the best you could hope to achieve might be 25 percent. If you want a decent society, therefore, the only practical thing to do is constantly to hammer high ideals into the heads of the populace. So it makes no sense to talk about the atheists as the down-to-earth thinkers. When it comes to behavior modification, they are the most impractical of people and the most ignorant of human psychology.

An example of the sort of thing Berkeley is talking about, to use one of his own examples, would be legalized gambling. Berkeley rejects the whole notion of a private vice which is, at the same time, a public virtue. Lowering public standards of morality does not produce general satisfaction in society, but only the desire for yet lower standards. Allow people to be licentious in one way, and what happens? They start looking for new avenues of lascivious behavior. The "something-for-nothing" attitude fostered by gambling, for instance, soon leads to other forms of unrealistic expectations. In due time the behavior of the whole society slowly disintegrates into a corrupt paganism. What is behind legalized gambling anyhow? Merely a shortsighted economic expedient used by irresponsible politicians looking for easy money with which to buy votes, influence, and armies. For these reasons, thinks Berkeley, the whole atheistic approach to public affairs is destructive. The sooner such an attitude is eliminated from society the better.[3]

What better way could be found for discrediting the atheists than by removing the very foundation of their materialism? As it happened, due to an internal necessity of their own system of the world, the materialists rather conveniently supplied the means for their own destruction. Based upon the primary-secondary sense quality distinction, Berkeley showed that there can be no such thing as a material world as described by the materialists. Thus, following the same line of reasoning which derived reductionistic materialism from Parmenides in the first place, Berkeley rather neatly transmuted it into a reductionistic *im*materialism. As a result of his intellectual victory Berkeley fully expected a general moral transformation to take place also.

As we know from history, of course, such a change did not occur. Was this because the good and well-meaning bishop was not scientific enough? I really don't think that this can be said. Remember that Berkeley never denied the *apparent* reality of the material world. All he did was to explain it away. It was now no longer an objective thing. Is Skinner unscientific for having done exactly the same sort of thing in reverse? To claim that Skinner was right and Berkeley was wrong might itself be a sign of certain unscientific prejudices.

Perhaps the best way to resolve such a conflict is to declare them both wrong. Failing this, one might declare them both right, but in such an abstract manner that perfectly nothing of a pragmatic nature can really flow from either view. Then how will anyone know which view to act on? Faith! To act on either position requires a faith in the words of the master. Since each one is beyond the pale of experiential confirmation or refutation, the words of the leaders in each camp must be regarded as a kind of Holy Writ if we are to get any sort of action out of such theories. Our actions would then be based upon faith rather than reason. The situation has been well put by Herbert Spencer.

> The interpretation of all phenomena in terms of Matter, Motion, and Force is nothing more than the reduction of our complex symbols of thought to the simplest symbols; and when the equation has been brought to its lowest terms the symbols remain symbols still. Hence the reasonings contained in the foregoing pages afford no support to either of the antagonistic hypotheses respecting the ultimate nature of things. Their implications are no more materialistic than they are spiritualistic; and no more spiritualistic than they are materialistic. Any argument which is apparently furnished to either hypothesis is neutralized by as good an argument furnished to the other. The Materialist, seeing it to be a necessary deduction from the law of correlation, that what exists in consciousness under the form of feeling is transformable into an equivalent of mechanical motion, and by consequence into equivalents of all the other forces which matter exhibits, may consider it therefore demonstrated that the phenomena of consciousness are material phenomena. But the Spiritualist, setting out with the same data, may argue with equal cogency that if the forces displayed by matter are cognizable only under the shape of those equivalent amounts of consciousness which they produce, it is to be inferred that these forces, when existing out of consciousness, are of the same intrinsic nature as when existing in consciousness; and that so is justified the spiritualistic conception of the external world, as consisting of something essentially identical with what we call mind. [4]

The materialist, in our case Skinner, thinks in terms of explaining all mental phenomena by reference to physical transformations of energy of one sort or another. The spiritualist, in our case Berkeley, on the other hand, thinks in terms of explaining all physical phenomena by reference to psychic transformations of ideas. Like the mixing of an acid and a base in chemistry, the results that come from such a combination of extremes is not an eternal battle between giants but is instead nothing but a rather unproductive, watered down, neutralized soup with little or no flavor.

In effect this means that neither of these two extreme paradigms is really rationally secure. Instead of resting secure in either one, all your energy must go into keeping it from becoming the other! Sooner rather than later the intelligent investigator of the human person will wonder if it is really worth it.

CHANGING TIMES

We live in changing social conditions. More and more the first and second, and even to some extent the third, positions on the human person are filtering into all aspects of our lives. It can safely be expected that as time goes on, the growing changes in our mental evaluations of ourselves will become more dominated by these views. This is even now becoming apparent in our legal system. Present laws are being altered and new ones introduced which are based upon a more materialistic view of the human person. The oppositions which now exist between those who want laws which reflect the spiritual nature of humankind and those who want to be strictly "modern" and "scientific" in their approach to people may well die out completely due to the complete victory of the first, second, or third position on the human person in the minds of the populace and the lawmakers. I state this simply as a fact.[5]

This sort of shift in values is usually referred to as the "secularization" of society and is usually thought to mean the elimination of religion. But in fact religion in some form cannot be pushed out of human life. Religion, in the very broad sense of an adherence to a set of values which transcend one's own momentary sensual interests, is necessary to the well-being of both individuals and society. Asking "What good is religion?" is like asking "What good is the mortar that holds together the bricks in a building?" Without something to relate people to each other in some type of long-lasting system there would be no society at all.

This is so true that where the need is not filled by some church independent of the state, the state itself assumes the religious function. Where independent religious influences are lacking, the state itself will set out the transcendental values its citizens are to follow. Wherever the first, second, or third position on the human person comes to dominate in a society, we can expect this to happen. Furthermore, in lieu of any personal spiritual transcendental values, we should not be surprised if the secular leaders take it into their heads that the best transcendental value for the people is the state itself. It is often pointed out that Marxism is a sort of religion. It substitutes, or at least attempts to substitute, for traditional religious institutions. It is often overlooked, however, that this can happen with any non-"religious" philosophy of the human person, for example, the "Liberal Creed" in North America. Such systems are usually more or less oppressive in that the state itself becomes the primary object of devotion. Close to home this shows up in such things as the difficulty encountered in obtaining "public" money for "private" education. Another example is the way the tax collector simply refuses to admit that your money is *your* money. Such thoughts are considered to be quite "unpatriotic."[6]

On this score those in the "Free World" are generally very unsophisticated. People such as president Harry Truman, who in 1945 thought he could handle the Marxists without knowing the first thing about them philosophically, and Joseph Raymond McCarthy would be good examples of such ignorance in high places. Great peals of laughter must have echoed through the halls of the University of Moscow in the early 1950s as Senator McCarthy was gaining worldwide fame for his anticommunist investigations. The reason for this laughter was well founded, for while the senator was out chasing after a few communists in the army, civil service, and Hollywood, the Hegelian philosophical foundations for the Marxist view of the human person, and consequently for the political revisions implicitly contained in such a view, were being openly taught in practically every biology classroom in the whole "Free World." For his part, Truman thought of the communistic states as just so many old-fashioned dictatorships, while for his part McCarthy naively believed that he could kill the Marxist species by pulling a few hairs out of its tail. Both men failed to see the unique characteristics of what they were dealing with, namely, nonreductionistic materialism.

The sad part of this situation, from the academic viewpoint, is that the vast majority of those engaged in teaching things about the human person do not know any more than the politicians. They have some vague notions in their heads (or in their souls) about what science is supposed to be all about, or about what this or that well-known name has said concerning the human person, but at no time do they ever acquire a comprehensive view of what the total spectrum of possible positions really is. My claim of course is that if and when such an analysis is actually undertaken, in a logical way, certain general features of the case will emerge. These are the paradigms I have given. Without deciding here which of the possible theories is right or wrong, it should be clear by now to anyone who has been reading these pages from the beginning that at least the following points are by and large true:

1. There are well-defined, mutually exclusive positions on the human person.
2. Their number is small.
3. They have a rational and intrinsic relationship to each other.
4. They are not momentary and haphazard creations, but rather perennial possibilities with well-established internal logics of their own.
5. They possess certain definite consequences which cannot be avoided in the long run.
6. It *is* possible to discover in a scientific way the order that exists in the area of what it means to be a human person.

THE ELUSIVE MIDDLE WAY

Now there is one more point to make, namely, that no one of the possible theories can claim to be the true via media with respect to all other possible hypotheses. Just as there is no one scientific method, but rather a multiplicity of different levels or layers to science, so there is no one happy medium represented by any one of the six theories. Regardless of what the advocates of any one of the six positions might assert, when the investigator observes the overall situation, he or she can see that all such claims *must* be unfounded. Once in command of a comprehensive view of things, the investigator can see that any claim on the part of any one of the theories to occupy exclusively the happy medium position must be quite arbitrary.

As a variation on this point, we can also see that, objectively speaking, there can be no convenient and comfortable moral compromise, no nicely neutral middle of the road ethical position. Like it or not, each human being must choose to emphasize either the flesh or the spirit. Claiming the benefits of the spirit in an otherwise materialistic philosophy of the human person is, at best, a form of nostalgia.

Such a claim would be parallel to someone's claiming that his position was the one and only scientific theory on the human person, and defending his claim by *defining* science so as to achieve an exclusive right to be called scientific in his approach to the human person. But obviously, as soon as such a claim is made, its advocate has forfeited the whole ball game. The whole point of being scientific as a general outlook on human rationality is to avoid arbitrariness. If nothing else, the scientist must be honest; he must let the chips fall where they may; he must not "fudge" the evidence. For a theorist to define science rather dogmatically in such a way as to eliminate automatically everyone else's view would be directly contrary to this basic premise of intellectual honesty.

Such arbitrariness must also be avoided when discussing the happy medium position with respect to the human person. As it turns out, according to my analysis, there is only one position which can lay claim to being the true happy medium. However, as my analysis of the classical sources in science, philosophy, and religion indicates, this position has not been maintained by any scientist, philosopher, or theologian of any great reputation.

Such a theory would fall between the third and fourth views on the human person. It would maintain that an immaterial form entirely mortal suddenly becomes immortal when its body disintegrates. In psychosomaticism without immortality the human soul is mortal from the moment it is generated out of its parents' sexual activity. In psychosomaticism with immortality the human soul is immortal from the very moment it is created by God in cooperation with the human parents. As you can see, an intermediate position would have to say that a mortal soul at some point becomes immortal.

How can such a thing be possible? Only by a deliberate act of God. But can it really be the case that the universe is really a pagan Aristotelian affair with Jehovah sort of tacked on to it in order to give immortality to those few souls who do good deeds?

True, I can imagine a situation in which someone, such as a Pomponazzi or a Husserl, says that, well, the soul is in fact immortal all along but that we cannot know it for sure here and now by natural reason alone. Possible—but beside the point. The point is that once skepticism is left behind anything positive said about the basic nature of the human person must fall within one of the six paradigms, and that the mortal-immortal soul thesis cannot be one of them.

Such a view is similar to the one already mentioned at the beginning of chapter 6. As you will recall, there I mentioned the apparent possibility of a soul created to be immortal suddenly becoming mortal. This would be the apparent true happy medium position in reverse. The two views are alike insofar as they each require a sudden reversal in the nature of the human soul. As you will further recall, though, such a position had to be rejected as too inconsistent for rational consideration. The same fate lies in wait for the mortal-immortal hypothesis.

Although proposed for consideration by several early Christian writers of the second century, the notion of a soul which is mortal at one time and immortal at a later time has never attracted the attention of any of the great thinkers of the past or present. Even though God certainly has the power to work such a wonder, anyone interested in maintaining a spiritual view of the human person is bound to be put off by the way such a view bounces back and forth between one type of nature for the soul and another.

For this reason such a view has not survived in any living and dynamic fashion. It has not become a part of our intellectual heritage in the twentieth century. Such a view is in no way intellectually satisfying. Moreover, in the light of the availability of the fourth, fifth, and sixth positions on the human person, it is quite unnecessary.

Finally, in the world today there is a plurality of paradigms on the human person. None of them is ever about to go away completely. But then neither are any really new ones about to appear on the scene, at least as far as is apparent from human history. Perhaps the best we can do for the time being is to continue to explore the domain of human experience in an effort to arrive at some worldwide consensus on the subject of human nature.

After this we may at long last be in a position to achieve a universal ethics. In that day, perhaps, not only will the nations of the world have many books filled with nice-sounding laws about human freedom, but they will actually put them into practice. As human beings, therefore, we must do what John Dewey wanted us to do when he said, "What the method of intelligence, thoughtful valuation will accomplish, if once it be tried, is for the result of trial to determine."[7] We must do it, however, with a circumspection Dewey himself was never able to command. Hopefully, as a result of our thoughtful reflection on the human person, our current states of conflict in the world will at least be lessened. That all problems can *ever* finally be resolved, in a practical way on a worldwide scale, is *too* much to hope for. So far as heaven on earth is concerned—*nunquam, et nunquam post hoc.*

Notes

CHAPTER 1

1. Examples of this would be C. W. Morris, *Six Theories of Mind* (Chicago, 1966); L. Stevenson, *Seven Theories of Human Nature* (New York, 1974); F. W. Matson, *The Idea of Man* (New York, 1976); M. Hollis, *Models of Man* (London, 1977). Also, M. J. Adler's work, *The Difference of Man and the Difference It Makes* (New York, 1971), although much better than most, still loses much clarity by trying to reduce all of the possible positions to just two: Humans differ from chimps either "in degree" or "in kind" (p. 63). This leads to further confusing consequences, such as playing down the importance of Hegel (see p. 59), and lumping together thinkers such as Plato, Aristotle, Aquinas, and Hegel (see pp. 54-55).

2. Illustrations of this would be J. A. Mann and G. F. Kreyche (eds.), *Reflections on Man* (New York, 1966); W. L. Kelly and A. Tallon (eds.), *Readings in the Philosophy of Man* (New York, 1967); H. Parkin (ed.), *The Social Animal* (London, 1969); C. C. Hughes (ed.), *Make Men of Them* (Chicago, 1972); F. S. Hulse (ed.), *Man and Nature* (New York, 1975).

3. Skinner, for instance, does not like being called a reductionist, while someone in the second paradigm is very likely to want to call anyone to the "right" a vitalist.

CHAPTER 2

1. *About Behaviorism* (New York, 1974), p. 249.
2. Ibid., p. 239.

3. Ibid., p. 251.

4. Ibid., p. 225.

5. Ibid., p. 241.

6. Ibid., p. 245.

7. See *Behaviorism* (New York, 1925), pp. 16-18.

8. On the central position held by Parmenides see E. Gilson, *Being and Some Philosophers*, 2nd ed. (Toronto, 1952).

9. See Lucretius, *De Rerum Natura*, Book I.

10. See especially René Descartes, *Meditations*, VI.

11. Lucretius, *De Rerum*, Book II, 730.

12. Ibid., Book II, 842.

13. On the importance of reductionism in early modern science see A. N. Whitehead, *Science and the Modern World* (New York, 1925), chapter 9, and E. Meyerson, *Identity and Reality* (New York, 1962).

14. On the early history of "scientific" psychology see E. G. Boring's work *A History of Experimental Psychology* (New York, 1929, and subsequent editions), and Edna Heidbreder's *Seven Psychologies* (New York, 1961).

15. *A Philosophical Essay on Probabilities*, Trans. from the 6th French ed. by F. W. Truscott and F. L. Emory (New York, 1951), p. 4.

16. *Beyond Freedom and Dignity* (New York, 1971), p. 205.

17. Ibid., p. 211.

18. See *De Rerum Natura*, Book II, 216, and Book III, 177-322.

19. See *A History of Science*, Vol. I (Cambridge, Mass., 1952), pp. 590-591.

20. Cf. Lucretius, *De Rerum*, Book III, 741ff., wherein he uses the observable facts of heredity to prove that mind is transmitted along with body in the process of reproduction. In our century the early behaviorists wanted to play down the role of heredity, but later ones have found this impossible to maintain.

Another small but telling indication of reductionism in modern times, related to this point of quantity *having* to become the essence of things because there's simply nothing else to appeal to, is the way in which many people today have come to say that "Big is beautiful." This can, of course, be seen in cars and buildings, but it also shows up in more subtle ways. For instance, why worry about saving the blue rorqual whales? Because they're the *largest* mammals in the world. Granted, but how does that make them any *better* than mice? It would seem, almost unconsciously, that quantity in and of itself has become something of importance in modern ecology. But more of this later.

21. *About Behaviorism*, p. 226.

22. See Hobbes's *Leviathan: or the Matter, Form, and Power of a Common-*

wealth, Ecclesiastical and Civil, first published in London in 1651. Earlier, in 1628, Hobbes did a translation of Thucydides in order to help publicize the evils of democracy. On his personal life see S. I. Mintz, *The Hunting of Leviathan* (London, 1962).

23. *Science* 185 (6 September 1974), p. 813.

24. See D. Hume, "My Own Life, Written By Himself," *On Human Nature and the Understanding,* ed. by A. Flew (New York, 1962), pp. 304-310.

25. This attack was first started by Hume's contemporary Thomas Reid in 1764. More recent comments along the same lines have been made by H. A. Prichard.

26. D. Hume, *On Human Nature,* p. 145.

27. D. Hume, "An Abstract of A Treatise of Human Nature," *On Human Nature,* p. 298.

28. D. Hume, *On Human Nature,* p. 143. This line of reasoning is most developed in his *An Inquiry Concerning the Principles of Morals* which Hume, in his autobiography, calls his best work.

29. See the "Appendix" to Hume's *A Treatise of Human Nature.*

30. H. Driesch, *The Science and Philosophy of the Organism* (London, 1908), pp. 284-285.

31. The same must also be true of someone such as the entomologist E. O. Wilson. Sociobiology is to biology as behaviorism is to psychology. Despite what some individual sociobiologists may personally wish to believe to the contrary, the transference of all individual human responsibility to one's minute material parts and social conditioning is quite destructive to women's rights, race equality, and human liberty.

CHAPTER 3

1. See K. Freeman, *Ancilla to the Pre-Socratic Philosophers* (Oxford, 1962).

2. See R. W. Sellars, "The New Materialism," *A History of Philosophical Systems,* ed. by V. Ferm (New York, 1950), p. 418.

3. See Ibid., p. 425.

4. See Ibid., p. 420.

5. Ibid., p. 425.

6. See M. R. Cohen, *A Preface to Logic* (New York, 1961), p. 210.

7. John Dewey, *Experience and Nature,* 2nd ed. (New York, 1929; Dover Reprint, 1958), p. 45.

8. Ibid., p. 48.

9. See Ibid., p. 249.

10. See Ibid., p. 264.

11. Ibid., p. 292.

12. Ibid., p. 262.

13. Ibid., p. 273.

14. Ibid., p. 262.

15. Ibid., p. 295.

16. Ibid., p. 74.

17. Ibid., p. 255.

18. Ibid., p. 295.

19. See E. Mayr, "Footnotes on the Philosophy of Biology," *Philosophy of Science* 36 (June 1969), p. 197.

20. Ibid., p. 201.

21. T. Dobzhansky, *The Biology of Ultimate Concern* (New York, 1967), p. 58.

22. Ibid., p. 130.

23. R. W. Sellars, p. 424. This is basically the same position as that held by the Marxists.

24. J. Dewey, *Experience and Nature*, p. 262.

25. See Edmund W. Sinnott, *The Biology of the Spirit* (New York, 1955), pp. 102ff.

26. Ibid., p. 104.

27. Ibid., p. 126.

28. Ibid., p. 164.

29. J. Dewey, *Experience and Nature*, p. 254.

30. Ibid., p. 293.

31. R. W. Sellars, p. 424.

32. T. Dobzhansky, "Species of Drosophila," *Science* 177 (25 August 1972), p. 664.

33. J.-P. Sartre, *Being and Nothingness*, trans. by H. E. Barnes (New York, 1966), p. 526; see also p. lxxx.

34. See Ibid., pp. 527-543.

35. See Ibid., pp. 539, 542.

36. See Ibid., pp. 537, 541.

37. G. Marcel, *The Philosophy of Existentialism*, trans. by M. Harari (New York, 1964), p. 83.

38. In recent years Sartre's intellectual efforts have been almost entirely political. If one thing doesn't work, try another. Others also, such as A. J. Ayer, have made a similar transition. In his *Language, Truth and Logic* Ayer is a decidedly Humean reductionist. However, since the realization in the 1950s that Logical Positivism could not possibly be more than partially true, Ayer has taken a turn towards James and Dewey. But what is pragmatism if not the application of evolutionary thinking to human knowledge? Can anything be absolutely true? No. Why? Because until the future is entirely completed we can

never really know for sure who or what will ultimately survive. Now, since actual survival is the only standard we have for *deserved* survival, by definition we can never know what is absolutely good and true.

39. See M. Merleau-Ponty, *Les Adventures de la Dialectique* (Paris, 1955) and *The Phenomenology of Perception*, trans. by C. Smith (New York, 1962).

40. See *The Essential Writings of Merleau-Ponty*, ed. by A. L. Fisher (New York, 1969), p. 164. This selection in Fisher's edition is the final chapter in the work *La Structure du Comportement*, 4th ed. (Paris, 1960).

41. Fisher, in his Introduction to *The Essential Works*, thinks that Merleau-Ponty may well have died reconciled to the Catholic church. This is because, following his death in May 1961, he was given a Catholic funeral. This may be so, but it may only indicate that his family had some influence over the local clergy.

42. See A. L. Fisher (ed.), *The Essential Works*, pp. 140-153.

43. Ibid., p. 154.

44. Ibid., pp. 154-156.

45. Ibid., pp. 156-159.

46. Ibid., pp. 159-164. For these reasons he must reject Kant who still kept a thing-in-itself untouched by the soul. See Ibid., p. 162, note 41, and p. 163.

47. Ibid., p. 166.

48. Ibid., pp. 167-176.

49. See A. L. Fisher's Introduction to *The Essential Works*, p. 8.

50. See T. Langan, *Maurice Merleau-Ponty's Critique of Reason* (New Haven, Conn., 1966), pp. 182-188.

51. S. J. Gould, Book Review in *Science* 188 (23 May 1975), p. 826.

52. C. Darwin, *The Origin of Species*, 6th ed. (London, 1872; New York: Modern Library Reprint), p. 160.

53. Ibid., p. 373.

54. G. Hegel, *Logic*, trans. by W. Wallace (New York, 1959), Chapter 7, #86, 2.

55. Ibid., #88, 5. Hegel's use of the term "pantheism" was unusual even at the time that he wrote. For at least a hundred years previous to Hegel's career pantheism had meant any identification of God and the world. By restricting pantheism to materialism, however, he did prevent the title from being applied to his own doctrine.

56. G. Sarton, *A History of Science* (Cambridge, Mass., 1952), Vol. I, p. 275.

57. G. Hegel, *Logic*, #88, 1.

58. Ibid., 2.

59. Ibid., #106.

60. Ibid., #108.

61. Ibid., #109.

62. F. Engels, *Dialectics of Nature* (London, 1955), p. 84.

63. See Ibid., p. 88.

64. J. Bronowski, "New Concepts in the Evolution of Complexity," *Synthèse* 21 (1970), p. 243.

65. J. Dewey, *Experience and Nature*, p. 252.

66. See Ibid., pp. 262-3.

67. See Ibid., p. 273.

68. Ibid., pp. 336-7.

69. H. L. Bergson, *Creative Evolution* (New York, 1944), pp. 32-33.

70. G. A. Wetter, *Dialectical Materialism*, trans. by P. Heath (New York, 1958), p. 133.

71. See J. Stalin, *Marxism and the Problems of Linguistics* (Moscow, 1954).

72. C. Darwin, *The Descent of Man*, 2nd ed. (London, 1874; New York: Modern Library Reprint), p. 541.

73. Ibid., p. 398. Italics added.

74. See *Origin of Species*, p. 360.

75. See *Fundamentals of Marxism-Leninism* (Moscow, 1963), pp. 70ff.

76. The twentieth century political situation is further complicated by the fact that some Hegelians have seen Fascism as the only possible outcome of the war between the classes. When the classes conflict, a new entity, different from either one of the two classes, should emerge as the new synthesis. This would be the State, as apotheosized in a Hitler or Mussolini for example. See E. Gilson, *The Unity of Philosophical Experience* (New York, 1937), pp. 287-289.

77. *Fundamentals of Marxism-Leninism*, p. 709.

78. Ibid., p. 714.

79. J. Dewey, *Experience and Nature*, p. 263.

80. See M. S. Dworkin (ed.), *Dewey on Education* (New York, 1971) for a chronological reprinting of the main shorter texts.

81. As an aside, consider how this "liberal," totalism, holistic, paradigm subtly imitates religious practices in the case of personal income taxes (even in the best of "free" societies), thereby giving the semblance of an empiricistic individualism (Darwin) in an otherwise pantheistic system of paternalistic salvation (Hegel). In order to collect taxes the government must pry into your personal affairs in a very detailed way. This rather gross invasion of privacy is certainly a violation of one of your (supposed) most precious rights. Nevertheless, it is a necessary means to the money-getting goal. How can this contradiction between your (supposed) right to privacy and the necessary means for tax collection be reconciled? Compromise. "You tell me all about your money," says the government, "and I'll promise to keep it top secret. No one will ever know about it except for a small handful of people who must know (and, of

course, the computer)." One is reminded of the religious practice of confession in which secrecy is exchanged for candor. When it comes to money, secular leaders can be very "religious."

CHAPTER 4

1. S. Kierkegaard, *Concluding Unscientific Postscript*, trans. by D. F. Swenson and W. Lowrie (Princeton, N.J., 1971), p. 101.

2. Ibid., p. 272n.

3. Ibid., p. 277. Cf. Ibid., p. 265. Elsewhere (p. 297) he imagines Socrates (who seems to be his ideal of a true philosopher precisely because he acted instead of writing books) engaged in a dialogue with Hegel. It would be as easy as pie, thinks Kierkegaard, for the Greek genius to destroy Hegel's pretensions to view things *sub specie aeterni* by simply insisting that Hegel consider his own mundane, finite, miserably human condition. The Pure Thought cannot be thought by an impure thinker.

4. See G. Wetter, *Dialectical Materialism* (New York, 1958), p. 552.

5. In his Preface to the second edition of *Capital* Marx says of Hegel's dialectic: "With him it is standing on its head. It must be turned right side up again, if you would discover the rational kernel within the mystical shell."

6. See G. Wetter, *Dialectical Materialism*, p. 557.

7. If physicists at the beginning of the scientific revolution had tried to use the Alice in Wonderland language which is so common today, they would have been largely ignored. The fact that they can do so today indicates just how greatly respected they have become since then. That the slippage may occur in the other direction, i.e., from Aristotle to Hegel, once the supernatural separate heavens have been removed, should also be noted here. For example, in history Pierre Bayle (1647-1706), a fideistic Calvinist in religion and a skeptic in philosophy, saw Strato, the third head of the Lyceum, as turning to pantheism. Apparently Hume was greatly impressed by Bayle's evaluation of the intrinsic tendencies of Aristotelianism. It may even be conjectured that Hume, if he had been a more original thinker, may indeed have adopted nonreductionistic materialism as an alternative to Aristotelianism. Instead he opted for the "crass" deterministic materialism of the atomists. See his *Dialogues Concerning Natural Religion,* ed. by N. K. Smith (Indianapolis, 1947), pp. 35-36, 80-86, 174-175.

8. See *Categories*, chapters 2, 4.

9. See Ibid., chapter 5.

10. *Physics*, VII, 4, 248 a 13-15.

11. Ibid., 249 b 1-4.

12. See Ibid., 249 b 25.

13. See *Metaphysics*, VII, 11, 1036 b 29 - 1037 a 4. At first sight the term

"intelligible matter" appears very strange, since for Aristotle matter in and of itself is unintelligible. Here, however, he is not referring to prime matter but to secondary matter, i.e., prime matter as informed by its essential quality.

14. See *Categories*, chapter 6.

15. See Ibid., chapter 8. Cf. also *Physics*, VI, 4, 5; *The Generation of Animals*, IV, 6, 774 b 30-35; *The History of Animals*, II, 17, 508 b 4-6. Qualities such as force, power, mass, and the like must also be regarded as not open to direct quantification.

16. *Metaphysics*, VII, 17, 1041 b 17-26.

17. W. R. Thompson, *Science and Common Sense* (Albany, N.Y., 1965), p. 164.

18. See V. E. Smith, *Idea-Men of Today* (Milwaukee, 1950), pp. 398 ff.

19. W. R. Thompson, *Science*, p. 168.

20. Ibid., p. 170.

21. *The Parts of Animals*, I, 1, 641 a 4. Thus to talk about a "dead organism" would be a contradiction in terms.

22. W. R. Thompson, *Science*, p. 171.

23. See *The History of Animals*, VIII, 1, 588 b 4-30.

24. W. R. Thompson, *Science*, p. 173.

25. See Ibid., p. 163.

26. See *On Generation and Corruption*, II, 9, 335 b 8-29; see also Ibid., I, 2, 315 b 25-30.

27. *On the Soul*, I, 1, 403 b 6-8.

28. Ibid., II, 2, 413 a 14-15.

29. *Metaphysics*, III, 4, 999 a 27-28. Cf. *The Parts of Animals*, I, 4, 644 a 24-26.

30. *Physics*, I, 8, 191 a 24-25.

31. Ibid., I, 8, 191 a 32-33.

32. See *Metaphysics*, I, 5, 986 b 27.

33. Ibid., I, 6, 987 a 29-30. In his work *The Sophist* (241d) Plato calls Parmenides his chief intellectual father.

34. *On Generation and Corruption*, I, 8, 325 a 26-27.

35. *Metaphysics*, XIV, 2, 1089 a 4.

36. See Ibid., VI, 1.

37. Cf. *On Generation and Corruption*, I, 8, 325 a 13-15: "Reasoning in this way, therefore, they were led to transcend sense perception and to disregard it on the grounds that one should stick to reasoning, and so the world must be One and Immobile."

38. *Physics*, I, 2, 185 a 31. Aristotle allowed for a hierarchy of essential qualities beginning with the forms of the four primitive elements (earth, air,

fire, water) and building upwards to visible macrocosmic substances. See *The Parts of Animals*, II, 1, 646 a 14-24.

39. *Physics*, I, 9, 192 a 31-32. Cf. also *On Generation and Corruption*, I, 4, 320 a 3-4; *Metaphysics*, VI, 2, 1027 a 14-15 and VII, 3, 1029 a 19-21.

40. See *Physics*, IV, 9, 217 a 20-35. Also see *Metaphysics*, VII, 3, 1029 a 15, and *Physics*, I, 2, 185 b 4.

41. See *Physics*, I, 7, 191 a 8-11.

42. See *Physics*, I, 8, 191 b 28-29. A few lines later Aristotle may be making a pun on Parmenides' "Way of Truth" when he says that people would be better off following his (Aristotle's) "road" or "way." See the beginning of Parmenides' poem for the comparison.

43. Saint Thomas Aquinas, *Commentary on the Metaphysics of Aristotle*, trans. by J. P. Rowan (Chicago, 1961), Vol. II, Book VII, 2, 1287, p. 500. The reference is back to chapter 2 of Book IV. See also M. J. Adler, *Dialectic* (New York, 1927), pp. 214-215.

44. *Metaphysics*, IV, 5, 1010 a 22-25. Cf. Ibid., XI, 6, 1063 a 22-29.

45. See *On Generation and Corruption*, I, 3, 317 b 16-18.

46. *Metaphysics*, I, 9, 991 a 8-10.

47. See *The Parts of Animals*, I, 1, 641 b 15-25.

48. See *Physics*, III, 1, 201 a 10-14.

49. *Metaphysics*, XII, 2, 1069 b 19-20.

50. See *On the Soul*, II, 4, 415 b 8-30.

51. *Metaphysics*, VII, 15, 1040 a 5.

52. Ibid., VIII, 3, 1043 b 24. Cf. Ibid., IX, 6, 1048 a 35.

53. See Ibid., VII, 8, 1033 b 10; VII, 15, 1039 b 26.

54. Ibid., VIII, 3, 1043 b 16-19.

55. Ibid., VII, 9, 1034 b 16-18.

56. Ibid., IX, 7, 1049 b 24-26.

57. Ibid., XII, 3, 1069 b 35 - 1070 a 2.

58. Ibid., XII, 6, 1072 a 9-10.

59. Ibid., XII, 7, 1072 b 14.

60. In his younger years Socrates followed the natural philosophers. Later, however, he became very much disappointed in them. See *Phaedo*, 96a-100a.

61. See V. E. Smith, *Science and Philosophy* (Milwaukee, 1965), pp. 109, 240-241.

62. See *On the Soul*, I, 5, 411 b 19-30; II, 2, 413 b 13-23.

63. See *The Generation of Animals*, III, 4, 755 a 22-35 and *The History of Animals*, VI, 13, 567 a 29-567 b 6.

64. See *The History of Animals*, VIII, 1, 588 b 4-23 and *The Parts of Animals*, IV, 5, 681 a 12-15.

65. *On The Soul,* II, 4, 415 a 29 - 415 b 2.
66. Ibid., I, 3, 407 b 24-25.
67. Ibid., II, 2, 414 a 19-21.
68. F. L. Peccorini, "Aristotle's Agent Intellect: Myth or Literal Account?" *The Thomist* 40 (1976), pp. 505-534.
69. *On the Soul,* II, 2, 414 a 14-21.
70. Ibid., III, 5, 430 a 20-25.
71. *On the Generation of Animals,* II, 3, 736 b 27-29.
72. *Nicomachean Ethics,* X, 7, 1177 b 26 - 1178 a 2.
73. Ibid., III, 2, 1111 b 22-24. Some followers of Aristotle in the modern day would still like to leave open the question of personal immortality in hylomorphism. Based upon the texts, though, there is no justification for such an attitude. See for example H. B. Veatch, *Aristotle* (Bloomington, Ind., 1974), p. 127.
74. J. Dewey, *The Quest for Certainty* (New York, 1929), p. 290.
75. *Metaphysics,* IX, 5, 1048 a 8.
76. *Nicomachean Ethics,* V, 8, 1135 a 23-26.
77. Ibid., VI, 2, 1139 a 32 - 1139 b 5.
78. See Ibid., X, 9, 1181 b 10-11.
79. Ibid., X, 8, 1180 a 9-11.

CHAPTER 5

1. A. C. Pegis, *At the Origins of the Thomistic Notion of Man* (New York, 1963), p. 49.
2. B. Suits, "Aristotle on the Function of Man," *Canadian Journal of Philosophy* 4 (1974), p. 25.
3. See *Metaphysics,* VI, 1, 1026 a 15-33.
4. *Summa Contra Gentiles,* IV, 54, #2. (Hereinafter referred to as *S.C.G.*)
5. *Summa Theologiae,* I, 8. (Hereinafter referred to as *S.T.*)
6. Ibid., I, 8, ad 2.
7. See Ibid., I, 8, ad 2.
8. See Ibid., II-II, 180, 3 and 188, 5.
9. Ibid., I, 68, 1.
10. Ibid., I, 101, 1.
11. See Ibid., I, 101, 2.
12. Cf. G. Ricciotti, *The Life of Christ,* trans. by A. I. Zizzamia (Milwaukee, 1947), p. 392. Cf. also Aquinas' analysis of John 6:70: "Dicit autem, *Credimus, et cognovimus,* quia prius est credere quam cognoscere: et ideo si prius cognoscere quam credere vellemus, non cognosceremus, nec credere valeremus, ut dicit Augustinus. Isa. 7, 9, secundum aliam litteram: 'Nisi

credideritis, non intelligetis'.'' Parma ed., X, chapter 6, Lecture 8, #10, p. 424.

13. Cf. the remarks of E. Gilson, "Education and Higher Learning," *A Gilson Reader,* ed. by A. C. Pegis (Garden City, N.Y., 1957), p. 325, note 5: "One of the most revolutionary effects of Christianity was to call *all men,* slaves or not, ignorant or learned, to the most liberal type of knowledge, which is that of truth embraced for its own sake. Faith made it accessible to all."

14. See *S.T.,* I, 75, 6. See also his *Disputed Questions on the Soul,* Article 14.

15. See *S.T.,* I, 76, 5, ad 1.

16. E. Gilson, *The Elements of Christian Philosophy* (New York, 1963), p. 229.

17. *S.C.G.,* II, 68, #6.

18. *On the Soul,* trans. by J. P. Rowan (St. Louis, 1949), Art. 14, ad 7.

19. Ibid., ad 11.

20. Ibid., ad 17.

21. Ibid., Art. 14 corpus; see also *S.T.,* I, 75, 2.

22. *S.C.G.,* II, 52, #2.

23. Ibid., II, 52, #3.

24. E. Gilson, *Elements,* pp. 230-231.

25. See *S.T.,* I, 29, 1.

26. See Ibid., I, 62, 5.

27. See Ibid., I, 75, 2, ad 2.

28. E. Gilson, *Being and Some Philosophers,* 2nd ed. (Toronto, 1952), p. 186.

29. *S.T.,* I, 85, 7.

30. See *S.C.G.,* II, 68, #6.

31. *S.T.,* Supplement, 79, 1.

32. See *S.T.,* I, 76, 5, ad 3.

33. See Ibid., I, 75, 3.

34. E. Gilson, *The Philosopher and Theology,* trans. by C. Gilson (New York, 1962), p. 74.

35. Ibid., p. 76.

36. Ibid., p. 83.

37. See Ibid., chapter V.

38. See *On Being and Essence,* trans. by A. Maurer (Toronto, 1949), chapter 4.

39. E. Gilson, *Being and Some Philosophers,* p. 187.

40. *S.T.,* I, 4, 1, ad 3.

41. Ibid., I, 29, 3.

42. See Ibid., I, 77, 1.

43. See Ibid., I, 84, 7 and II-II, 8, 1. In the latter place we read: "To speak about understanding implies an intimate knowledge, because *intelligere* means *intus legere* [to read within]. And this is obvious from a consideration of the difference between the intellect and the senses. Sense knowledge is concerned with external sensible qualities, while the intellect penetrates to the very essence of things. The object of the intellect is what a thing is, as said in *De Anima*, 3."

44. See W. N. Kellogg, "Communication and Language in the Home-Raised Chimpanzee," *Science* 162 (25 October 1968), pp. 423-427.

45. See D. Premack, "Language in Chimpanzee?" *Science* 172 (21 May 1971), pp. 808-822.

46. *S.T.*, I, 118, 2.

47. Ibid., ad 2. Cf. Ibid., I, 45, 8.

48. Ibid., I, 46, 2.

49. Ibid., I, 118, 3, ad 2.

50. See Ibid., I, 69, 2; 70, 1, ad 4; 70, 3.

51. Ibid., I, 71, ad 1.

52. Ibid., I, 73, 1, ad 3.

53. Ibid., I, 91, 4, ad 3.

54. On this particular point, E. C. Messenger, in his otherwise excellent and admirable work, would seem to be a little off the mark. See his *Evolution and Theology* (New York, 1932), chapter 16, pp. 208-216. Could it be that he was writing at a time when it was still fashionable to think of Aquinas as an Aristotelian?

55. T. Dobzhansky, *The Biology of Ultimate Concern* (New York, 1967), p. 125.

56. P. A. Harcombe and P. L. Marks, Editorial in *Science* 194 (22 October 1976).

57. From the fact that species have disappeared it cannot be deduced that the elimination of species is to be encouraged. In a well-balanced ecological system any disruption of the *status quo* could well have unfortunate effects upon human beings. This is a fact, even if it was not clearly seen by Aristotle and Aquinas. As George Sarton has pointed out concerning ecology, "Superstitions turn in circles and lead nowhere, but the rational questions that were asked twenty-three centuries ago by men of science such as Aristotle and Theophrastos are still exercising and fertilizing the minds of men today." *A History of Science*, I, p. 567. What Sarton himself never seemed to appreciate was the reason *why* men of science cannot be ecologists and atheistic evolutionists simultaneously.

58. *S.T.*, I, 118, 2, ad 2. Cf. *S.C.G.*, III, 22, #7.

59. See *On the Generation of Animals*, II, 3, 737 a 27.
60. See *The City of God*, XIX, 25.
61. See *S.T.*, I, 96, 3 and 4; see also I-II, 94, 5, ad 3. This refers to the way things *should* be. For comments on the more usual situation in 1270, see *S.T.* II-II, 61, 3.
62. Aquinas, *On Kingship*, trans. by G. B. Phelan (Toronto, 1949), p. xxxix.
63. T. I. Cook, *History of Political Philosophy from Plato to Burke* (New York, 1936), p. 224.
64. *S.T.*, I-II, 105, 1.
65. T. I. Cook, *History*, p. 225. It might be thought from this that the American founding fathers derived their inspiration from such a view. Perhaps Aquinas was the first Whig. Historically speaking, however, their inspiration came more from John Locke whose view of secular-religious relations was predicated on skepticism rather than rational optimism. Aquinas: Where reason is strong but a religious unity is lacking toleration is in order. Locke: Reason always was, is, and will be very weak and powerless in deciding which religion is the true one and so toleration is in order. See Locke's *Letter on Toleration* [1689], Gough ed., p. 136. Both Aquinas and Locke would have looked upon each other as hypocrites; Locke, because Aquinas put toleration last instead of first; and Aquinas, because Locke was merely making a virtue out of a necessity. Exactly how much Locke knew of Aquinas is not known.
66. Saint Thomas Aquinas, "Sermon for the Feast of St. Martin," *Thomas Aquinas: Selected Writings*, ed. by M. C. D'Arcy (New York, 1950), p. 4.
67. See V. J. Bourke, *Aquinas' Search for Wisdom* (Milwaukee, 1965), pp. 191-194.

CHAPTER 6
1. A. O. Lovejoy, *The Great Chain of Being* (New York, 1960), p. 326.
2. Ibid., p. 316. In contrast to this Lovejoy pits the evolutionary view which says that "there is more in the effect than was contained, except as an abstract unrealized potentiality, in the cause." (p. 317) Lovejoy's modification between commas is another small illustration of how easy it is to slip from position two to position three. For Aristotle potencies were as real as actualities and thus he escaped Parmenides' conundrum. Lovejoy finds himself having to say the same sort of thing if he would avoid the unqualified assertion that effects must exceed their causes.
3. Ibid., p. 45.
4. Ibid., p. 322. Note that in the dispute between Fichte, the man of faith, and Schelling, the pantheist, Hegel sided with the latter.
5. Ibid., pp. 79-80.

6. H. Cairns, "Introduction," *Plato: The Collected Dialogues,* ed. by E. Hamilton and H. Cairns (New York, 1963), p. xxv.

7. See A. N. Whitehead, *Process and Reality* (New York, 1929), pp. ix, 63, 126.

8. M. J. Adler, *Dialectic* (New York, 1927), p. 233.

9. A. Koyré, "Galileo and Plato," *The Roots of Scientific Thought,* ed. by P. P. Wiener and A. Noland (New York, 1960), p. 159.

10. Ibid., p. 166.

11. E. Gilson, *History of Christian Philosophy in the Middle Ages* (New York, 1955), p. 804, note 82.

12. Ibid., p. 94. See also his *God and Philosophy* (New Haven, Conn., 1941).

13. A. E. Taylor, *Plato,* 6th ed. (New York, 1961), p. 522.

14. Ibid., pp. 450-451.

15. Ibid., p. 454.

16. See *Phaedo,* 81ce. See also the *Philebus,* 32ff.

17. T. M. Robinson, *Plato's Psychology* (Toronto, 1970), p. 158.

18. Ibid., p. 155.

19. See *Euthuphro,* 6; *Gorgias,* 503.

20. See *Phaedo,* 83a; *Republic,* 409c; *Sophist,* 228.

21. According to de Vogel the "Neoplatonism" of Plotinus was in fact already very strong both in Plato himself and in the intervening time period between Plato and Plotinus. See her article "On the Neoplatonic Character of Platonism," *Mind* 62 (1953), pp. 43-64.

22. The academic turn toward skepticism began with Arcesilaus (315-240 B.C.). He asked how a completely material thing locked up in the sense world, as human beings were said to be by the Stoics for instance, could be sure about anything in the material world, even that it existed. See E. Zeller, *The Stoics, Epicureans and Sceptics* (New York, 1962), chapter 23 and W. T. Jones, *A History of Western Philosophy,* 2nd ed., Vol. I (New York, 1970), p. 351.

23. G. Sarton, *A History of Science,* Vol. I (Cambridge, Mass., 1952), p. 402, note 17.

24. See Aristotle, *Metaphysics,* XIII, 4, 1078b30-1079a4; see also I, 9, 990 b 1.

25. Such misunderstandings about Plato are quite widespread. Even someone such as E. R. Dodds leaves his readers with the impression that Plato's insistence upon the independence of mind is merely a superstitious carryover from oriental mysticism. See his *The Greeks and the Irrational* (Boston, 1957), chapter 7.

26. J. Dewey, *The Influence of Darwin on Philosophy* (Bloomington, Ind., 1965), pp. 15-16.

27. A. N. Whitehead, *The Function of Reason* (Boston, 1959), p. 31.

28. See *Phaedo*, 76e; *Meno*, 72c; *Theaetetus*, 185. See also *Philebus*, 59ac; *Timaeus*, 28a, 52a; *Cratylus*, 440.

29. See *Phaedo*, 74b; *Sophist*, 252c, 257a.

30. The first systematic treatment of self-reflection in terms of its philosophical significance was performed by Proclus (411-485), the last important leader of the Academy. See his *Elements of Theology*, trans. by E. R. Dodds (New York, 1933), pp. 17-21.

31. See *Charmides*, 171d; *Phaedo*, 65c; *Theaetetus*, 188c, 200b.

32. As indicated by the beginning of the fifth part of the *Discourse*, Descartes looked upon the situation then as we today would look upon government PR men trying to cover up a flying saucer landing. It's not very scientific, but it is understandable in terms of the government's concern over what it conceives to be the common good.

33. As reprinted in *Descartes: Philosophical Writings*, ed. by E. Anscombe and P. T. Geach (London, 1966), p. 275.

34. Some modern physicists feel inclined to do just that. See W. Heisenberg, *Physics and Philosophy* (New York, 1962), pp. 70-71, 160-161.

35. Kant's general plan of calling upon the mind for the "informing" of the chaos of sensation is still very much alive today as a theory of cognition. See A. L. Blumenthal, *The Process of Cognition* (Englewood Cliffs, N.J., 1977).

36. I. Kant, *Critique of Pure Reason*, trans. by N. K. Smith (New York, 1965), p. 113.

37. Kant regarded his answer to Hume's skepticism as simple yet hard to find. See Kant's *Prolegomena to Any Future Metaphysics*, trans. by L. W. Beck (Indianapolis, 1950), pp. 20, 25.

38. I. Kant, *Critique of Pure Reason*, p. 377.

39. Ibid., p. 354. The primitiveness of Descartes's *cogito* is so obvious to Kant that he calls it a tautology. Moreover, the difference between "inner" thoughts and "outer" appearances is so clear that it has been the most universally used basis for maintaining the soul's immateriality. See Ibid., pp. 337-339.

40. Ibid., p. 341.

41. Ibid., pp. 359-361.

42. See Ibid., p. 325, note *a*.

43. I. Kant, *Critique of Practical Reason*, trans. by L. W. Beck (Indianapolis, 1956), pp. 126-128.

44. Ibid., p. 127.

45. See Ibid., pp. 134-142. In his old age Kant seems to have pulled more and more into himself—and pulled God along with him. He wanted to exalt God as the completely other, but ended up thinking that maybe God is really

the same as Kant himself. He states: "God is not a being outside me, but only a thought in me. God is the morally practical self-legislative reason." *Kants Opus Posthumum,* ed. by E. Adickes (Berlin, 1920), p. 819, sec. 341. This, I'm afraid, is like saying, "Yes, Virginia, there *is* a Santa Claus; he really exists in your own mind and heart."

46. See Lauer's Introduction to E. Husserl, *Phenomenology and the Crisis of Philosophy,* trans. by Q. Lauer (New York, 1965), p. 31, note 36.

47. See E. Husserl, *Ideas,* trans. by W. R. B. Gibson (New York, 1962), Part I, chapter 2. See also his *Cartesian Meditations,* trans. by D. Cairns (The Hague, 1960), pp. 4-6.

48. E. Husserl, *Cartesian Meditations,* p. 5.

49. See E. Husserl, *Ideas,* pp. 74-82, 85, 135, 141, 154, 204-213, 230.

50. Ibid., pp. 16-17, 229. Intentionality for Husserl includes acts of the will and the emotions, for example, experiencing joy.

51. Ibid., p. 166.

52. Ibid., pp. 113-115, 149-151. See also *Cartesian Meditations,* pp. 141-148.

53. E. Husserl, *Ideas,* p. 144.

54. Ibid., p. 142.

55. Ibid., p. 139.

56. Ibid., p. 134.

57. Ibid., pp. 128-129.

58. Ibid., p. 18.

59. Husserl also called his *Ideas* "Meditations" (p. 101).

60. P. Pomponazzi, "On the Immortality of the Soul," *The Renaissance Philosophy of Man,* ed. by E. Cassirer, P. O. Kristeller, J. H. Randall, Jr. (Chicago, 1956), p. 306.

61. D. Cairns, "Phenomenology," *A History of Philosophical Systems,* ed. by V. Ferm (New York, 1950), p. 358.

62. *Summa Theologiae,* I, 75, 1. The "many ways" can be found in the *Summa Contra Gentiles,* II, 65.

63. Ibid., I, 3, 1.

64. See Ibid., I, 84, 6.

65. See Aristotle, *Metaphysics,* I, 9, esp. 992b.

66. See *Phaedo,* 81d; *Gorgias,* 523a; *Philebus,* 34, 38e; *Phaedrus,* 248e; *Republic,* 614a; *Timaeus,* 91d; *Laws,* 959b.

67. When a Buddhist talks about the migration of "persons," what migrates? According to traditional Buddhist doctrine the person is composed of five "heaps" or "aggregates" of traits, namely, body, and the four mental traits of sense knowledge, emotions, intellectual knowledge, and overall self-reflection. Whether or not this means a radical pluralism or a radical monism is another question. Regardless of the answer, however, all agree that this com-

bination of physical and mental "heaps" has no long-term stability. The traits come and go in various degrees as the person—who ultimately has no truly independent existence apart from Brahma—passes in and out of Brahma (Nature). In this way each last moment of existence can precondition the next moment so that it is possible for the body to break down while the other traits pass on, regroup, and reconstitute a new creature in a new body. This will continue until the "thirst" for life is finally eliminated.

This doctrine puts Buddhism into a very peculiar position. It would seem to be both pantheistic, in the second-paradigm way, and vitalistic at the same time. This means that it has a foot in each of two different camps, with two other views coming in between! But this is an impossible synthesis. (See R. A. Gard, *Buddhism* [New York, 1963], pp. 18, 101-103.)

68. See E. Mayr, *Animal Species and Evolution* (Cambridge, Mass., 1963), pp. 5-6.

69. On Whewell's "induction" as compared with its more naive form as found in J. S. Mill see A. Ellegard, "Darwin's Theory and Nineteenth-Century Philosophies of Science," *The Roots of Scientific Thought*, ed. by P. P. Wiener and A. Noland (New York, 1960), pp. 537-568.

70. W. Whewell, *The History of the Inductive Sciences*, I, p. 87.

71. See Ibid., I, pp. 76-77, 91-92.

72. Ibid., II, p. 564.

73. Ibid., II, p. 565.

74. See Ibid., II, pp. 566-567.

75. See G. Sarton, *A History of Science* (Cambridge, Mass., 1952), Vol. I, pp. 412, 413, 415, 419.

76. See on education: *Laws*, 804c; on slaves: *Laws*, 777; *Politicus*, 309a; on lies and genetics: *Republic*, 389, 459-461; *Laws*, 773-774; on isolation: *Laws*, 950d; on censorship: *Republic*, 401-402; on religion: *Laws*, 828; on population: *Laws*, 737-740; on capitalism: *Laws*, 742-745.

As part of his plan to have the city-state imitate the Ideas Plato wanted a completely stable economy. This meant having an absolutely secure currency. Long before the twentieth century he realized the usefulness of a central bank and wage and price controls. To achieve his goal, money supply, interest rates, foreign exchange, and the amount of cash any one individual could hold were all to be fixed within narrow limits.

CHAPTER 7

1. Some texts avoid definitions entirely. Instead, matter is reduced to mass, and mass is called a scalar quantity. The latter is then called a static magnitude, such as volume and weight—which puts us right back where we started from.

2. See A. Einstein, "Notes on the Origin of the General Theory of Relativity," *Essays in Science* (New York, 1934), pp. 78-84.

3. The latest edition of Berkeley's works is *The Works of George Berkeley, Bishop of Cloyne*, ed. by A. A. Luce and T. E. Jessop, 9 vols. (London, 1948-1957).

4. Below, any numbers referring to the *Principles* represent these sections.

5. Later Hume said they could because they were capable of existing alone. See *A Treatise of Human Nature*, I, iv, 5. Berkeley lived long enough to write an answer to Hume but did not. Why? Could he see that Hume was right? All we have from the latter part of his life is his *Siris*, a work which takes a mystical, neo-Platonic turn.

6. See J. Locke, *An Essay Concerning Human Understanding*, II, viii, 23. See also Sir Isaac Newton, *Opticks*, 4th ed. (London, 1730), Book III, Part I, Query #31.

7. For an analysis of Hume's reasoning see F. F. Centore, "Hume, Reid, and Skepticism," *Philosophical Studies* (forthcoming).

CHAPTER 8

1. E. Heidbreder, *Seven Psychologies* (New York, 1961), p. 426.

2. See Ibid., p. 428.

3. This aspect of Berkeley's thinking is brought out more clearly in his *Alciphron, or the Minute Philosopher* than in his *Principles* or *Dialogues*. It was written while he was residing for several years (1728-1731) in Newport, Rhode Island, where he had gone in the hope of ultimately founding a Christian school in Bermuda. Its three editions appeared in early 1732, late 1732, and 1752. Alciphron was a lawyer who became a "freethinker." Berkeley's choice was fitting in that lawyers tend to ignore questions of right and wrong and to think instead merely in terms of legal conventions. Often they justify this by claiming that morality *is* nothing but convention. Berkeley regarded such a view as a belittling of human nature and the work of pygmy minds. Hence the term "minute" in the subtitle. It comes from a line in Cicero's *Cato Maior de Senectute*, xxiii, 85: "If when dead, as some petty (minute) philosophers think, I am to be without sensation, then I have no fear that these philosophers when dead will have the last laugh on me." The main point of the *Alciphron* can be put in a nutshell: Things will go well for people to the extent each person *does* practice what God preaches, and to the extent that each person *does not* practice what the atheist preaches.

4. H. Spencer, *First Principles*, 4th ed. (New York, 1880), p. 470.

5. Every period of "cultural lag" has its interesting aspects. These days we observe those who want both abortion and pollution control simultaneously. The former, these days, usually depends upon accepting either the reduction-

istic or nonreductionistic materialism paradigm of the human person, while the latter depends upon rejecting them. Can you really have it both ways at once? A clear-sighted view of the options should soon render those who think you can as extinct as the dodo.

6. It may also happen that a "religious" society will also be oppressive. However, as history shows, where this occurs, it is not because there exists an independent church but because church and state have been identified either officially or in effect. This is necessarily the case where the religion does not have a separate organization and hierarchy, as for example in some Protestant groups in the past and in Islam, so that it must use political force in order to achieve its ends on earth.

7. J. Dewey, *Experience and Nature* (New York, 1958), p. 437.

Bibliography

Abelson, R. *Persons.* New York, 1977.

Adler, M.J. *Dialectic.* New York, 1927.

———. *The Difference of Man and the Difference It Makes.* New York, 1971.

Agassi, J. *Towards a Rational Philosophical Anthropology.* The Hague, 1977.

Aquinas, T. *Summa Theologica and Summa Contra Gentiles.* 6 vols. Rome, 1894.

———. *On Being and Essence.* Trans. A. Maurer. Toronto, 1949.

———. *On Kingship.* Trans. G. B. Phelan. Toronto, 1949.

———. *In Joannem Evangelistam Expositio.* Ed. Parma. Vol. 10, 279-645. New York, 1949.

———. *Thomas Aquinas: Selected Writings.* Ed. M.C. D'Arcy. New York, 1950.

———. *On the Soul.* Trans. J.P. Rowan. St. Louis, 1951.

———. *Commentary on the Metaphysics of Aristotle.* Trans. J.P. Rowan. 2 vols. Chicago, 1961.

Aristotle. Passim Loeb Classical Library, 24 vols. Cambridge, Mass., 1926-1970.

———. *The Basic Works of Aristotle.* Ed. R. McKeon. New York, 1941.

Armstrong, D.M. *A Materialist Theory of the Mind.* New York, 1968.

Augustine, A. *Basic Writings of St. Augustine.* Ed. W.J. Oates, 2 vols. New York, 1948.

Ayer, A.J. *Language, Truth and Logic.* 2nd ed. New York, 1945.

———. *The Concept of a Person and Other Essays.* London, 1963.

————. *The Origins of Pragmatism.* London, 1974.

Azar, L. "The Elusive One." *Philosophical Studies* 16 (1967), 104-115.

Baisnee, J.A. "Two Catholic Critiques of Personalism." *The Modern Schoolman* 22 (1945), 59-75.

Bennett, J.B. "The Disembodied Soul," *Process Studies* 4 (1974), 129-132.

Bergson, H.L. *Creative Evolution.* New York, 1944.

Berkeley, G. *The Works of George Berkeley, Bishop of Cloyne.* Ed. A.A. Luce and T.E. Jessop. 9 vols. London, 1948-1957.

Bernstein, R.J. "Why Hegel Now?" *The Review of Metaphysics* 31 (1977), 29-60.

Blakeley, T.J. *Soviet Scholasticism.* Dordrecht, 1961.

Blumenthal, A.L. *The Process of Cognition.* Englewood Cliffs, N.J., 1977.

Boring, E.G. *A History of Experimental Psychology.* 2nd ed. New York, 1950.

Bourke, V.J. *Aquinas' Search for Wisdom.* Milwaukee, 1965.

Bowler, P.J. *Fossils and Progress.* New York, 1976.

Broad, C.D. *The Mind and Its Place in Nature.* London, 1925.

Bronowski, J. "New Concepts in the Evolution of Complexity." *Synthèse* 21 (1970), 228-246.

Bury, J. B. *The Idea of Progress.* London, 1920.

Cahn, S. M., ed. *New Studies in the Philosophy of John Dewey.* Hanover, N.H., 1977.

Campbell, G. T. "Sartre's Absolute Freedom." *Laval Théologique et Philosophique* 33 (1977), 61-91.

Cassirer, E. *An Essay on Man.* New Haven, Conn., 1944.

————; Kristeller, P. O.; and Randall, J. H., Jr., eds. *The Renaissance Philosophy of Man.* Chicago, 1948.

Centore, F. F. "Neo-Darwinian Reactions to the Social Consequences of Darwin's Nominalism." *The Thomist* 35 (1971), 113-142.

————. "Mechanism, Teleology, and Seventeenth Century English Science." *International Philosophical Quarterly* 12 (1972), 553-571.

————. "A Note on Wittgenstein as an Unwilling Nominalist." *The Thomist* 37 (1973), 762-767.

————. "Atomism and Plato's *Theaetetus.*" *The Philosophical Forum* 5 (1974), 475-485.

————. "The Possibility of Metaphysics." *Philosophical Studies* 23 (1975), 31-48.

————. "Hume, Reid, and Skepticism." *Philosophical Studies* (forthcoming).

Chisholm, R. M. *Person and Object.* LaSalle, Ill., 1976.

Chroust, A.-H. "Aristotle's Doctrine of the Uncreatedness and Indestructibility of the Universe." *The New Scholasticism* 52 (1978), 268-279.

Cohen, M. R. *A Preface to Logic.* New York, 1961.

Collins, J., ed. *Readings in Ancient and Medieval Philosophy.* Westminster, Md., 1960.

Cook, T. I. *History of Political Philosophy from Plato to Burke.* New York, 1936.

Cooper, B. "Hegelian Elements in Merleau-Ponty's *La Structure Du Comportement.*" *International Philosophical Quarterly* 15 (1975), 411-423.

Dagenais, J. J. *Models of Man.* The Hague, 1972.

Darwin, C. *The Origin of Species and The Descent of Man.* New York, n.d.

DeGeorge, R. T. *Patterns of Soviet Thought.* Ann Arbor, Mich., 1966.

Delaney, C. F. *Mind and Nature.* Notre Dame, Ind. 1969.

DeMarco, D. *Abortion in Perspective.* Cincinnati, 1974.

Desan, W. *The Marxism of J.-P. Sartre.* Garden City, N.Y., 1965.

Descartes, R. *The Method, Meditations and Philosophy of Descartes.* Ed. J. Veitch. Washington, D.C., 1901.

——. *Descartes: Philosophical Writings.* Ed. E. Anscombe and P. T. Geach. London, 1966.

deVogel, C. J. "On the Neoplatonic Character of Platonism and the Platonic Character of Neoplatonism." *Mind* 62 (1953), 43-64.

Dewey, J. *The Quest for Certainty.* New York, 1929.

——. *Experience and Nature.* 2nd ed. New York, 1929.

——. *The Influence of Darwin on Philosophy.* Bloomington, Ind., 1965.

——. *Dewey on Education.* Ed. M. S. Dworkin. New York, 1971.

Dewey, R. E. *The Philosophy of John Dewey.* The Hague, 1978.

Dobzhansky, T. *The Biology of Ultimate Concern.* New York, 1967.

——. "Species of Drosophila." *Science* 177 (25 August 1972), 664-669.

Dodds, E. R. *The Greeks and the Irrational.* Boston, 1957.

Doncell, J. F. *Philosophical Anthropology.* Mission, Kan.,1967.

Driesch, H. *The Science and Philosophy of the Organism.* London, 1908.

Dupré, L. "Idealism and Materialism in Marx's Dialectic." *The Review of Metaphysics* 30 (1977), 649-685.

Dutt, C., ed. *Fundamentals of Marxism-Leninism.* Moscow, 1963.

Edelstein, L. *The Idea of Progress in Classical Antiquity.* Baltimore, Md., 1967.

Edwards, P., ed. *The Encyclopedia of Philosophy.* 8 vols. in 4. New York, 1972.

Einstein, A. *Essays in Science.* New York, 1934.

Engels, F. *Dialectics of Nature.* London, 1955.

Evans, J. *Aristotle's Concept of Dialectic.* London, 1977.

Eysenck, H. J. *The Inequality of Man.* London, 1973.

Fabre, J. H. *The Wonders of Instinct.* London, 1918.

Ferm, V., ed. *A History of Philosophical Systems.* New York, 1950.
Feuer, L. S., ed. *Marx and Engels.* Garden City, N.Y., 1959.
Flew, A., ed. *Body, Mind, and Death.* New York, 1967.
Fothergill, P. G. *Historical Aspects of Organic Evolution.* London, 1952.
Freeman, K. *Ancilla to the Pre-Socratic Philosophers.* Oxford, 1962.
————. *The Pre-Socratic Philosophers.* 2nd ed. Oxford, 1966.
Freud, S. *The Future of an Illusion.* London, 1928.
————. *A General Introduction to Psychoanalysis.* Trans. J. Riviere. New York, 1952.
Friedman, M. *The Hidden Human Image.* New York, 1974.
Fromm, E., ed. *Marx's Concept of Man.* New York, 1961.
Gard, R. A. *Buddhism.* New York, 1963.
Garrett, H. E. *Great Experiments in Psychology.* New York, 1941.
Gasman, D. *The Scientific Origins of National Socialism.* London, 1971.
Gelin, A. *The Concept of Man in the Bible.* Trans. D.M. Murphy. Staten Is., N.Y., 1968.
Gilby, T. *The Political Thought of Thomas Aquinas.* Chicago, 1963.
Gilson, E. *The Unity of Philosophical Experience.* New York, 1937.
————. *The Spirit of Mediaeval Philosophy.* New York, 1940.
————. *God and Philosophy.* New Haven, Conn., 1941.
————. *Being and Some Philosophers,* 2nd ed. Toronto, 1952.
————. *History of Christian Philosophy in the Middle Ages.*New York, 1955.
————. *A Gilson Reader.* Ed. A. C. Pegis. Garden City, N.Y., 1957.
————. "Autour de Pomponazzi." *Archives D'Histoire Doctrinale et Littéraire du Moyen Age* 28 (1961), 163-279.
————. *The Philosopher and Theology.* New York, 1962.
————. *Elements of Christian Philosophy.* New York, 1963.
————. *D'Aristotle a Darwin et Retour.* Paris, 1971.
Godelier, M. *Perspectives in Marxist Anthropology.* London, 1977.
Gould, S. J. "Book Review." *Science* 188 (23 May 1975), 824-826.
Gray, J. G. *Hegel and Greek Thought.* New York, 1968.
Gruber, H. E. *Darwin on Man.* New York, 1974.
Haller, J. S. *Outcasts From Evolution.* Urbana, Ill., 1971.
Hammond, A. L. "Artificial Intelligence." *Science* 180 (29 June 1973), 1352-1353.
Hanfling, O. *Body and Mind.* London, 1973.
Harcombe, P. A., and Marks, P. L. "Editorial." *Science* 194 (22 October 1976).
Hartman, E. *Substance, Body, and Soul.* Princeton, N.J., 1977.
Hegel, G. *The Logic of Hegel.* Trans. W. Wallace. London, 1892; reprinted London, 1959.
Heidbreder, E. *Seven Psychologies.* New York, 1961.

Heisenberg, W. *Physics and Philosophy.* New York, 1962.
Hilgard, E. R. *Divided Consciousness.* New York, 1977.
Hobbes, T. *Leviathan.* Chicago, 1949.
Hollis, M. *Models of Man.* London, 1977.
Huertas-Jourda, J. *The Existentialism of Miguel de Unamuno.* Gainesville, Fla., 1963.
Hughes, C. C., ed. *Make Men of Them.* Chicago, 1972.
Hulse, F. S., ed. *Man and Nature.* New York, 1975.
Hume, D. *An Inquiry Concerning the Principles of Morals.* LaSalle, Ill., 1938.
————. *Dialogues Concerning Natural Religion.* Indianapolis, 1947.
————. *A Treatise of Human Nature.* Garden City, N.Y., 1961.
————. *On Human Nature and the Understanding.* Ed. A. Flew. New York, 1967.
Husserl, E. *Cartesian Meditations.* Trans. D. Cairns. The Hague, 1960.
————. *Ideas.* Trans. W.R.B. Gibson. New York, 1962.
————. *Phenomenology and the Crisis of Philosophy.* Trans. Q. Lauer. New York, 1965.
Huxley, T. H. *Evolution and Ethics.* New York, 1895.
Hyppolite, J. *Studies on Marx and Hegel.* New York, 1973.
James, W. *The Principles of Psychology,* 2 vols. New York, 1890.
————. *Human Immortality,* 2nd ed. New York, 1898.
Jones, T. B., and Kamil, A. C. "Tool-Making and Tool-Using in the Northern Blue Jay." *Science* 180 (8 June 1973), 1076-1077.
Jones, W. T. *A History of Western Philosophy,* Vol. I. New York, 1970.
Jung, C. *Modern Man in Search of a Soul.* London, 1933.
Kainz, H. P. *The Philosophy of Man.* Washington, D.C., 1977.
Kant, I. *Kants Opus Posthumum.* Ed. E. Adickes. Berlin, 1920.
————. *Prolegomena to Any Future Metaphysics.* Trans. L. W. Beck. Indianapolis, 1950.
————. *Critique of Practical Reason.* Trans. L. W. Beck. Indianapolis, 1956.
————. *Religion Within the Limits of Reason Alone.* Trans. T. M. Greene and H. H. Hudson. New York, 1960.
————. *Critique of Pure Reason.* Trans. N. K. Smith. New York, 1965.
————. *Anthropology From a Pragmatic Point of View.* Trans. M. J. Gregor. The Hague, 1974.
Kellogg, W. N. "Communication and Language in the Home-Raised Chimpanzee." *Science* 162 (25 October 1968), 423-427.
Kelly, W. L., and Tallon, A., eds. *Readings in the Philosophy of Man.* New York, 1967.
Kierkegaard, S. *Concluding Unscientific Postscript.* Trans. D. F. Swenson and W. Lowrie. Princeton, N.J., 1971.
King-Farlow, J. *Self-Knowledge and Social Relations.* New York, 1978.

Koehler, W. *The Task of Gestalt Psychology*. Princeton, N.J., 1969.
Koestenbaum, P. *The New Image of the Person*. Westport, Conn., 1978.
Konecsni, J. *A Post-Kantian Anthropology*. Washington, D.C., 1978.
Kuhn, T. S. *The Essential Tension*. Chicago, 1978.
Langan, T. *Maurice Merleau-Ponty's Critique of Reason*. New Haven, Conn., 1966.
LaPlace, P. S. *A Philosophical Essay on Probabilities*. Trans. F. W. Truscott and F. L. Emory. New York, 1951.
Lauer, Q. *The Triumph of Subjectivity*. Bronx, N.Y., 1958.
Leuret, F., and Bon, H. *Modern Miraculous Cures*. London, 1957.
Levin, M. E. *Metaphysics and the Mind-Body Problem*. New York, 1979.
Locke, J. *An Essay Concerning Human Understanding*. Ed. J. W. Yolton. 2 vols. New York, 1961.
――――. *The Second Treatise of Government and a Letter Concerning Toleration*. Ed. J. W. Gough. 3rd ed. Oxford, 1966.
Loewenberg, B. J., ed. *Darwin, Wallace and the Theory of Natural Selection*. Cambridge, Mass., 1959.
Lovejoy, A. O. "The Paradox of the Thinking Behaviorist." *The Philosophical Review* 31 (1922), 135-147.
――――. *The Great Chain of Being*. New York, 1960.
――――. *Reflections on Human Nature*. Baltimore, Md., 1968.
Luckmann, T. *The Invisible Religion*. New York, 1970.
Lucretius. *De Rerum Natura*. Trans. W. H. D. Rouse. Cambridge, Mass., 1959.
Maher, M. *Psychology*. 9th ed. London, 1919.
Mann, J. A., and Kreyche, G. F., eds. *Reflections on Man*. New York, 1966.
Marcel, G. *The Philosophy of Existentialism*. Trans. M. Harari. New York, 1964.
Marcell, D. W. *Progress and Pragmatism*. Westport, Conn., 1974.
Margolis, J. *Persons and Minds*. Dordrecht, 1978.
Maritain, J. *Christianity and Democracy*. Trans. D. C. Anson. New York, 1944.
――――. *Scholasticism and Politics*. Garden City, N.Y., 1960.
Martland, T. R. *The Metaphysics of Wm. James and J. Dewey*. New York, 1969.
Marx, K. *Capital*, Vol. I. New York, 1947.
Matson, F. W. *The Idea of Man*. New York, 1976.
Mayr, E. *Animal Species and Evolution*. Cambridge, Mass., 1963.
――――. "Footnotes on the Philosophy of Biology." *Philosophy of Science* 36 (1969), 197-202.
――――. *Evolution and the Diversity of Life*. Cambridge, Mass., 1976.
McAlister, L.L., ed. *The Philosophy of Franz Brentano*. London, 1976.

McGovern, A. F. "Should a Christian be a Marxist?" *Proceedings of the American Catholic Philosophical Association* 51. Washington, D.C., 1977, 220-230.

McMullin, E., ed. *The Concept of Matter in Greek and Medieval Philosophy*. Notre Dame, Ind., 1965.

———, ed. *The Concept of Matter in Modern Philosophy*. Notre Dame, Ind., 1978.

Merleau-Ponty, M. *Les Adventures de la Dialectique*. Paris, 1955.

———. *The Phenomenology of Perception*. Trans. C. Smith. New York, 1962.

———. *Signs*. Trans. R. C. McCleary. Evanston, Ill., 1964.

———. *The Essential Writings of Merleau-Ponty*. Ed. A. L. Fisher. New York, 1969.

Messenger, E. C. *Evolution and Theology*. New York, 1932.

Meyerson, E. *Identity and Reality*. New York, 1962.

Midgley, M. *Beast and Man*. Ithaca, N.Y., 1978.

Miller, J. "Merleau-Ponty's Marxism." *History and Theory*. 15 (1976), 109-132.

Mintz, S. I. *The Hunting of Leviathan*. London, 1962.

Morris, C. W. *Six Theories of Mind*. Chicago, 1966.

Munro, D. J. *The Concept of Man in Early China*. Stanford, Calif., 1969.

Mure, G. R. G. *A Study of Hegel's Logic*. New York, 1959.

Nelson, B. "Machine Translation." *Science* 155 (6 January 1967), 58-59.

Newton, I. *Opticks*, 4th ed. London, 1730.

Nott, K. *Philosophy and Human Nature*. New York, 1971.

Owens, J. *A History of Ancient Western Philosophy*. New York, 1959.

———. *An Elementary Christian Metaphysics*. Milwaukee, 1963.

———. *An Interpretation of Existence*. Milwaukee, 1968.

———. *The Doctrine of Being in the Aristotelian Metaphysics*, 3rd ed. Toronto, 1978.

Pannenberg, W. *What Is Man?* Philadelphia, 1970.

Parel, A., ed. *Calgary Aquinas Studies*. Toronto, 1978.

Parkin, H., ed. *The Social Animal*. London, 1969.

Parsons, H. L., ed. *Marx and Engels on Ecology*. Westport, Conn., 1977.

Pascal, B. *Pensées*. Brunschvicg, ed. Paris, 1958.

Pasch, A. "Dewey and the Analytical Philosophers." *The Journal of Philosophy* 56 (1959), 814-826.

Patterson, F. "Conversations with a Gorilla." *National Geographic* 154 (October 1978), 438-465.

Peccorini, F. L. "Aristotle's Agent Intellect: Myth or Literal Account?" *The Thomist* 40 (1976), 505-534.

Pegis, A. C. *At the Origins of the Thomistic Notion of Man*. New York, 1963.

Peters, F. E. *Greek Philosophical Terms.* New York, 1967.

Plato. Passim Loeb Classical Library, 12 vols. Cambridge, Mass., 1914-1935.

————. *Plato: The Collected Dialogues.* Ed. E. Hamilton and H. Cairns. New York, 1963.

Popper, K. R. *Conjectures and Refutations,* 2nd ed. London, 1965.

————, and Eccles, J. C. *The Self and Its Brain.* New York, 1977.

Premack, D. "Language in Chimpanzee?" *Science* 172 (21 May 1971), 808-822.

————. *Intelligence in Ape and Man.* New York, 1976.

————, and Woodruff, G. "Chimpanzee Problem-Solving: A Test for Comprehension." *Science* 202 (3 November 1978), 532-535.

————, and Kennel, K. "Paper-Marking Test for Chimpanzee: Simple Control for Social Cues." *Science* 202 (24 November 1978), 903-905.

Prichard, H. A. *Knowledge and Perception.* New York, 1970.

Proclus. *The Elements of Theology.* Trans. E. R. Dodds. New York, 1933.

Rabil, A. *Merleau-Ponty.* New York, 1967.

Rader, M. *Marx's Interpretation of History.* New York, 1979.

Reeves, J. W., ed. *Body and Mind in Western Thought.* New York, 1958.

Reid, T. *An Inquiry into the Human Mind.* Ed. T. Duggan. Chicago, 1970.

Ricciotti, G. *The Life of Christ.* Trans. A. I. Zizzamia. Milwaukee, 1947.

Robinson, T. M. *Plato's Psychology.* Toronto, 1970.

Rorty, A. O., ed. *The Identities of Persons.* Berkeley, Calif., 1976.

Rosenthal, D. M., ed. *Materialism and the Mind-Body Problem.* Englewood Cliffs, N.J., 1971.

Roslansky, J. D., ed. *The Uniqueness of Man.* Amsterdam, 1969.

Ross, W. D. *Aristotle.* New York, 1961.

Rothblatt, B., ed. *Changing Perspectives on Man.* Chicago, 1968.

Royce, J. E. *Man and Meaning.* New York, 1969.

Rumbaugh, D. M., ed. *Language Learning by a Chimpanzee.* New York, 1977.

Ryle, G. *The Concept of Mind.* New York, 1949.

Salmon, W. C. "Why Ask, Why?" *Proceedings and Addresses of the American Philosophical Association* 51 (1978), 683-705.

Sarton, G. *A History of Science,* 2 vols. Cambridge, Mass., 1952-1959.

Sartre, J.-P. *Existentialism and Human Emotions.* New York, 1947.

————. *Being and Nothingness.* Trans. H. E. Barnes. New York, 1966.

Sayre, K. M. *Cybernetics and the Philosophy of Mind.* Atlantic Highlands, N.J., 1976.

Scheler, M. *Man's Place in Nature.* Trans. H. Meyerhoff. New York, 1962.

Schilpp, P. A., ed. *The Philosophy of John Dewey.* Evanston, Ill., 1939.

Seifert, J. "Essence and Existence: Part II." *Aletheia* 1 (1977), 371-459.

Shaw, G. B. *Man and Superman.* London, 1956.

Shealy, C. N. *Occult Medicine Can Save Your Life.* New York, 1977.

Sinaiko, H. W. "Letter on computer translations to the editor." *Science* 174 (17 December 1971), 1182, 1184.

Sinnott, E. W. *The Biology of the Spirit.* New York, 1955.

Skinner, B. F. *Walden Two.* New York, 1948.

————. *Beyond Freedom and Dignity.* New York, 1971.

————. *About Behaviorism.* New York, 1974.

————. "Letter to the editor." *Science* 185 (6 September 1974), 813.

Smith, V. E. *Idea-Men of Today.* Milwaukee, 1950.

————, ed. *Philosophy of Science.* Jamaica, N.Y., 1960.

————. *Science and Philosophy.* Milwaukee, 1965.

————, ed. *Philosophical Problems in Biology.* Jamaica, N.Y., 1966.

Somjee, A. H. *The Political Theory of John Dewey.* New York, 1968.

Spector, M. *Concepts of Reduction in Physical Science.* Philadelphia, 1978.

Spencer, H. *First Principles,* 4th ed. New York, 1880.

————. *Illustrations of Universal Progress.* New York, 1889.

Spiegelberg, H. *The Phenomenological Movement,* 2nd ed. The Hague, 1965.

Stalin, J. *Marxism and the Problems of Linguistics.* Moscow, 1954.

Stevenson, L. *Seven Theories of Human Nature.* New York, 1974.

Strasser, S. *The Soul in Metaphysical and Empirical Psychology.* Pittsburgh, 1962.

Strawson, P. F. *Individuals.* London, 1959.

Suits, B. "Aristotle on the Function of Man." *Canadian Journal of Philosophy* 4 (1974), 23-40.

Synan, E. A. *The Popes and the Jews in the Middle Ages.* New York, 1965.

Taylor, A. E. *Plato,* 6th ed. New York, 1961.

Taylor, C. *Hegel.* London, 1975.

Teilhard de Chardin, P. *The Phenomenon of Man.* New York, 1961.

Thompson, W. R. *Science and Common Sense.* Albany, N.Y., 1965.

Thorpe, W. H. *Learning and Instinct in Animals.* London, 1956.

————, and Zangwill, O. L. *Current Problems in Animal Behaviour.* London, 1961.

Turner, D. *Commitment To Care.* Old Greenwich, Conn., 1978.

Twain, Mark. *What Is Man?* Berkeley, Calif., 1973.

Tymieniecka, A.-T. *Phenomenology and Science in Contemporary European Thought.* New York, 1962.

Ullman, W. *Medieval Foundations of Renaissance Humanism.* Ithaca, N.Y., 1977.

Van Doren, M. *The Noble Voice.* New York, 1947.

Van Note, C. "Letter on endangered species to the editor." *Science* 201 (29 September 1978), 1174.

Veatch, H. B. *Aristotle.* Bloomington, Ind., 1974.

Vesey, G. *Personal Identity.* Ithaca, N.Y., 1977.

Vlastos, G. *Plato's Universe.* Seattle, Wash., 1975.

Vrooman, J. R. *René Descartes: A Biography.* New York, 1970.

Watson, J. B. *Behaviorism.* New York, 1925.

Weiner, B. *Theories of Motivation.* Chicago, 1973.

Wetter, G. *Dialectical Materialism.* Trans. P. Heath. New York, 1958.

Whewell, W. *The History of the Inductive Sciences,* 2 vols. New York, 1859.

Whitehead, A. N. *Science and the Modern World.* New York, 1925.

————. *Process and Reality.* New York, 1929.

————. *The Function of Reason.* Boston, 1959.

Wiener, P. P., and Noland, A., eds., *The Roots of Scientific Thought.* New York, 1960.

Wilhelmsen, F. D. "The I and Aquinas." *Proceedings of the American Catholic Philosophical Association* 51. Washington, D.C., 1977, 47-55.

————. *Christianity and Political Philosophy.* Athens, Ga., 1978.

Wilson, E. O. *Sociobiology.* Cambridge, Mass., 1975.

————. *On Human Nature.* Cambridge, Mass., 1978.

Wisdom, J. *Other Minds.* New York, 1952.

Woodruff, G.; Premack, D.; and Kennel, K. "Conservation of Liquid and Solid Quantity by the Chimpanzee." *Science* 202 (1 December 1978), 991-994.

Young, R. M. *Mind, Brain and Adaptation in the Nineteenth Century.* New York, 1970.

Zaner, R. M. *The Way of Phenomenology.* New York, 1970.

Zeller, E. *The Stoics, Epicureans and Sceptics.* Trans. O. J. Reichel. New York, 1962.

Zurcher, J. R. *The Nature and Destiny of Man.* Trans. M. R. Bartlett. New York, 1969.

Index to Proper Names

Index to Subjects

About the Author

F.F. Centore is Associate Professor of Philosophy at St. Jerome's College, University of Waterloo, in Ontario, Canada. His works include the coauthored *Philosophy Today* and *Hooke's Contributions to Mechanics* as well as many scholarly articles.